The Legacy of Positivism

The Legacy of Positivism

Michael Singer

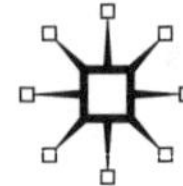

First published 2005 by
PALGRAVE MACMILLAN
Houndmills, Basingstoke, Hampshire RG21 6XS and
175 Fifth Avenue, New York, N.Y. 10010
Companies and representatives throughout the world

PALGRAVE MACMILLAN is the global academic imprint of the Palgrave Macmillan division of St. Martin's Press, LLC and of Palgrave Macmillan Ltd. Macmillan® is a registered trademark in the United States, United Kingdom and other countries. Palgrave is a registered trademark in the European Union and other countries.

ISBN-13: 978–1–4039–9402–8
ISBN-10: 1–4039–9402–1

This book is printed on paper suitable for recycling and made from fully managed and sustained forest sources.

A catalogue record for this book is available from the British Library.

Library of Congress Cataloging-in-Publication Data
Singer, Michael, 1942–
　　The legacy of positivism / Michael Singer.
　　　　p.　cm.
　　Includes bibliographical references and index.
　　ISBN 1–4039–9402–1 (cloth)
　　1. Positivism.　I. Title.
　　B831.S52 2005
　　146′.4 – dc22　　　　　　　　　　　　　　　　　　　　2005049582

10　9　8　7　6　5　4　3　2　1
14　13　12　11　10　09　08　07　06　05

Printed and bound in Great Britain by
Antony Rowe Ltd, Chippenham and Eastbourne

Contents

Acknowledgements vii

Introduction viii

PART I THE POSITIVISM OF AUGUSTE COMTE

1 The Philosophy of Positivism 3
  i. Comte and his works 3
  ii. The origins of positivist philosophy 7
  iii. The law of three stages 11
  iv. The evolution of scientific thought 15

2 The Structure of a Positive Science 19
  i. Juridical and scientific laws 19
  ii. The epistemology of a positive science 22
  iii. Laws and causes 24
  iv. The predictive power of science 26

3 Positivist Social Reorganization 32
  i. Order and progress 32
  ii. The theory of social reorganization 35
  iii. The practice of social reorganization 38
  iv. Society and the individual 40
  v. Positivist morality in theory and practice 43

PART II THE DEVELOPMENT OF POSITIVISM THROUGH MILL AND LITTRÉ

4 Comte and Mill 51
  i. Harmony and discord 51
  ii. Mill's empiricism 55
  iii. Mill's theory of induction 60
  iv. Comte's epistemology 65
  v. Differences over induction 67

5 The Critic and the Disciple 72
  i. Mill as critic 72
  ii. Littré as disciple 77

6 The Structure of the Legacy of Positivism   84
   i.   Positivism as creed: diversions from the legacy   84
   ii.   The received view of the legacy   90
   iii.   The legacy in method   93
   iv.   The legacy in structured explanation   96
   v.   The legacy in scientific autonomy   97
   vi.   The legacy regarding benefit to humanity   100
   vii.   The legacy in prescriptive human science   102
   viii.   The legacy in moral non-science   107

PART III   THE LEGACY OF POSITIVISM IN LAW

7 The Legacy of Positivism in the Autonomy of Law   113
   i.   Introduction to Part III   113
   ii.   Law in Comte's positivism   117
   iii.   The claim of law as a science   122

8 Aspects of the Legacy of Positivism in Law   128
   i.   From the legacy of positivism to legal positivism   128
   ii.   Law and morality in adjudication under legal positivism   135
   iii.   The human sciences in law   138

Notes and References   143

Bibliography   181

Index   187

Acknowledgements

I am especially grateful to Courtney W. Howland, who read numerous drafts and patiently engaged in many discussions of positivism over several years. Her invaluable insights are reflected at many points throughout this book and have substantially influenced its overall structure. I also thank Amanda Perreau-Saussine, Frank Stewart and the anonymous reader for Palgrave Macmillan publishers for their extensive and helpful comments on an earlier version of Part I, and the School of Law of King's College London for providing me the great privilege of a stimulating and supportive scholarly environment.

MICHAEL SINGER

Introduction

The legacy of positivism as I define and describe it in this book is a mode of thought so widely pervasive as to pass generally unremarked. It ultimately derives from the combined philosophical and socio-political theory known as positivism that was extensively developed in the nineteenth century. However, this legacy is not a consequence, direct or indirect, of consciously adopting positivism, as a theory or otherwise. Rather, it is the substance of certain positivist ideas as they have become pervasively woven into modern thought, whether we are mindful of them or not.

This mode of thought has philosophical, ethical, sociological, political and jurisprudential ramifications that may seem disparate until I demonstrate that they are built on a common epistemological foundation. In the present book I investigate this foundation and chart the derivation of various present-day strands of thought from it, both theoretically and historically. The process that I describe has not previously been recognized in its entirety in the literature of the subject. In consequence, accounts of positivism have often lacked focus or been selective, and so have failed to explain fully the developments that have stemmed from positivism and the connections between them. Thus, there has been no satisfactory account of this important vein of intellectual history that has, at the same time, presented a theoretical framework providing insight into the modern thought structures that have their genesis in positivism.

Part I, comprising the first three chapters, gives an account of Auguste Comte's positivism. As is well known, Comte applied the term *positif*, from which 'positivism' derives, to describe a doctrinal structure that he set forth in the early nineteenth century in France. This combined a descriptive philosophy with a stringently prescriptive social and political doctrine. There are already many descriptions of this structure in the literature, but my justification for presenting yet another is that my account focuses on those aspects of Comte's structure of significance for the later developments that concern me.

Moreover, many of the existing accounts of Comte's work that might otherwise have served stray too far from his texts to be reliable. Of these, the French sources tend to paraphrase selected aspects of Comte's ideas into their texts without citation, while the English sources at best offer citation to indifferent translations. Consequently, they often directly mislead. I rely entirely on Comte's original texts. For the convenience of the reader I quote from them in English (giving my own translations) in my text, but the original French is always available in the notes. I deal similarly with all writers in languages other than English to whom I refer.

The term 'positivism' has long been contested and its application in any case has often been a matter of controversy. Indeed, some present-day scholars' usage of 'positivism' would make the term inapplicable to Comte's doctrinal structure. Nevertheless, Comte is an important, influential and indeed pivotal figure in the development of the mode of thought that concerns me. A clear sense of this development comes from starting with his doctrines, and looking backwards for their roots and forwards for their legacy.

In Chapter 1, I indicate the main sources, as well as the philosophical and social roots, of Comte's thought. Of course, it is rarely possible to determine clear origins for any stream of thought or to set out an uncontentious account of its historical development. However, it is sufficient for my account to chart the emergence of Comte's positivism from the confluence of several major European social and philosophical developments that – at least with hindsight – are already discernible in the seventeenth century. These include an Enlightenment-inspired focus on human progress, on reason as the foremost guide to progress, and on the corpus of human knowledge as the unified product of reason. The social effects of rapid developments in science had brought a more focused view of the lineaments of human reason. The confluence of these ideas that led to positivism was developed in the work of French writers of the late eighteenth century and came to fuller fruition in the work of Comte.

In developing his thesis, Comte systematized a number of ideas that were already widely mooted at the time. He took up the existing term *positif* and enlarged its meaning to suit his scheme. He ascribed to it five senses that were to characterize the positivist method: investigating only matters with which human minds can actually cope; directing all investigations towards improving the human condition; seeking certainty and universal agreement in all matters; seeking the level of precision that the area of investigation permits and that human needs demand; and focusing all efforts on the constructive reorganization of society. In this connection, he framed his *law of three stages*, which states that each branch of human knowledge becomes positive after having necessarily begun with a theological stage and subsequently passed through a transitional metaphysical stage.

Comte held that different branches of knowledge become positive in a specific order, depending on the complexity of the phenomena that they treat. On this basis he presented the sciences as a hierarchy, beginning with mathematics and astronomy and progressing to biology. He continued the hierarchy by introducing the idea of a new discipline of *sociology* – the study of human society as a science – for which his work is widely known. He argued that the law of three stages applied as fully to sociology as to any other branch of knowledge, so that it too would eventually develop into a positive science.

Comte's view of the positive sciences depended strongly on the concept of a scientific *law*. In preparation both for examination of this and for Part III, I begin Chapter 2 with a discussion of the earlier sense of law, the juridical sense, in relation to the scientific. A historical account shows how science shifted from a prescriptive sense of law, derived from a juridical notion of the universe obeying the edicts of a deity, to a descriptive sense from which the positive sciences developed.

Returning to the scientific context, I discuss the structure of a positive science in Comte's scheme. Many of his contemporaries, and many later thinkers as well, believed that all sciences would ultimately be reducible to mathematical formulation. However, taking a view closer to modern sentiments, Comte recognized that this would not be feasible for the human sciences, including biology and, even more so, sociology. Rather (using modern terminology), each science develops its own defining epistemological variant of the overall positive method, so no science can be epistemologically reduced to those below it in the hierarchy.

I next discuss a crucial distinction that Comte drew between the positive stage and its theological and metaphysical predecessors. He saw these earlier modes of viewing the world as concerned with determining the primary or ultimate *causes* of phenomena, and thereby leading to inconclusive and futile discussions of no benefit to humanity. However, positivism would confine itself to the *laws that relate* phenomena, and these could be conclusively determined by positive scientific investigation.

Moreover, determining these laws would benefit humanity, because, Comte insisted, scientific laws enable the prediction of the future from the past. Since the human sciences would eventually become positive, they would then be able to predict the future just as the physical sciences do. This would benefit humanity by permitting methodical determination of the steps needed to ensure desirable social and political development. Comte now declared that ensuring this was to be the goal of the positivist human sciences. This allowed him to shift sociology from a descriptive to a prescriptive science, and thus provided the bridge between his philosophical and his socio-political scheme.

Chapter 3 describes the social and political aspects of Comte's positivism. These took the form of an ambitious proposal for a thorough-going reorganization of society to propel it towards the desired positive state. Comte later extended his proposal for reorganization into a kind of religion, his so-called religion of humanity. His proposed reorganization was aimed at avoiding social upheavals along the road to the positive state, which Comte, influenced by the events of the Revolution and its aftermath, particularly stressed. This led him to declare that the primary goal in reorganization was to achieve progress while maintaining order.

Comte regarded the task of social reorganization as immensely difficult. For such a task, a substantial plan would be needed before anything could be done. In Comte's terms, theory must precede practice in social reorganization. Since this theory would be so important, it could be entrusted only to experts in developing theory – that is, to the scientists. Their conclusions would be scientific conclusions, and as such as unassailable as the conclusions of the physical sciences. This led Comte to reject the principle of freedom of individual opinion in social and political matters.

This rejection typified Comte's view of the relationship between society and the individual in the positivist scheme. He regarded people as lacking natural morality, so that close and continuing organization of all spheres of human thought and activity, reinforced by the strong pressure of public opinion, would be needed to promulgate and maintain positivism in practice.

Comte paid particular attention to the need to develop a positivist moral sense in society, and consequently elevated morality from being a part of sociology to being a science in its own right. This placed it at the summit of the hierarchy of the sciences, serving as a link between positivist philosophy and positivist politics. Positivist morality was to be socially oriented, and Comte recognized that promulgating it through society would require not only scientific exposition but also subjective inculcation. This would take place through education and in the family setting. The latter would be the particular province of women, for whom Comte stipulated an exclusively family-oriented role based on a stereotypical view of women's nature.

In Comte's positivist scheme, morality would thus have a twofold nature. As a science, it would rely on sociology's determinations of what was good for society, and on this basis would determine what was right for human beings to do. But as subjectively inculcated, each person would directly experience it as prescribing what was right, without reference to sociological determinations. Expressed in the terminology of modern moral philosophy: in positivist *philosophy*, 'the good' is prior to 'the right', whereas in positivist *politics*, 'the right' is prior to 'the good'.

Part II, comprising Chapters 4 to 6, considers the roles of John Stuart Mill and Émile Littré in the development of positivism. In Chapter 4 I discuss the relationship between Comte and Mill. Mill, although known as a liberalist, became an ardent supporter of Comte. He accepted Comte's ideas of the hierarchy of the sciences, the law of three stages, and the eventual accession of every branch of human knowledge to the positive, or scientific, stage. He agreed with Comte that the development of the study of human society as the new science of sociology would be largely a task for experts, whose authority the mass of people would be bound to accept. His considerable political and intellectual influence contributed greatly to developing Comte's reputation and making known the works in which he had presented these ideas.

Mill later diverged from Comte regarding key aspects of the latter's scheme for social reorganization, particularly its rejection of individual freedom. I argue that fundamental philosophical differences between Comte and Mill inevitably led to this political divergence, despite their sharing goals important to them both. These differences can be expressed in terms of their respective epistemologies. Analysis of Mill's epistemology is complicated by his professing sceptical empiricism, but in practice adopting a naïve realism crucial to his development of his theory of logic. The core of this theory was his general theory of logical induction. This rested on his stipulation that the processes whereby human beings form classifications and generalizations (these processes being the essence of induction) are initially natural, and develop thereafter in a proper fashion through experience. However, Comte – taking an approach in fact closer to present-day sensibilities – viewed these processes as contextual and always resting on a prior theory, and thus by no means natural or based on some generic form of experience.

As a result of this difference, Comte and Mill saw human society's path to the positive state in sharply different terms. For Mill, achieving the positive state was consistent with individual liberty, because experience would lead every person (or at least every educated person) to proper positive thought. But Comte could not trust experience in such a general way. In his view, humanity would stay on the path towards the positive state only if constrained by tight social control. Otherwise it would likely stray, causing the social upheavals that he feared.

Chapter 5 considers the critical positions that Mill and Littré took towards Comte's thesis. Mill found himself in a quandary regarding Comte. He wanted to continue to support, intellectually and politically, the aspects of Comte's positivism with which he had long agreed. However, he abhorred Comte's scheme for reorganizing society. Moreover, adverse reaction in many quarters against this scheme was threatening to bring positivism in its entirety into disrepute. Consequently, he was faced with the task of rescuing the aspects of Comte's positivism that he supported from association with Comte's scheme for social reorganization.

I argue that Mill had not come to terms with the profound epistemological difference between himself and Comte, and consequently was unable to frame substantive arguments against Comte's socio-political scheme. He was reduced to making a general and an *ad hominem* attack on Comte. His general attack was to ridicule Comte for following through with his reasoning in sociology regardless of common sense. This criticism clashed with Mill's commitment to developing sociology as a science. His *ad hominem* attack was to focus on Comte's mental deterioration in his last years and stretch this to encompass all of the later works in which he had developed his socio-political scheme. On this basis Mill could split Comte's life, and thereby Comte's work, into two parts. He portrayed the younger Comte as an admirable theoretician who had created the important philosophy of positivism. He portrayed the older Comte as a pathetic figure of failed intellect whose socio-political doctrines were best ignored. However, this criticism ignored the fact that Comte had already set out the framework of his socio-political scheme in earlier works.

Mill's criticism was analytically unsatisfactory, but it adequately served both his philosophical and his political goals. Philosophically, he could retain his commitment to the development of sociology as an authoritative predictive science. Politically, his dismissal of Comte's later work effectively guarded against his socio-political scheme either adversely influencing the philosophy of positivism or being put into effect.

The next section of this chapter deals with the contribution of Émile Littré, a sometime follower of Comte who split from him and developed positivism in a different vein. I do not consider whether the ideas that Littré set down were original to him or rather reflected the spirit of his time. Littré, like Mill, accepted some aspects of Comte's work while rejecting others, but made the division in a different way. He rejected Comte's introduction into positivist doctrine of the subjective sense that was to form the basis of moral inculcation. In addition, unlike Mill, he argued that it was impossible to achieve extensive predictive power in the human sciences, thus rejecting a key aspect of Comte's philosophical structure. As a result, it would be impossible to implement Comte's scheme of social reorganization in the way that he had intended, with the entire future course of development of society predetermined.

Littré insisted that he was not rejecting positivism but purifying it of errors that Comte had introduced. He saw himself as remaining loyal to the true spirit of positivism as Comte had established it and that Comte by various doctrinal developments had later betrayed. He also rejected Mill's approach, dismissing Mill as a critic of positivism while he himself was a disciple.

Littré stressed that what was most important in positivism was the positive *method*, rather than any specific set of doctrines. This was to be essentially the scientific method as Comte had envisioned it, with each science developing its own defining epistemological variant. This would allow sociology to be regarded as a positive science, despite its having only very limited predictive power. The lack of predictive power meant that sociology could only guide society regarding general trends rather than plan its development in detail. However, Littré insisted that this remained a supremely important role. Within this role, sociology would continue to be a prescriptive science.

Littré's development affected the role of morality in the positivist scheme. Since sociology would now offer only fairly general conclusions, morality as a science could develop from them only fairly general principles of conduct that would be insufficient to support a comprehensive inculcated morality. In any event, without Comte's subjective sense positivism would have no means of subjectively inculcating morality. This broke Comte's link between theory and practice. Also, it entailed that 'the good' would be prior to 'the right' in positivism, both philosophically and politically.

In Chapter 6 I describe and critique the extensive legacy of positivism in modern thought. However, I begin by discussing some viewpoints that have become associated with positivism, but have not substantially affected modern thought. Although I therefore do not include them within the legacy of positivism, it is helpful to discuss them because they have come to define the attitudes – usually adverse – of many people towards positivism. Some of these attitudes date back to Comte's era, and relate to the extreme systematization of his scheme, the more unappealing aspects of his proposals for social reorganization and the influence of his religion of humanity. Although, as I discuss, Comte's focus on systematization may have somewhat influenced modern thought, otherwise these aspects of positivism have not done so. Consequently, they are essentially irrelevant to its legacy.

I consider here also the widely held view that positivism supports the idea of neutral and objective observation being possible. On this basis, positivism has been criticized as narrow and conservative. However, Comte had insisted that any observation rests on a prior theory, and this in fact is opposed to a belief in neutral and objective observation. Consequently, I do not regard such a belief as deriving from Comte's positivism, and so do not include it within the legacy of positivism.

Other adverse attitudes to positivism relate to more current issues. One stems from rejection of logical positivism. However, I show that this is not relevant to the legacy of positivism in modern thought because, as is well known, logical positivism has little in common with positivism as developed by Comte and Littré. Indeed, logical positivism's rejection of value-statements as unverifiable directly opposes Comte's goal of developing sciences of humanity capable of deriving value-statements as scientific laws.

A further source of adverse attitudes to positivism is a longstanding association between positivism and extreme political conservatism. I discuss the two most important contexts in which this association appears. One derives from a perceived opposition between Comte and Marx, and leads to the view that positivism is the theoretical foundation for modern capitalism. However, I show that this view is not based on any reasonable interpretation of Comte, and anyway is irrelevant to the aspects of positivism that have entered modern thought as its legacy. The other derives from Latin American political thought, stemming from nineteenth-century attempts to implement positivism as a socio-political system in much of the region. Although these developments were initially largely progressive in intent, positivist political forces later became associated with repressive regimes. This has led to a retrospective association between positivism and political conservatism. However, I show that there is no connection between this history and the legacy of positivism in modern thought.

I begin the description of the legacy of positivism with the aspects of modern thought that have previously been recognized as influenced by Comte. These include a belief in the certainty and accuracy of the physical sciences, which we rely on in day-to-day life however philosophically suspect it may be. They further include a demand for scientific standards of explanation in all fields, including the humanities disciplines, and aspiration to scientific status as the goal of these disciplines. I illustrate these aspects of modern thought with examples from recent writings in the human sciences.

All the other aspects of the legacy of positivism that I describe have not previously been recognized as such. They derive from various facets of the thought of Comte as developed by Littré that I discussed in previous chapters. What I describe as the legacy in *method* appears in the general recognition that each of the sciences, including the human sciences, must develop its own modes of investigation and proof. This is closely linked with the broad – and somewhat uneasy – recognition that our observations, particularly in the human sciences, depend on a prior sense of theory. Here I illustrate these aspects of modern thought with examples from recent writings in anthropology.

The remaining aspects of the legacy of positivism that I describe do not derive directly from Comte's positivism but from the developments of it that Littré set down. What I describe as the legacy in *structured explanation* insists that the human sciences are capable, at least in principle, of explaining all events. However, it separates explanation from prediction in the human sciences, allowing that they are capable of predicting only general trends, not specific events. This raises the question of how the validity of explanations is to be tested, and it appears that each human science must determine its own tests internally. Here my illustration is from recent writings in history.

As a result of abandoning predictive power in the human sciences, Comte's tight, hierarchical and socially mandated relationships between them become attenuated. Taking this together with the legacy in method, the result is to allow each of the human sciences a high degree of separateness and independence. The result is what I describe as the legacy in *scientific autonomy*. My illustrations of this come from recent writings in history and sociology. I note that this aspect of the legacy, taken together with the aspects previously discussed, entails that the conclusions of any human science are validated within the internal structure of that science only, and cannot on this basis claim universal validity.

The legacy regarding *benefit to humanity* appears in a widespread, although admittedly not universal, sense that the sciences should pursue the benefit of humanity. This should be considered together with the legacy in *prescriptive human science*. In this aspect of modern thought, the human sciences follow Littré's mandate to offer guidance to society. At this point I consider how the human sciences move from deriving explanations of events to framing normative conclusions about the benefit of humanity. I show that they achieve this by using a claim of exclusive scientific expertise to equate the desired normative conclusion with a universally accepted normative conclusion. I argue that this may entail an illegitimate claim of universal validity for conclusions validated within the internal structure of a particular science. I illustrate this with an example from anthropology that, I argue, demonstrates the problems with, and the need for further critique of, the aspects of the legacy of positivism that have come to us through the ideas that Littré set down.

Finally, I consider what I describe as the legacy in *moral non-science*. Littré's abandonment of Comte's subjective sense eliminated any prospect of the kind of 'scientific' foundation for morality that Comte had promised. I argue that this has influenced modern thought in two ways. First, it is widely accepted that the human sciences cannot derive conclusions to serve as the foundation for moral principles. Second, moral reasoning – the process of reasoning entailed in justifying moral principles or in developing a structure of morality – has become detached from the modern idea of science. I discuss and illustrate this with different perspectives on investigating and discovering truth. However, I do not claim that it would in some fashion be 'better' if moral reasoning followed the methods of modern science, except in cases where moral principles are promoted on the basis of predicted specific benefits.

Part III, comprising Chapters 7 and 8, considers the influence of the legacy of positivism on reasoning and analysis within the juridical context and on modern thought about how the juridical process operates within society. Although this influence stems from aspects of the legacy of positivism that I already discussed in Chapter 6, the specialized nature of legal analysis and the immediate and substantial effect of judicial decisions in society make separate treatment in the juridical context desirable.

Chapter 7 begins with a detailed introduction to this part of the book, so I need only outline the topics here. Following this introduction in Chapter 7, I first discuss Comte's view of law as, essentially, a collection of rules that, together with public opinion and inculcated morality, would maintain order in society. I then consider the nineteenth-century claim that law should be regarded as a science. I argue that this claim would have been untenable under Comte's scheme, but could be more readily sustained under Littré's development, which stressed the internal structure of a discipline rather than its place in any external structure.

In the first two sections of Chapter 8, I discuss the influence of the legacy of positivism on a sampling of the broad and fragmented range of doctrines known as legal positivism. I focus on the claim of epistemological autonomy that legal positivism makes for the legal system, and on the view of legal positivism regarding the relationship between law and morality in adjudication. I show the epistemological connection from the legacy of positivism to legal positivism here, and consequently critique aspects of the position of legal positivism. The final section of Chapter 8 considers the application of conclusions of the human sciences in adjudication. I argue that this shows a double influence of the legacy of positivism, and apply my critique of Chapters 6 and 7 to call for greater caution in this regard.

Part I
The Positivism of Auguste Comte

1
The Philosophy of Positivism

i. Comte and his works

In 1822, Auguste Comte, then twenty-four years of age, published a plan for the total intellectual, social and political reorganization of society.[1] He had studied mathematics at the École Polytechnique in Paris, and had read widely in the sciences and in French political philosophy of the eighteenth century. He was to devote his life to his work on the doctrines that became known as positivism, continuing until shortly before his death in 1857. In the extensive *Cours de Philosophie positive*, published mainly in the 1830s, he developed positivism as a combined philosophical and socio-political structure. The philosophical aspects of the structure consisted of purportedly descriptive theories of human knowledge and society. The socio-political aspects were prefigured in the early work referred to above, and following their adumbration in the *Philosophie positive* they were fully developed in the later *Système de politique positive*. These aspects were explicitly normative, and directed towards the goal of systematically implementing his philosophical theories as the modes of thought and action of human society. Comte's later works further developed positivism as an explicitly religious framework – the so-called religion of humanity – for the propagation and social implementation of the positivist philosophical and political structure.

In so far as it is feasible to separate these philosophical, socio-political and religious aspects of Comte's work, it may be said that the philosophical aspects captured the spirit of many of the most notable thinkers of the times and brought Comte great acclaim. They were later subjected to considerable criticism but nonetheless have been widely influential to an extent that is often not clearly recognized. However, the socio-political aspects of Comte's work quickly led to controversy. They gained Comte a number of followers, but they also alienated many prominent scholars and political personages, among them some of Comte's most influential supporters. The adverse reactions cost Comte his official positions and left him to spend his last years in impoverished dependence on the support of charitable sympathizers with the philosophical aspects of his earlier work.[2]

Whether indeed it is feasible to separate Comte's work into its philosophical, socio-political and religious aspects has long been a contested matter. This in fact combines two kinds of issues – essentially, a conceptual and a textual issue – that have not always been well distinguished. The first is to what extent it is possible to derive viable separate philosophical, socio-political and religious doctrinal structures from the totality of Comte's conceptual edifice, without regard to whether Comte intended these structures to be identified and considered separately. The second issue is to what extent such structures are separately identifiable within Comte's corpus of work as distinct texts or parts of texts, or even as distinct textual themes. The interplay of enquiries into these two issues over the years has affected the reception of and responses to Comte's work, and to a considerable extent has thereby fashioned the various views taken of positivism today.

It is difficult in discussing Comte to avoid reference to the problems that his texts pose. Putting aside the dullness and prolixity of his writing and the great length and repetitiveness of his works, of which many have justifiably complained,[3] there remain two pervasive problems that intertwine issues of style and substance and so give rise to serious difficulties of interpretation. The first problem concerns Comte's contextual use of certain language terms that were in common use in his era and remain so today. These are terms signifying themes that the established social order traditionally treats as oppositional, including, for example, the opposition between rationalism and romanticism, and between conservatism and revolution. Comte employs these terms in non-standard ways that confuse and undermine the sense of opposition that has been traditionally taken for granted. This can make it difficult to gain a clear sense of his meaning.[4] In my view, it seems likely that Comte's non-standard contextual usage of these traditionally oppositional terms is purposeful. They represent themes that, as we shall see, he wishes to harmonize in his positivist scheme, and this suggests that his purpose is to overcome linguistic constraints on the expression of his thesis. However, awareness of this does not make his works any easier to read or his arguments any easier to summarize.

The second problem is that in Comte's meandering and repetitive works any given idea is likely to occur in several places and to be painstakingly developed in subtly different ways in each of them. Some of these differences may represent shifts in Comte's viewpoint over the long course of his work. Other differences may merely represent shifts in emphasis. Yet other differences may stem from Comte's use in different places of different terms that he seems to have regarded as synonyms, so such differences are likely to be more apparent than real. In some cases there can be no definitive conclusion regarding what Comte thought on a particular matter. Indeed, it is noteworthy that the development of positivism after Comte saw numerous schisms among various factions that all claimed to possess the true understanding of his vision and to be his true followers, which suggests that any wholly uncontroversial assessment of every aspect of his work can hardly be expected.[5]

In others cases, reaching a definitive conclusion regarding what Comte thought requires following the development of the matter in question through his various works, and taking into account his shifts in emphasis and usage. In this way it may be possible to offer a balanced synopsis and assessment closely based on selected passages of his works that fairly represent the trend of his thought on the issues in question. Plainly, it would be hazardous to rely on translations of Comte's works for this, especially since there is no wholly satisfactory translation of any of his works available.[6] Unfortunately, as I have noted in the Introduction, many of the existing accounts of Comte's work in English do rely on translations. The accounts in French obviously do not present this problem, but unfortunately many of them rely on paraphrases of selected aspects of Comte's ideas into their texts, often without citation. The results of both approaches are unreliable and often directly misleading.

I rely entirely on Comte's original texts, and quote rather than paraphrase. The resulting fidelity of presentation justifies the relatively high density of quotations. For the convenience of the reader I quote in English in my text, but give Comte's original French text in the notes for immediate reference in every case. The translations throughout are my own. I have tried in every case to convey the sense of the original, as evinced by its context, rather than be bound by the literal form of words. I deal similarly with all writers in languages other than English to whom I refer.

Both of the pervasive problems with Comte's texts that I have mentioned should be viewed in the broader context of his utter rejection of the French literary and philosophical tradition of writing in a detached tone rich with allusions to a common culture of learning and scholarship. Rather, his works present an impression of being treatise, manifesto, lesson and sermon combined.[7] In my view, this results from Comte's aim of creating a combined and all-encompassing philosophical and socio-political scheme and pursuing its implementation. Thus, he does not choose to adopt the traditional manner of literary or scholarly writing because he simply has no interest in reasoning with the learned reader as an equal participant in such a tradition. On the contrary, he sets out to convert the reader into a disciple of his positivist doctrines and an active participant in the creation of the new positivist order in accordance with these doctrines. The reader's response to this mode of presentation – whether, for example, she embraces or resists new terminological usages in the treatise, or whether she feels inspired or browbeaten by its sermonizing – may depend on whether she approaches the text as a disciple or not.

Despite the difficulties in reading Comte, the influence of his writings has been considerable. He succeeded in putting together a package of philosophical, socio-political and quasi-religious ideas in a way that rejected various aspects of the received wisdom of his era, and at the same time used a diverse collection of relatively new and socially influential ideas (some original, some not) to form a cohesive scheme. In effect, his works purported to set out what the best knowledge and ideas of his day meant for the history, present state and future development of human society. He claimed to be telling humanity what its situation had been and what it then was, and in consequence what in the future it ought to be. Moreover, he set out the measures that should be taken if the desired future was to be realized.

Comte's scheme challenged not only the existing socio-political order but also many of the then current proposals for creation of a new order. His influence and popularity were such that this challenge could not be simply ignored. Rather, it had to be met and countered, and a process of selective adoption and adaptation of Comte's proposals largely accomplished this. As we shall see, this process eventually reached the point of departing from much of Comte's proposed structure. Indeed, much of what Comte thought crucial to his scheme was abandoned, and much that was introduced under the rubric of positivism he would surely have abhorred. But nevertheless the process took place in relation to Comte's work, and so cannot be understood independently of understanding Comte's work. Put simply, we must understand Comte's scheme to understand the historical and intellectual process of diverging from it.[8]

ii. The origins of positivist philosophy

Among the most direct influences on the early development of Comte's thought was the social theorist Henri de Saint-Simon. Comte was his secretary for several years in the early 1820s, and his earliest works first appeared as essays in Saint-Simon's publications. These works contain several of the major ideas that Comte was later to develop into the philosophical part of his positivist thesis, and Saint-Simon clearly influenced them substantially. Indeed, some of these ideas can be readily traced to earlier works of Saint-Simon, although generally they appear there in rudimentary form.

Comte later broke away from Saint-Simon and wholly denied his influence. Yet he was perfectly willing to acknowledge his debt to his own and Saint-Simon's predecessors in Enlightenment thought, particularly that of seventeenth- and eighteenth-century France and England.[9] In its philosophical aspects, Comte's achievement was to bring together in a single, systematic thesis and advance further a number of already closely interconnected ideas that stemmed from this thought. One of these ideas was a commitment to the inevitability of human progress, which held that humanity had developed from an initial state of primitive savagery and would ultimately aspire to the highest levels of civilization. Condorcet had expressed this enthusiastically:

> The time will yet come when the sun will shine on an earth of none but free men who recognize no other master than their own reason; when tyrants and slaves . . . will exist only in history and on the theatrical stage.[10]

This demonstrated remarkable optimism considering his circumstances at the time as a fugitive from the Revolution. In addition, Condorcet's reference to human reason indicates another idea of primary importance at the time. Enlightenment thinkers, in a view particularly associated with Immanuel Kant, contrasted reason with faith and superstition and insisted that the use of reason would guide humanity not only to a correct view of the physical world but also to right moral action. A third, equally fundamental idea was that all human knowledge should be viewed in its totality as a unified corpus. This idea was given quite literal interpretation by the Encyclopaedists of the mid-eighteenth century under Denis Diderot and Jean d'Alembert.

A further stimulus to thinkers of the time was a collection of ideas developing under the rubric of *science*. This developing idea of science encompassed a method, process and body of knowledge that its protagonists viewed as founded on empirical observation. Such observation was to take place, where feasible, in the context of controlled experiments that would refine the processes of observation and ensure their reliability. The method of science further required systematic classification of the results of observations and rigorous logical deduction of the consequences of these results. Then, processes of logical induction were to be applied, whereby general laws of behaviour were to be extracted from the results of the observations. These laws were ideally to be expressed in mathematical terms and, where feasible, were to be tested by further experiment.

In the present chapter, devoted to the historical development of positivism, I take for granted a naïve sense of the idea of science and the idea of logical induction. I discuss these more fully in subsequent chapters.

These aspects of the scientific method are already to be found in the works of Francis Bacon, even if in rudimentary form.[11] On the value of scientific experiments, Bacon states that 'experiments permit far greater refinement than the senses, as long as they are focused on the matter in question and skilfully thought out and applied. Consequently we do not rely greatly on the direct, unmediated use of the senses, but set things up so that the senses adjudge the experiment and the experiment adjudges the matter in question.'[12] This is all well and good, but it finesses the point that the *use* of experiments to obtain knowledge was highly controversial in Bacon's time. The scientific development of induction from the results of experiments represented a major change from earlier times in the perceived relationship between observations of phenomena and general laws of behaviour. Bacon stands at a crux between the earlier approach, going back to Plato and Aristotle, which still prevailed in his own time, and the scientific method that he advocates and that would become increasingly prevalent in the coming two centuries. It would be hard to improve on his statement of the distinction between these approaches:

There are – and can only be – two ways to investigate and discover truth. The one leaps from particular sense experiences to the most general statements, which it then treats as inviolable axioms and the source of any intermediate assertions. This is the current way. The other elicits basic principles from particular sense experiences, and generalizes from them steadily and step by step, reaching the most general principles only at the culmination of the process. This is the proper way, but it has not been followed.[13]

A good illustration of the two approaches is the development, in the centuries following Bacon, of observational astronomy in opposition to the medieval worldview that was based on the Aristotelian scheme. I discuss this in Chapter 2. For the present, I note only that the use of induction to extract general laws of behaviour from the results of observations is certainly well established by the time that Isaac Newton, a century later, could baldly declare that '[i]n the experimental sciences propositions are inferred from [observation of] phenomena and generalized [into laws] by induction'.[14]

The idea prevalent by the time of Comte was that science, understood in the terms discussed above, constituted a powerful force for the development of human knowledge and the progress of human society. The power of science had already been well recognized by the eighteenth century, although thinkers were divided as to its social value. In the middle of the century Jean-Jacques Rousseau had famously declared that 'the more our sciences and our arts advance towards perfection, the more our souls become corrupted'.[15] Closer to Comte's own time, Condorcet was among the most enthusiastic proponents of the social value of scientific knowledge, and insisted that 'we can find . . . in observing the progress that the sciences . . . have made to this point . . . the strongest grounds for believing that nature has set no limit to our expectations'.[16]

In general, the scientific advances of the early nineteenth century engendered widespread optimism. Scientific theory was demonstrating ever more astonishing explanatory and predictive capacities. The technical applications of science in agriculture, industry, public health and medicine came increasingly to drive substantial improvements in prosperity, comfort and health. These were far more visible and impressive than a variety of concomitant, arguably detrimental developments such as industrial pollution and increasingly lethal weaponry. In sum, science – increasingly being viewed as a single body of knowledge – came to be seen as the embodiment of human progress and as the power of human reason made manifest.

In Comte's time the French term *science positive*, based on *positif* as meaning definite or fact-based, was coming into use to denote the sciences developed in this way. Thus Comte is able to introduce it as a term already known.[17] He extrapolates from this basic meaning in a way that will enable him to develop the concept of 'positive' in philosophical and political context. Specifically, he gives five senses for *positif* that should be seen not as a linguistic analysis of the term but as a guide to the aims of his scheme. Note that although I shall use the English 'positive' for *positif* in my translations, its common usage by no means captures all of these senses that Comte ascribes to *positif*.

The first of the five senses is:

> The word 'positive' denotes that which is real rather than chimerical. In this regard, it corresponds fully to the new philosophical spirit that is characterized by its constant devotion to scientific investigations with which our minds can actually cope, and that pays no heed to the impenetrable mysteries that obsessed humanity in earlier times.[18]

The second sense is:

> The word 'positive' . . . indicates the contrast between the useful and the futile. Thus it reminds us of the proper purpose of all sound philosophical theorizing: the continuing improvement of our actual condition, individual and social, rather than the worthless satisfaction of mere academic curiosity.[19]

The third sense is:

> The word 'positive' . . . is often used to describe the opposition between certainty and indecision. Thus it indicates the characteristic ability of positive philosophy to generate individual and social harmony, in place of the ill-defined doubts and interminable discussions to which earlier modes of thought gave rise.[20]

The fourth sense is:

> The word 'positive' . . . sets precision against vagueness. This sense recalls the constant tendency of the genuine positive spirit to reach in every case the degree of scientific precision that the phenomena under investigation permit, and that our true needs demand. This contrasts with the general vagueness characteristic of earlier philosophies, under which the only discipline in thought resulted from continuing repression on the claimed basis of supernatural authority.[21]

The fifth sense is:

> The word 'positive' . . . contrasts with *negative*. With this sense it declares one of the most important characteristics of this true

modern philosophy: that it is destined by its nature not to destroy but to reorganize the human social order.[22]

I shall refer to these five senses of 'positive' at various points in the sequel.

iii. The law of three stages

In his philosophical framework, Comte developed and extended the synthesis of knowledge that I discussed in the previous section with two ideas on which he would build the basic structure of positivism. I discuss the first of these in the present section, and the second in the next section.

Comte framed an idea that he presented as explanation and justification for the primacy of human reason in the progress of humanity:

> In studying ... the total development of human intelligence in its various spheres of activity, from its first and simplest stage up to our own time, I believe that I have discovered a great fundamental law ... This law states that each of our important concepts and each branch of our knowledge passes successively through three distinct theoretical stages: the theological or fictitious stage; the metaphysical or abstract stage; the scientific or positive stage.[23]

In the theological stage, the defining concept for human thought is 'the great notion of Deity'.[24] Comte describes human thought during this stage as follows:

> In the theological stage, the human mind essentially directs its investigations ... towards obtaining absolute knowledge. It therefore explains phenomena as the product of the direct and continuous action of a greater or lesser number of supernatural agencies, the arbitrary intervention of which explains all the apparent anomalies of the universe.[25]

In the metaphysical stage, the defining concept for human thought is 'the vague idea of Nature'.[26] Comte describes human thought during this stage as follows:

> In the metaphysical stage, which is basically only a simple general modification of the theological, the supernatural agencies are

replaced by personalized abstractions...regarded as capable of causing all observed phenomena by themselves. Thus the explanation of observed phenomena consists of assigning to each phenomenon its corresponding abstract entity.[27]

Finally, 'in the positive stage, the notion of Humanity will be the primary source of a complete mental restructuring'.[28] Comte will in due course develop the notion of humanity in his scheme of social reorganization, which I discuss in Chapter 3, and in his religion of humanity. He characterizes human thought in the positive stage as scientific:

Finally, in the positive stage, the human mind will recognize the impossibility of obtaining absolute knowledge and give up the search for the origin and destination of the universe . . . Rather, it will focus entirely on discovering the actual laws of the universe, using an appropriate combination of reasoning and observation.[29]

This clearly draws on the senses that Comte gives to 'positivism', as discussed in the previous section. I explore its implications for Comte's scheme in Chapter 2.

There will be no regression from the positive to the metaphysical or theological stage. 'The positive spirit . . . has left no other unified system of thought possible than that which will result from its own universal ascendancy. Each new branch of knowledge that becomes positive can never again return to theology or metaphysics, because as positivism increases its range its philosophy will become more and more embedded into the general common sense.'[30]

Comte sees these three stages as representing 'three kinds of philosophies . . . that are mutually exclusive. The first is the necessary point of departure for human understanding, and the third is its fixed and definitive final state. The second plays a merely transitional role.'[31] Nevertheless, Comte regards the transitional modification that the metaphysical stage provides as crucial for human philosophical and social development:

Human understanding can develop only by the smallest steps and so could not have passed sharply and directly from the theological to the positivist stage. The theological and positivist philosophies are so fundamentally incompatible, with their conceptual structures so radically opposed, that the human mind could not have abandoned the former and adopted the latter without pausing at an intermediary, hybrid stage that thereby allowed a gradual transition.[32]

Thus the metaphysical stage is in fact developmentally necessary as a precursor for the positivist stage.

Comte does not tire of restating this theme, insisting on 'the utter incompatibility of positivism with any kind of theological worldview ... the impossibility of any lasting reconciliation between the two philosophies, whether in terms of method or doctrine, so that all doubt on this subject can be readily dispelled'.[33] Consequently, it is plain that in his scheme the positivist mode of thought and the positivist approach to the socio-political order will wholly supplant the theological and metaphysical.[34]

Note that Comte does not assert that the claims made by theology and metaphysics were false, and then argue that theology and metaphysics are to be abandoned because of this. As he is surely aware, to assert the falsehood of theological and metaphysical claims would run counter to the ethos of positivism, since the falsehood as much as the truth of such claims falls into the category of questions beyond the power of the human mind to determine. For this reason, Comte is bound to reject atheism as much as any theology, and does so in strong terms:

> Atheism ... tends to prolong the metaphysical state indefinitely with its unceasing pursuit of new solutions of theological problems, instead of dismissing all investigations of matters inaccessible to us as utterly futile. The true positive spirit ... is ... incompatible with the arrogant dreams of an unfathomable atheism regarding the formation of the universe, the origin of animals, and so forth.[35]

Comte adjudges the atheism of his own time as a doctrine that not only rejects any notion of a deity but also seeks some alternative, mechanistic explanation of the creation and development of the universe.[36] This is plainly contrary to the ethos of positivism, so that Comte can bluntly declare that '[f]ar from relying on the support of present-day atheists, positivism is bound to find in them its natural enemies'.[37]

Rather than rejecting the doctrines of theology and metaphysics as false, Comte insists that they are to be abandoned because they have failed to deal with the problems that beset humanity. In his view, the current situation therefore demands that positivism must 'not fight against backward beliefs except on the basis of its own general ability better to satisfy all moral and social needs'.[38] He observes in this connection that '[u]ndoubtedly no one has managed to prove logically the non-existence of Apollo, Minerva and so forth . . . but this has in no way prevented humanity from irrevocably abandoning such ancient beliefs once they finally became unsuited to its overall situation'.[39]

Note also that Comte ejects theology and metaphysics from the positivist world only as philosophical structures and foundations for ordering society. They are still part of social and moral history, and we shall see in Chapters 2 and 3 that Comte regards the history of any human society as important for understanding its present circumstances and future development. Consistently with this, he also rejects atheism for 'the blind hatred of the past that it inspires'.[40] In sum, his goal is to supersede theology and metaphysics but not to eradicate them from human social and historical awareness. He presents this as a limited relativist aspect of positivism:

> The absolutist nature of the ancient doctrines, whether theological or metaphysical, necessarily caused each of them to adopt a negative stance towards all the others. It is, on the contrary, in accordance with the relative spirit of the new positive philosophy that it can always appreciate the genuine worth of the theories that most oppose it. Nevertheless, this never leads positivism to make any pointless concession that might affect the clarity of its views or the steadfastness of its decisions.[41]

However, in practice Comte rarely considers anything to be worth adopting from earlier doctrines other than certain organizational aspects of the medieval (Roman Catholic) Church, about which he enthuses.[42]

Comte further observes that 'the different branches of our knowledge cannot be expected to have passed through the three great developmental phases at equal speed, and so cannot be expected to reach the positive stage simultaneously'.[43] In the next section, I discuss Comte's view of the order in which the sciences reach the positive stage.

Comte's law of three stages impressed many thinkers of the time, including John Stuart Mill, as expressing a profound historical and social truth. Whether it actually is true is hardly relevant to the present study, and I merely note in passing that there seems little evidence to support it. We surely cannot accept Comte's claim to have derived the law from empirical study of humanity from its earliest stages of development through to the present day.[44] Note also that Comte gives no reason why the third, positive stage should be, as he claims, the final stage. Even putting aside evidentiary concerns, it is hard to see how the conclusion that the positive stage is final could be derived from empirical study, which could surely only show the positive stage to be the ultimate achieved *so far*. This issue has received some attention in recent years, and I discuss it in Chapter 4 in the context of Comte's epistemology.

iv. The evolution of scientific thought

In this section I discuss the second of the two ideas on which Comte built the philosophical structure of positivism. This was that science itself went through a process of evolution whereby the range of application of scientific thought would be classified, ordered and extended. He developed this idea in the *Philosophie positive*, beginning with an examination of the development of mathematics as a positive science and continuing through the range of the sciences. This, he insisted, did not entail an examination of these individual sciences themselves:

> There can be no question here of a series of special courses on each of the main branches of natural philosophy . . . It is a *course of positive philosophy*, and not of positive sciences, that I propose to undertake. This is solely a matter of considering each of the basic sciences in terms of its relation to the positive system as a whole and in terms of its essential character; that is, as expressed in its fundamental methods and main results.[45]

In the first three volumes of the *Philosophie positive*, Comte progressed in this fashion from mathematics to the physical sciences, including astronomy and optics, and then to chemistry and biology. This completed the examination, in relation to positivist philosophy, of the sciences that, according to Comte, were already positive or well on the way to positivism. Note that Comte does not see this as a rigid classification with clear boundaries of separation between the sciences. Rather, he states:

> Indeed, the divisions that we establish between our sciences, although not arbitrary (as some believe them), are essentially artificial. In reality, the subject of all our researches is a single unified subject. We divide it up only in order to separate the difficulties from one another, so as to improve our prospects of solving them.[46]

Nevertheless, the order that he gives for the sciences – first mathematics, then the physical sciences, and so forth – expresses a hierarchical classification fundamental to his thesis. It gives the historical order in which the sciences have become, or will become, positive, a matter that Comte relates to the complexity of the phenomena that the respective science treats:

> The sciences have become positive, one after the other, in the order ... of the greater or lesser complexity of the phenomena that they treat ... Thus, first astronomical phenomena, being the most simple, and then successively physics, chemistry and physiology were developed into positive theories, the latter only recently.[47]

Moreover, this hierarchy corresponds naturally to the relational structures between the sciences in their positive state. Comte states that 'the primary goal that one must keep in sight in all encyclopaedic work is to arrange the sciences in their natural sequential order in accordance with their mutual dependency. In this way one can expound them successively without being dragged into even the smallest vicious circle.'[48] Thus, this hierarchy expresses the fact that each science will draw on the concepts and results of the sciences preceding it in the classification, but not on the concepts and results of the sciences following it in the classification.

Furthermore, the hierarchy is crucial for the further development of Comte's theory, providing him with a framework for extending the reach of the scientific method to new areas of thought, specifically to what came to be known as the human sciences. In the fourth volume of the *Philosophie positive* Comte introduced *sociology* (*sociologie*), a term of his own creation to denote the study of human society through the application of scientific thought.[49] Sociology as Comte initially defined it included the entire range of the human sciences, from history to moral science, and he stipulated that it was to be 'the last of the fundamental sciences'.[50] However, he later amended his schema to separate out moral science, placing it above sociology in the hierarchy, and then deemed this to be the last of the fundamental sciences. I discuss Comte's science of morality in Chapter 3.

Four points should be noted. First, to a considerable extent Comte's hierarchy expresses the current generally accepted view of the relationship between the various sciences. Thus, the philosopher of science Rom Harré offers an uncontroversial illustration from the physical sciences:

When Pasteur tested the hypothesis that the spores of anthrax bacilli were carried to the surface of the earth by earthworms, he had to assume the laws of optics because he had to trust the microscope. Failure to find the spores in the digestive tracts of worms might have been due to an unknown optical effect, just as his success in finding them depended on assuming that what he saw with the microscope was really an enlarged view of some very small things.[51]

Second, to a considerable extent the current generally accepted view of the relationship between the sciences accepts the idea of a hierarchy extending from the physical to the human sciences. Thus, the historian E. H. Carr observes:

[T]he historian is entitled to rely on what have been called the 'auxiliary sciences' of history – archaeology, epigraphy, numismatics, chronology, and so forth. The historian is not required to have the special skills which enable the expert to determine the origin and period of a fragment of pottery or marble, to decipher an obscure inscription, or to make the elaborate astronomical calculations necessary to establish a precise date. These so-called basic facts, which are the same for all historians, commonly belong to the category of the raw materials of the historian rather than of history itself.[52]

Note also that nothing in Comte's hierarchy or in any current view requires each science to draw *only* on the science immediately below it. Thus, for example, history (as part of sociology in Comte's scheme) is higher in the hierarchy than biology, because it needs to draw on the results of biology, and biology is likewise higher than chemistry. But history is free to draw directly on the results of chemistry, as, for example, it might do if the historical development of science were the topic for investigation.

Third, the basic idea of extending the reach of scientific thought was not original to Comte but had been widely mooted for some time. Comte himself traced the idea back to 'the noble aim suggested by Bacon' of extending the scientific method to moral and social conceptions.[53] Closer to Comte's era, Condorcet had already proposed that various aspects of human affairs, including history and politics, could be studied by the method of the sciences, although Comte dismissed Condorcet's efforts and insisted that a fresh start must be made.[54] And Mill observed in his critique of Comte and positivism that various political philosophers and political economists were already convinced that social phenomena conform to laws that could be discovered by, essentially, the scientific method. However, he acknowledged Comte's contribution in developing such a conviction into a structured thesis.[55]

Fourth, Comte went beyond his precursors in proposing to develop sociology not only as the study of human affairs but also as a plan for the reorganization of society. To do this he developed his concept of a positive science in a way that allowed him to shift sociology from a descriptive to a prescriptive enterprise. I discuss his development of positive science in the next chapter, and go on in Chapter 3 to consider how he made the move from description to prescription.

2

The Structure of a Positive Science

i. Juridical and scientific laws

In the previous chapter I used the term 'law' exclusively in the sense of a *scientific* law. That is, roughly speaking, as a descriptive statement of coherence in the behaviour of real-world entities that has been derived by inductive reasoning from observations. But it is convenient at this stage to interrupt the discussion of Comte's thesis to note that 'law' also has a *juridical* sense. This, again roughly speaking, is the sense of an authoritative prescription governing or authorizing conduct. In every language that I know there is a single term reasonably equivalent to 'law' that similarly encompasses both the scientific and juridical senses. Moreover, in all these languages the juridical sense was conceptually and linguistically prior to the scientific, by many centuries.

The term 'law' in English originated with the sense of *placing* or *setting down*. It soon derived the sense of a commandment that is set down by authority, human or divine.[1] Thus, the first sense was essentially juridical law. However, in so far as divine authority had not only prescribed human conduct but also ordered the material universe, it was easy to extend the notion of divine law to encompass the material universe. 'The "laws of nature", by those who first used the term ["laws"] in this sense, were viewed as commands imposed by the Deity upon matter.'[2] This was typically the medieval view of the universe, as based on the Aristotelian scheme supported by the Roman Catholic Church. It rested squarely on the structural premise of a perfect deity as the creator of the universe, and permitted the deduction of laws of nature.

This premise was particularly fruitful in astronomy. An immediate deduction was that a perfect deity would create perfect celestial bodies and ordain that they move in perfect figures. Since the circle was the most perfect figure, the orbit of any planet must be a circle. (The scheme was later modified to improve the fit with observational data, but the modified scheme retained the perfection of circles.) Moreover, since the earth was central in the divine scheme and the planets were perfect as celestial bodies, the earth must lie at the centre of every circular planetary orbit. These then were laws of nature derived from the basic structural premise. They provided a coherent worldview resting firmly on fundamental postulates about the inherent nature of things.

But it took some time before 'law' came to be used for the results derived from scientific investigations. To understand why, consider some crucial results of the early seventeenth century derived from astronomical observations: Kepler's three famous discoveries regarding planetary motion. It is enough here to consider the first of these, that the planets travel not in circles about the earth as centre but in ellipses about the sun as focus.[3] Nowadays we call this Kepler's first law of planetary motion, but it is not surprising that at the time it did not in itself suggest extrapolating 'law' from the juridical to the scientific context. While its close fit with observational data rapidly won it widespread acceptance, it did not provide a structural sense of the universe. Kepler offered no profound explanation for elliptical orbits, which therefore appeared as an inexplicable isolated fact that contradicted the Aristotelian scheme without offering a viable alternative to it.

Scientific astronomy could compete with the Aristotelian scheme only when it began to produce deeper results that revealed structural coherence in the universe. The most important of these was the conclusion, largely due to Isaac Newton, that the gravitational attraction between two bodies is inversely proportional to the square of the distance between them. This offered a coherent fundamental principle that could readily be seen as the manifestation of a divine prescription, and thus in terms of the action of a law. Via this route the sense of 'law' was extrapolated from the juridical to the scientific context, beginning in the latter part of the seventeenth century and becoming established in the eighteenth.[4] Newton's conclusion itself quickly became known as the inverse-square law of gravitational attraction. Newton later succeeded in deriving Kepler's conclusions from the inverse-square law,[5] whereupon they took their place within a comprehensive schema and were also regarded as laws.

In the seventeenth century the fledgling scientific approach surely gained social and political credibility by this association with the established prestige of law. It must also have gained intellectual credibility, as this association would have suggested that a scientific law applied fairly and without bias would provide as predictable and reliable a route to reaching the truth as supposedly would a juridical law similarly applied, each in its respective context. This of course does not deny the possibility of scepticism regarding the application of laws, in either the juridical or the scientific context.

A gradual shift in focus followed. Scientists may well have continued to believe in a divine prescription underlying the laws that they discovered, but they became less concerned with trying to derive conclusions directly from the presumed nature of the divine prescription. Although Kepler himself continued to seek scientific explanations in terms of some divinely ordained notion of perfection or harmony in the universe,[6] in due course the kind of religious mysticism that forms a theme within his works disappeared from scientific writings. Rather, scientists came to focus on their data and the conclusions they derived from them by induction, in a form of writing increasingly familiar to modern science. In this way, the sense of prescription disappeared from scientific laws, and they became perceived as purely descriptive.

Somewhat later the term 'positive' came to be applied to scientific laws, but it had long since been applied to juridical laws. The term originated with the sense of *placing* or *setting down*, and soon acquired the sense of being certain and precise.[7] It quickly came to be associated with law, and in due course 'positive law' came largely to mean law that had been explicitly laid down, particularly by human authority, rather than natural law. 'By the end of the twelfth century, the canonists had created the term *ius positivum*, or positive law, to describe law promulgated by a human legislator.'[8] (The fact that in the expression 'positive law' the two words have similar origins of meaning stems from the quirk of the English language that 'law' serves for both an individual edict and the juridical system.)[9] This usage supported the idea that the application of positive law was certain and precise. Thus, when applied to the newly developing sciences it supported a similar idea of their certainty and precision.

Before leaving the subject of juridical laws, which I shall take up again in Part III, I note a danger of terminological confusion in how different disciplines, and even different writers within disciplines, tend to use 'law' and certain other closely associated terms, particularly 'norm', 'principle' and 'rule'. In jurisprudence, many writers distinguish these notions, but rarely give clear definitions. Very roughly speaking, they appear to use 'norm' for general prescriptive or deontological guidance, 'principle' for somewhat more specific guidance, 'law' (in the sense of individual edict) for a more specific stipulation, and 'rule' for a narrow and precise stipulation. However, some writers allow the use of 'norm' for virtually any prescription, even one so specific as a verdict in an individual case; these writers may reserve 'rule' for a prescription that can be applied repeatedly in a range of cases. Yet other writers use 'rule' for a prescription, whether general or specific, that is deemed to be binding by virtue of a supposedly authoritative source having declared it, but 'principle' for a prescription that is deemed to be binding by virtue of some claimed intrinsic merit. In general these are often vague and sometimes inconsistent distinctions, and unsurprisingly many of the various arguments based on them tend to be shaky.

Other disciplines appear not to draw quite the same range of distinctions, although again clear definitions are rare. Very roughly speaking, moral philosophy uses 'norm' much as does jurisprudence in the first sense given above, that of a general prescription, but often uses 'rule' in a sense that seems largely to cover the spectrum that 'principle', 'law' and 'rule' together cover in jurisprudence. Here again, arguments are built on these vague distinctions and they tend to be shaky. In the physical sciences, 'norm' is rarely if ever used; 'principle' is confined largely to matters of scientific method; 'law' is used for descriptive statements of coherence derived from induction, whether broad or narrow; and 'rule' is often used for heuristically derived statements of coherence, although it may also be used in the same sense as 'law'. Physical scientists do not generally base arguments on these or similar differences. However, philosophers of science sometimes do so, and in particular Mill – with a shaky argument – criticized Comte for failing to distinguish narrow laws ('empirical laws' in Mill's terminology) from broader laws ('causal laws') in his theory.[10]

From now on, until Part III, I use 'law' only in the scientific and not the juridical sense. This sense will be refined in the following sections.

ii. The epistemology of a positive science

I noted in Chapter 1 that a common view in Comte's era was that scientific laws were ideally to be expressed in mathematical terms. This view developed in regard to the physical sciences, but a number of thinkers hoped for a similar development regarding the sciences of humanity that were being mooted. This hope persisted. Bertrand Russell, recalling his youth in the intellectual context of the 1880s, stated: 'I liked to think of the applications of mathematics to the physical world, and I hoped that in time there would be a mathematics of human behaviour as precise as the mathematics of machines.'[11] In some of the human sciences (economics is a clear example) efforts to establish a complete mathematical formulation continued through much of the twentieth century.

Comte certainly recognizes the fundamental importance of mathematics, declaring that '[i]t is through mathematics that positive philosophy began its formation, and it is from mathematics that we have the *positive method*'.[12] He even writes regarding mathematics that 'from a purely logical point of view, this science is . . . universal. For there is no question whatsoever that cannot ultimately be framed in terms of determining quantities in their relations to one another, and consequently as reducible, in the final analysis, to a simple question of numbers.'[13]

However, Comte now distinguishes actual from logical possibilities. Although *logically* all phenomena are describable in mathematical terms, Comte continues that 'to obtain an appropriate idea of [the actual role of] mathematical science . . . it is no less vital to consider the major real limitations that, in view of the weakness of our intelligence, sharply restrict its zone of effective application'.[14] Otherwise humanity will waste its efforts 'in a chimerical search for an impossible perfection'.[15] This would be contrary to the first of the five senses that Comte ascribes to 'positive', as I discussed in Chapter 1.

Thus, taking human capabilities into account, Comte argues that '[t]he essential condition for phenomena to allow description by mathematical laws *capable of being discovered* is clearly that the various quantities entailed in their description can take the form of fixed numbers'.[16] This, he concludes, precludes a mathematical formulation for the biological sciences, because 'a particular characteristic of physiological phenomena . . . is that they show an extreme numerical instability . . . under the influence of a host of circumstances . . . so that any idea of fixed numbers, and so of mathematical laws *that we could hope to establish*, entails a genuine contradiction with the special nature of this class of phenomena'.[17] Comte further insists that since 'every idea . . . of a mathematical law has already been rejected in biology . . . it must *a fortiori* be utterly excluded from the yet more complex investigations of sociology'.[18]

We have seen in Chapter 1 that each science will draw on the concepts and results of the sciences preceding it in Comte's hierarchical classification. But since the laws of a discipline such as astronomy can be expressed largely in mathematical terms whereas those of sociology cannot, it follows that sciences higher in the hierarchy cannot draw their *entire* conceptual framework from those lower in the hierarchy. Comte accepts this as part of an important general principle:

> Each science in its process of development has subjected the general positive method to modifications determined by the phenomena specific to that science . . . Only thus has each science acquired its defining character, which must never be confused with that of any other fundamental science.[19]

In modern usage, *each science develops its own epistemology* by modifying and extending the epistemologies of the sciences below it in the hierarchy.

Comte uses the term 'materialism' (*matérialisme*) for the contrary view that all sciences have the same epistemology, or that each science can be reduced to those below it in the hierarchy. He rejects this as entailing 'the imminent disruption of the higher studies under the blind domination of the lower'.[20] He finds regrettable evidence of this 'materialism' at every step in the hierarchy, including 'in the constant tendency of the most eminent biologists to conceive social science as a simple corollary or appendix of their own'.[21] His particular basis for rejecting 'materialism' in the step from biology to sociology is that it ignores 'the indispensable primacy of historical analysis' in the sciences of human behaviour.[22] This is remarkably consonant with present-day sentiments, and I discuss it further in Chapter 4.

iii. Laws and causes

Comte continues the development of his scheme by declaring a fundamental limitation on positive thought and investigation:

> Our proper studies are strictly confined to the analysis of phenomena to discover their effective *laws*, that is the constant relationships of succession or similarity between them, and have nothing whatsoever to do with their inner nature, nor their *cause*, whether primary or ultimate . . . Every hypothesis that oversteps these limits of the positive sphere can produce nothing but interminable discussions, as it claims to pronounce on questions that are necessarily insoluble for our intelligence.[23]

The rejection of activities that are beyond human intelligence and that lead to interminable discussions is in accord with the senses of positivism that Comte gives, as I discussed in Chapter 1. The specific rejection of investigation into the causes of phenomena is directed against the theological and metaphysical precursors of positivism, as quickly becomes clear from Comte's major illustration of the distinction he wishes to draw. He takes Newton's inverse-square law, as discussed in the previous section, as his example of analysis in terms of laws. This provides a suitable context because Comte regards astronomy as a firmly established positive science. He declares:

> We say that the general phenomena of the universe are *explained* – to the extent that they are subject to explanation – by Newton's law of gravitation because, on the one hand, this beautiful theory shows us all the immense variety of astronomical facts as being nothing but the consideration from different points of view of one and the same fact: the constant attraction of all objects towards each other in direct proportion to their masses and in inverse proportion to the square of the distance between them. And, on the other hand, this general fact is presented to us as a simple extension of a phenomenon that is eminently familiar to us, and that, by reason of this alone, we regard as perfectly known: the weight of bodies on the surface of the earth. As for determining what this attraction and this weight are in themselves, or what their causes are, these are questions that we regard as quite insoluble, that are not the concern of positive philosophy, and that we rightly leave to the imagination of theologians or the subtleties of metaphysicians.[24]

In contrast to the Newtonian analysis of astronomical phenomena, we have seen that the Aristotelian scheme offered an analysis in terms of the perfection of the creator as an ultimate cause. This is just the kind of approach that Comte rejects. The limitation that he imposes is a strong one, under which a sufficient explanation for phenomena – and indeed all that can possibly count as an explanation – is merely one that gives a coherent description of the succession of related events. Put otherwise, '[t]he true spirit of positivism consists above all of always substituting the determination of *how* [phenomena are related] for the determination of *why* [they occur]'.[25]

There are three obvious problems with Comte's approach. The first is terminological. Comte wishes to distinguish the investigation of causes from the investigation of relationships of succession, but in common parlance the term 'cause' (in both French and English) is itself widely used in specifying relationships of succession between phenomena. It can specify such a relationship directly, as in 'imbibing alcohol causes intoxication', or it can do so indirectly by introducing a further phenomenon that underlies the relationship, as in 'the rotation of the earth about its axis causes the succession of day and night'. Consequently, I try to avoid the common usage of 'cause' in discussing Comte's work, although it is not easy to do so. Indeed Comte himself occasionally slips and uses 'cause' in its common sense, and also cannot avoid other essentially equivalent terms.[26]

The second problem is substantive. In many contexts, there is no clear distinction between a cause and a relationship of succession. Moreover, any distinction that there is may be unstable, since as science progresses an enquiry that would formerly have seemed a futile investigation into causes can later become a positive investigation into scientific laws. For example, gravitational attraction and terrestrial weight are no longer the irreducible concepts that they appeared to be in Comte's day.

The third problem is what is generally known as Hume's problem of induction. Hume's problem is that there is no absolute way to distinguish a relationship of succession between phenomena from a mere series of prior coincidences that, for all anyone knows, might not continue in the future. However, Comte seems to assume that this distinction can be made, thus in effect ignoring Hume's problem. I consider Comte's view of induction in Chapter 4, but note in the meantime that for Comte the task of identifying relationships of succession is necessarily one for each science to undertake in accordance with its epistemology. Arguably, no science can progress unless its epistemology in effect finesses Hume's problem.

Comte unreservedly applies his principle of analysing in terms of laws rather than causes to all the positive sciences. As I discussed in Chapter 1, he holds that the sciences of humanity will eventually become positive. They will therefore become subject to this principle. In this context the principle is of course considerably more controversial than in the area of observational astronomy.

iv. The predictive power of science

It will be helpful in this section to begin with a survey of certain aspects of the process of scientific investigation. This will raise a range of issues, of which some will be briefly discussed, others will be postponed for later consideration, and one will remain as the subject matter of this section.

Let us then imagine a scientist about to begin an investigation. The first issue concerns her initial mind-set; that is, whether her mind should be regarded as, say, a *tabula rasa* open to the inscription of any and all observations, or whether it already, even before beginning the investigation, possesses a developed worldview. I shall consider this question in the context of the epistemologies of Comte and Mill in Chapter 4.

The scientist now decides on her topic of investigation. The issue for this stage concerns whether she forms a tentative hypothesis regarding the expected results of her observations before she actually makes any observations. Nowadays this is of course normal procedure and constitutes a crucial stage of the dominant hypothetico-deductive method in scientific investigation. However, in the eighteenth and nineteenth centuries there was considerable controversy over whether such hypothesizing was proper for scientists, with a number of writers arguing that it led one astray and that only a mind devoid of all preconceptions could properly experiment, observe and reason.[27] This view survived at least in popular literary imagination well into the twentieth century.[28] Plainly, this issue is closely related to that of the initial mind-set of the scientist.

However, Comte's view is close to the modern scientific approach:

> [Without] the introduction . . . of hypotheses in natural philosophy . . . there would clearly be no effective way to set about discovering natural laws. But the use of this powerful device must be constantly subject to a fundamental condition . . . [which is] that one must imagine only hypotheses that by their nature are subject to positive verification.[29]

Combining this with Comte's views on laws and causes, as I discussed in the previous section, shows that under positivism it is acceptable, and indeed indispensable, to hypothesize about the laws governing phenomena. The observations or experiments that ensue will subject the hypotheses to positive verification. However, it is not acceptable to hypothesize about primary or ultimate causes. These are not subject to positive verification, so the hypothesizing is merely futile.

In this connection, Comte warns against the propensity of the physical sciences of his era to invent imaginary entities, such as the ether, as a supposed route to explaining phenomena. He sees this as overstepping the limits of positivism, and destined to lead only to endless discussions.[30] However, a problem with this is that imaginary entities can be essential in developing scientific laws. As it turned out, Comte was correct that the ether was a relatively worthless imaginary entity for this purpose. Yet electric and magnetic fields are equally imaginary entities that were extremely valuable in developing scientific laws. Comte does allow that in some cases it might be worthwhile to hypothesize entities under strict limitations.[31]

Next, the scientist carries out her observations, which in some cases will derive from experiments, and sets down the results. This raises issues of the reliability of observations, which I consider in Chapter 4. Following this, the scientist applies induction to formulate a scientific law from the results of her observations. Such a law might be narrow and specific or broad and general. She may now verify the law by checking that it holds in further situations that (she argues) are similar in appropriate respects to those from which the law has been derived. If the law survives the verification process it is deemed valid, at least in the current state of scientific knowledge. I consider the issues raised by these processes of induction and verification in Chapter 4, in relation to the epistemological differences between Comte and Mill.

The scientist has now derived a law that describes a structure of connections between phenomena or events. If we ignore laws expressed in probabilistic terms, as Comte does,[32] a scientific law tells us what, under given preconditions, happens. No specific time reference is implied in the verb 'happens' here, as I now discuss. A scientific law is not merely a restatement in structured terms of the particular observations from which it was derived. Rather, a properly derived and validated scientific law is claimed to apply in all situations similar in appropriate respects to those from which the law was derived. Thus, when Newton set down his law of gravitational attraction he presented it as applicable to all bodies in all places and at all times. He certainly did not consider it limited to the particular bodies that he had observed acting under its influence, and at the particular times that he had observed them.

Consequently, scientific laws will apply in situations yet to occur. Thus, they are able to tell us what, under given preconditions, *will happen*. That is, the law enables us to *predict* future events. For example, if the law in question is Newton's law of gravitational attraction it allows me to predict that if I drop a stone from a tower it will fall to earth.

But we can say more than this. Suppose that at some point in the past there was a situation satisfying the preconditions of some scientific law. Suppose also that this situation was sufficiently far in the past that the events that the law would predict would also have occurred in the past. Although all relevant events are in the past, we can still apply the law to tell us what *must have happened* at that past time. Thus, for example, if I dropped a stone from a tower yesterday morning the law tells me that it *must have fallen* to earth yesterday.

This analysis is the foundation of Comte's view of scientific prediction (*prévision*), which, as he understands it, is not confined to foretelling the future from the past. Rather, 'scientific prediction clearly applies equally to the present, the past and the future'.[33]

And we can say yet more. Suppose that when I dropped the stone from the tower yesterday morning I actually watched it as it fell to earth. I do not now need Newton's law of gravitational attraction to tell me that this happened. However, the law still has an application in this situation: it *connects* or *relates* the fact that I dropped the stone with the fact that it fell to earth. Put otherwise, the law of gravitational attraction *explains* the stone's falling to earth as a consequence of my dropping it from the tower. Thus, depending on when events occurred and what we know of them, scientific laws can be used for prediction or for explanation equally. This indeed is Comte's conclusion, that '[w]hether it is a matter . . . of explaining or predicting, everything always comes down to making connections. Every genuine connection . . . discovered between any two phenomena allows both explanation and prediction of one in terms of the other'.[34]

Despite this conclusion, the idea of predicting the future from the past plays a crucial role in Comte's scheme. He develops this role in several stages. First, he ties the idea of predicting the future from the past into the development of science:

> In fact, all men, however little advanced they may be, make true predictions, and always on the basis of the same principle: deriving knowledge of the future from knowledge of the past. For example, all of them predict the general effects of weight, as well as a host of other phenomena that are sufficiently simple and of sufficiently common occurrence for their effects and consequences to be obvious to the least accomplished and least observant onlooker. *In each person, the measure of his ability to predict is the extent of his scientific knowledge.* The astronomer who predicts the state of the solar system a great number of years ahead with perfect accuracy is engaging in exactly the same kind of predictive process as the savage who predicts the next sunrise. The only difference lies in the extent of their respective scientific knowledge.[35]

Having made this association between science and prediction, he passes easily to the next stage, which is to declare that the capacity to predict the future is the *test* of a positive science. Thus, he refers to 'this [capacity for] rational prediction that we have seen constitutes, in every respect, the primary character of true science'.[36] Note that Comte offers here only a negative test for a positive science: any philosophical structure that lacks predictive power cannot be a positive science. This test continues to have considerable support.[37] He does *not* offer any affirmative test for a positive science here. Specifically, he does not claim that no philosophical structure other than a positive science can have predictive power. This is understandable, since, as he is surely aware, he has no basis *within the positivist framework* for asserting the falsity of the various ambitious theological and metaphysical predictions that have been made. Thus, Comte does not claim that predictive power distinguishes positive science from theology or metaphysics.[38]

Next, Comte declares that 'it is the *aim* of every positive science to predict the future from the past'.[39] Positivism and predictive power are now essentially united. 'Thus, the true positivist spirit consists above all in observing in order to predict, and in studying what there is in order to determine from it what there will be, according to the general principle of invariability in the laws of nature.'[40]

Now he is ready to extend this unification of positive science with predictive power to the sciences of humanity. Comte was not the first to consider this. Condorcet had already declared:

> If humanity can predict with almost complete assurance the phenomena of which it knows the laws . . . why should one regard it as fanciful to trace out a likely picture of the future destiny of the human race, based on the events of its history? . . . [T]he general laws . . . that rule the phenomena of the universe are necessary and uniform. Why should this principle be less valid for the development of human intellectual and moral faculties than for other natural processes?[41]

Comte takes up this theme, declaring that '[i]t is thus clearly wholly in keeping with the nature of humanity that observation of the past should be able to reveal the future, in the political sciences just as in astronomy, physics, chemistry and physiology'.[42] Here of course the political sciences are representative of the social sciences as a whole. He concludes with the ultimate aspiration of positivism in this regard:

> The ultimate perfection of science, which will likely never be completely attained, consists, in regard to theory, of determining exactly . . . the advances made from one generation to another. This applies equally to the social order, every science, every art, and every part of

the political organization. And in regard to practice it consists of completely determining in every essential detail the social system that by the natural progress of civilization is bound to prevail.[43]

Finally, he begins to shift from the sciences of humanity as purely social description to the sciences of humanity as the basis for social action. He declares that 'one must view the study of nature as providing the true rational basis for the action of humanity on nature, for the knowledge of the laws of nature that allows us to predict phenomena clearly gives us the only way actively to modify phenomena to our advantage'.[44] In his well-known summary: '*science enables prediction; and prediction enables action*'.[45] Moreover, it now quickly becomes the goal of positivism 'to regulate the present in accordance with the desired future as deduced from the past'.[46] I explore the development of this theme in the next chapter.

3
Positivist Social Reorganization

i. Order and progress

I concluded the previous chapter with the observation that Comte uses the idea of prediction in the sciences to shift from the sciences of humanity as purely social description to the sciences of humanity as the basis for social action. This should remind us that even when Comte presents his thesis in theoretical terms he has his political goals in view and remains always focused on the realization of those goals. In the present chapter I explore his grand scheme of social reorganization for implementing the social developments that his philosophy has predicted.

As I discussed, Comte has stipulated that when the human sciences become positive they will be able to predict the future course of social development. Given that they become positive sciences, what they predict is bound to occur; this, after all, is the test for a positive science. Comte insists on this:

> The fundamental law that governs the natural progress of civilization strictly prescribes all the successive stages through which the human race is bound to pass in its process of development . . . The course of development of civilization that derives from this law is therefore essentially unalterable in its fundamental aspects. More precisely, none of the intermediate stages that it prescribes can be avoided, and no really retrograde step can be made.[1]

He further argues that failure to recognize this inevitable process has led to a false approach to history, in which:

One sees only individuals, and never the irresistible forces that drive them. Instead of recognizing the primary influence of civilization, history displays the efforts of these individuals who anticipated events as if they were the actual causes of the improvements that took place, and that would have taken place anyway, if just a little later, without their involvement . . . In short, following the ingenious expression of Mme de Staël, this kind of history mistakes the actors for the play. Such an error is of exactly the same kind as that of the Indians who attributed to Christopher Columbus the eclipse that he had predicted.[2]

This seems clear enough. But Comte has also stipulated that prediction enables action, which allows him to shift from descriptive philosophy to social prescription. The question is why he needs to shift. He has insisted that the course of social development is inevitable, as determined by positive laws, and this after all must remain the case whether or not we yet know these laws. So how can any action be necessary? What point is there in directing action towards a goal that is in any event inevitable?

The point, Comte argues, is that although no individual can much affect the course of social development, yet the actions of a mass of people can do so more substantially:

The course of civilization is somewhat modifiable in its rate of progress, and within certain limits, by various physical and moral causes that can be assessed. Among these causes are the actions of political groups. This is the only kind of way in which humanity can affect the course of its own civilization.[3]

In particular, Comte notes, a mass of people trying to oppose the inevitable process of social development can do substantial harm by causing social upheaval that may lead to violent revolution. He declares this implicitly, although nonetheless clearly, in a statement that 'the true and essential goal of practical politics is to avoid the violent revolutions that arise from opposition to the progress of civilization'.[4]

The prospect of revolution troubled Comte deeply, and it is reasonable to relate this to the political turmoil of late eighteenth- and early nineteenth-century France. In any event, the need to avoid revolution now becomes a guiding force in his work. Note that by declaring this need, and stipulating that it is the goal of practical politics, Comte has introduced his own substantive principle of what is good for humanity into the positivist scheme. This again assists him in shifting sociology from a descriptive to a prescriptive science of humanity.

Comte is therefore in search of a way to sustain society in its progress towards the positive state while avoiding revolutionary upsets in the social order. But looking back through a period of revolutionary crises, he observes that these have been conflicting goals:

> For the past half-century, in which the revolutionary crisis of modern societies has developed its true character, . . . a thoroughly reactionary approach has constantly ensured that all major social efforts are directed in favour of maintaining order. Meanwhile, the main efforts undertaken on behalf of achieving progress have always been carried out under radically anarchic doctrines . . . This is the profoundly vicious circle in which present-day society struggles so futilely.[5]

Indeed, Comte notes, 'since antiquity order and progress have been viewed as fundamentally irreconcilable'.[6]

Comte rejects this supposed opposition, declaring that '[n]o genuine, lasting state of social order can be maintained unless it is fully compatible with progress, and moreover there can be no substantial progress unless its end result is to consolidate the social order'.[7] However, the question remains whether it is in fact possible to achieve the harmony between order and progress that will allow society to escape its vicious circle. Comte now declares that this will be achieved by 'the positivist socio-political scheme, since what particularly characterizes it is its ability to unite order and progress as two wholly inseparable aspects of a single principle'.[8] Thus, 'the fundamental reconciliation between order and progress constitutes the distinguishing prerogative of positivism . . . The maintenance of order will become the permanent precondition for progress, while the achievement of progress will be the permanent goal of order.'[9]

Comte ties this reconciliation between order and progress into the structure of positive science. He begins by asserting a distinction between two kinds of scientific laws:

> For every category of events, the scientific laws must . . . be distinguished as of two kinds, according to whether they declare a relationship of similarity or harmony between phenomena that coexist, or whether they declare a relationship of inevitable succession between phenomena that follow one upon the other . . . this is the

basis of the fundamental distinction between *static* and *dynamic* analysis that is found in every discipline.[10]

His idea here is that the laws of similarity or harmony determine static relationships, whereas the laws of succession determine dynamic relationships. He can now connect the relationship between order and progress to the relationship between the two kinds of scientific laws. Introducing the division of scientific laws, Comte refers to it as 'a happy combination of stability and activity, from which result the simultaneous need for order and progress'.[11] Thus, static laws are to correspond to order and dynamic laws to progress. Under positivism, the two kinds of laws are brought together under the universal rubric of laws of relationship.[12] This corresponds to bringing together order and progress within the positivist scheme.

ii. The theory of social reorganization

Comte begins his analysis of how society should be reorganized by criticizing the attempts of the preceding period that, as I discussed in the previous section, he regards as one of continuing revolutionary crises. This period had seen the production of a number of popular constitutions, an approach that Comte sees as having completely misunderstood the gravity of the social situation:

> The great number of so-called constitutions that the people have brought forth since the beginning of the crisis period, and the excessive meticulousness of drafting that all of them to a greater or lesser extent display, would alone suffice to show . . . that up to now the nature and difficulty of forming a plan for social reorganization have not been recognized.[13]

Rather, he argues, a social system cannot be so readily constructed. In the spirit of his positivist system, he draws a parallel with the construction of a physical science:

> When any science whatsoever is reconstructed on a new theoretical basis . . . first of all the main principle is declared, discussed, and settled on. Then it takes an extended and laborious process to work out the structure that coordinates all the various parts of the science – a structure that no one, not even the discoverer of the principle, could have initially conceived. Thus, for example, after Newton had

discovered the law of universal gravitation it took nearly a century of extremely difficult work . . . to reconstruct astronomy on this law as foundation . . . If humanity always has to follow such a course in undertaking revolutions that, despite their importance and difficulty, nevertheless concern only a specific area, then it has been both frivolous and presumptuous to follow the course that has so far been taken in regard to the most general, momentous, and difficult of all revolutions – that which aims at completely recasting the social system![14]

Comte now introduces a crucial distinction. He declares that such inappropriate approaches to social reorganization have been taken because 'the people have not so far understood the great work of social reorganization. In seeking to specify in what way they have failed to recognize the nature of this work, one finds that they have viewed as purely *practical* a task that is really *theoretical*.'[15] He explains this distinction as follows:

The development of any plan of social organization necessarily comprises two categories of works that are completely distinct, both in their purpose and in the kind of human abilities that they demand. One, theoretical or spiritual, aims at developing the formative principle of the plan . . . and the system of general ideas that will guide society. The other, practical or temporal, determines how power is to be distributed and what administrative institutions should be set up; it does this in complete conformity with the true ethos of the system as already fixed by the theoretical part of the plan. Since the work of practice is based on the work of theory . . . the general enterprise must necessarily begin with the work of theory. It is . . . the most important and difficult part of the enterprise.[16]

He goes on to consider how the first, theoretical phase in the process of reorganization is to be carried out. He begins by observing that 'whenever society needs any kind of theoretical work done, it recognizes that it must go to the appropriate class of experts (*savants*)'.[17] As to what the appropriate class is, '[s]ince this is theoretical work, it is clear that . . . the experts engaged with the sciences of observation are the only ones with the capabilities and intellectual culture to satisfy the necessary conditions . . . Only the education . . . that results from the study of the sciences of observation can develop their natural theoretical capacity in the proper way.'[18]

It follows that Comte's scheme will exclude the great mass of the people from the theoretical phase of socio-political reorganization. Moreover, since the theoretical plan will serve as the foundation for the practice phase of reorganization, it follows that the great mass of the people will have little influence on the eventual structure of the new positivist order. So Comte's insistence that the theory phase should be the exclusive province of scientific experts will ultimately conflict with popular principles of social organization, and in particular with the principle of the sovereignty of the people.

Even this conclusion, which Comte fully recognizes, is not enough to give him pause. Indeed, he embraces this conclusion and relates it to the political history of human society. In his view, '[t]he doctrine of the sovereignty of the people . . . was created to combat the principle of divine right, which was the general political basis of the ancient system'.[19] The problem now is that 'the prevailing opinion among the people as to how society should be reorganized . . . presents the principles of mere criticism that were useful in destroying the feudal and theological system as if they were organic, creative principles'.[20] These principles of criticism are thus given an inappropriate role, which has a theoretical and a practical manifestation. 'The principle in its theoretical manifestation is the doctrine of unlimited freedom of conscience . . . The principle in its practical manifestation is the doctrine of the sovereignty of the people, which is nothing but the political application of the principle of unlimited liberty of conscience.'[21]

These doctrines are the manifestations of a view under which '[g]overnment is no longer regarded as the leader of society whose role is to bind all individual activities together and direct them towards a common goal, but rather as a natural enemy'.[22] As such, neither doctrine will be of value in the new positive order. 'The doctrine of the sovereignty of the people can no longer serve as the political basis of social reorganization, while the doctrine of freedom of conscience can no longer be its moral basis. Both were created as agents of destruction, and both are equally unsuited to serve as foundations.'[23]

Plainly, abandoning the principles of freedom of conscience and the sovereignty of the people would require a major shift away from commonly accepted attitudes. Again, this conclusion is not enough to make Comte even hesitate. He declares that 'it is absolutely impossible to reorganize the political order without first reconstructing human opinions and social customs. Thus our first social need is to systematize the entirety of human thought processes, in terms of both order and progress.'[24]

The doctrine of freedom of conscience will disappear in this reconstruction. In a strong statement, Comte declares that this accords with scientific principles:

> There is no freedom of conscience whatsoever in matters of astronomy, physics, chemistry and physiology, in the sense that everyone would find it absurd not to believe with confidence in the principles that competent men have established in these sciences. In so far as it is otherwise in politics, it is because the ancient principles have fallen away but new ones have not yet been formed. In the meantime, there are, strictly speaking, no established principles. But to convert this transitory fact into an absolute and eternal dogma, and to make a fundamental maxim out of it, is to declare that society must evermore remain without general governing principles . . . Such a doctrine should . . . be reproached as anarchy.[25]

Thus, once sociology has become a positive science it will be equally absurd to dispute its findings. Although this view shocked a number of people it also gained a good deal of support at the time, including that of Mill, as I discuss in Chapter 4.

iii. The practice of social reorganization

In Comte's scheme, as I discussed in the previous section, theory must largely be developed before practice. Since the development of theory had yet to begin, it would seem that Comte would be able to say very little about practice. He recognizes this in general principle, but makes what at first appears to be a narrow exception for setting out 'the various measures that will enable the fundamental reconstruction of society'.[26] He proceeds to this in considerable detail and at great length. His main concern is to ensure that the plan for the positive reorganization of society, as developed by the scientists in the theory phase, will be successfully propagated through society. This concern has several aspects. The first is the issue of which persons or classes should be given the task of propagating the plan. The second is the issue of whether some persons or classes will be more receptive than others to the new social order. The third issue is how the new social order should be maintained after it has been successfully propagated through society.

The task of propagating the plan requires the efforts of those who were charged with creating it:

Scientific experts are the only class who exercise unchallenged authority in matters of theory. Thus, independently of the fact that they alone are qualified to form the new organic doctrine, it is also the case that they alone have the moral authority to secure its recognition by the populace. No other authority could possibly overcome the prejudice that regards each individual as invested with the right to act as a sovereign independent moral agent.[27]

But Comte is aware that the moral authority of scientists will not alone ensure successful propagation. 'It is never possible to inspire the great mass of people with passion for any system by demonstrating to them theoretically that the inevitable course of civilization has led up to it and that it is now called for to govern society . . . The only way . . . is to present them with a lively description of how the new system is bound to improve the condition of humanity, considered from all points of view. There need then be no reference to the theoretical necessity and timeliness of the new system.'[28]

Under Comte's scheme, the task of creating this lively description and presenting it to the general populace 'is the role especially reserved for the fine arts in the general work of social reorganization'.[29] With this, he can set out a profile of the entire scheme, theoretical and practical, as follows:

> Thus, all the positive forces will cooperate in this vast enterprise. The scientific experts will work out the plan of the new system. The artists will contribute to its universal adoption. The industrial leaders will establish the practical institutions needed to put it into operation. These three great forces will combine in founding the new system and, when it is established, in ensuring its day-to-day operation.[30]

As to whether some persons or classes will be more receptive than others to the new social order, Comte feels that 'of all sectors of present society, the proletariat will surely be the best disposed . . . towards favourable reception of the new positivist philosophy, which will ultimately find there its principal source of support, both intellectual and social'.[31] He develops this confidence in the proletariat relatively late in his writings. According to Comte's erstwhile disciple Émile Littré, whom I discuss in Part II, it stemmed from the favourable impression that this class made on Comte in the Paris revolution of February 1848.[32] A more mundane explanation is that Comte was responding to changes in the composition of his public following. In his earlier years, around the

1820s, many eminent scientists and intellectuals were among his followers and attended his public lectures. However, by the 1840s many of these had abandoned him. From this time on, the audiences for his public lectures consisted mainly of workers.[33]

The issue of how the new social order is to be maintained after it has been successfully propagated through society is of great importance for Comte and takes up a large part of his works. He eventually presents three separate approaches, to be combined in the social order. The first approach, with which I conclude the present section, relies on societal pressure. The second approach, which I consider in the following sections, relies on developing an internal moral sense. Finally, the third approach employs governmental power in the form of law; I consider this in Part III.

The first approach demands continuing societal pressure in the form of public opinion. This is to play a crucial role in the restructured society:

> Public opinion ... must become the chief support for morality, including not only social morality but also the most private and personal morality. Public opinion will be able to reach heretofore private matters because in the positivist order every man will be pressed to live more and more in the public gaze, so as to permit effective public control of every aspect of life. The irrevocable collapse of religious illusions renders this public control indispensable to compensate for the lack of natural morality in most men, even the well educated.[34]

Comte refers to this as 'the empire of public opinion'.[35] Recall in this connection that in Comte's scheme all matters of social and moral importance are not to be debated endlessly but rather settled once and for all, so this empire will tolerate fixed opinions only.[36]

In so far as this pervasive action of public opinion depicts a peculiarly unattractive social order, it should be borne in mind that Comte views it as the means of avoiding continuing and violent social upheavals. As he sees it, this invidious choice results from 'the lack of natural morality'. His attempt to compensate for this lack within the positivist scheme is the subject of the following sections.

iv. Society and the individual

In associating the 'collapse of religious illusions' with 'the lack of natural morality', as I discussed in the previous section, Comte reflects a longstanding debate that had been particularly active in eighteenth-century France. A major theme of this debate was whether religion exercises an essential civilizing influence on society. Voltaire, among others, had explored whether a society of atheists could properly function, and had traced the discussion back to the influential work of Pierre Bayle at the end of the seventeenth century.[37] The views expressed in this long debate ranged from an optimistic belief in a benign human nature that requires nothing like religion to order it, to a pessimistic sense (sometimes claiming Machiavelli as its inspiration) that human nature is savage unless constantly repressed.

Comte's insistence on the need for 'public control of every aspect of life' makes it plain that he rejects the former view. It might also suggest that he comes close to embracing the second, but this would overstate his pessimism. Although he does not believe that human beings are naturally moral, he does believe that they can be made moral. This will be achievable under the positivist reorganization of society, because 'positivism . . . has an inherent capacity finally to systematize human morality, which is always the primary application for every true theory of humanity'.[38]

But Comte rejects the kind of morality that religion engenders, since, in his view, 'religious thought is in its nature essentially individual and never directly collective. From the perspective of religious faith, especially monotheism, . . . human society appears only as a collection of individuals . . . each wholly concerned with his own salvation.'[39] Rather, in keeping with the ethos of positivism, he will demand a socially oriented morality. His view of positivist social morality develops over the course of his work. At a relatively early stage, he introduces a positivist moral concept that he calls *sentiment social*. I translate this here as 'social awareness', but no English term wholly captures its sense. Comte's *sentiment social* plays on association with the common term *sentiment religieux*, which can be translated as religious feeling, fervour, sentiment or thought, depending on context.

Comte describes the nature and production of social awareness as follows:

Making the genuine historical method primary in social studies has . . . the happy property of spontaneously developing social awareness, by putting plainly into evidence . . . the inherent connections between the diverse events in human history that capture our . . . immediate attention . . . by reminding us of the real influence that these events have exercised on the gradual development of our own

> civilization . . . It is crucial . . . not to confuse such a sense of social
> solidarity with the mere sympathetic interest that any common,
> merely descriptive stories (indeed, even fictions) of human life
> arouse. The sense of social awareness under consideration here is
> deeper and more reflective, and, above all, flows from a scientific
> commitment.[40]

He insists that 'positivism . . . alone is capable of developing this social
awareness, which in turn is fundamental to the development of a proper
social morality'.[41] This sense will in due course extend through society.
'Although initially confined to the elite theoreticians, the new sense of
social awareness would eventually spread universally, albeit with lesser
intensity, as the general concepts of sociology became widely available
to the populace.'[42]

In giving a powerful role to public opinion, as I discussed in the previous section, and in viewing social awareness as fundamental to the
development of morality, Comte asserts the positivist focus on society
rather than the individual. The question arises whether his aim is the
complete subsumption of individual identity within social identity. On
this crucial issue for the development of positivist morality, Comte
conveys different impressions at different points in his works. On the
one hand, he declares:

> The positive spirit . . . is, as far as possible, directly social . . . The indi-
> vidual does not actually exist for it, but only humanity, because our
> entire development, in every aspect, is due to society. If the idea of
> *society* seems a mere intellectual abstraction, this is a result of the old
> modes of thought. In fact, the idea of the *individual* is really the intel-
> lectual abstraction, at least for the human species.[43]

But on the other hand, Comte elsewhere refers to 'definitively splitting
the human social order into its two essential modes of being: the one
collective, forming social existence and the other individual, forming
moral existence'.[44]

However, one can essentially resolve such statements by considering
Comte's scheme in its intended practice. He states the relationship
between societal and individual interests as follows:

> This requires, on the one hand, determining in every case exactly
> what is required to satisfy the needs of society, and, on the other
> hand, developing the corresponding mental dispositions in every
> individual member of society. This continuing dual function requires

above all a fundamental doctrine, an appropriate education, and a well-directed public spirit. It must therefore depend primarily on the philosophical authority which positivism will install at the summit of the society that is to be.[45]

As a result of this social development of the appropriate mental dispositions, 'the most complete exercise possible of general social desires will become the main source of personal satisfaction'.[46] In sum, regarding the moral rules of the positivist social order, Comte declares:

> All persons subject to these rules will have voluntarily approved them by virtue of their education, and their regular observance of them will deserve the name of liberty.[47]

Thus, the resolution of Comte's view of society and the individual is essentially that the individual continues to exist, but with virtually all opinions and moral sense societally engendered.[48] This may appear a daunting and even a chilling prospect in itself, before even going on to consider the substantive content of the opinions and moral sense to be inculcated. However, it is worth noting that intense socialization, insistence on fixed social and political opinions, continuing pressure of public opinion, and societal inculcation of moral sense are hardly unique to Comte's scheme. Rather, these have featured in various social orders and religions throughout the world and throughout recorded history. Even the extreme degree of societal shaping and control of the individual that Comte demands is by no means unique in human experience. Arguably, it is Comte's explicitness that makes his scheme appear particularly repellent. In so far as this is the case, any critiques to which Comte's scheme gives rise regarding the principles that should govern societal shaping and control of the individual could helpfully be applied in a variety of societal contexts.

v. Positivist morality in theory and practice

Comte sees that social implementation of the conclusions of the sciences of humanity presents difficulties that social implementation of the conclusions of the physical sciences does not. Thus, as I discussed in previous sections, he stipulates that maintaining general acceptance of society's moral rules will require the relentless pressure of public opinion, but he does not suppose that this will be needed to maintain general acceptance of Newton's inverse-square law of universal gravitation. The difference is that in regard to moral matters society must overcome each individual's powerful sense of self-regard, and redirect it towards the good of society as determined by the science of sociology.

Thus, morality as a science in terms of Comte's scheme is necessarily a different enterprise from sciences lower in the hierarchy. His recognition of this ultimately affects the entire development of his scheme. He had originally categorized morality as part of sociology; now it becomes a science in its own right, at the head of the hierarchy.[49] Moreover, it is to have a special role as a link between the philosophical and political structures of the positivist scheme. Comte makes a key declaration:

> The proper function of philosophy is to integrate all the aspects of human existence into a unified theoretical structure . . . Politics has sole charge of all development of practice. The science of morality is both the connecting link and the line of demarcation between these two principal functions of the great social organism. It thus constitutes a particularly distinctive application of philosophy and serves as a general guide for the development of politics.[50]

Let us consider what this is to mean. On the one hand, Comte insists that it does not affect the status of morality as a science:

> The positive approach will finally subject moral precepts to indisputable scientific proof. The scientific laws that result from genuine knowledge of our individual and social nature will allow us to make a precise, moral assessment, in private or public life, . . . of each affection, thought, action, or habit. Belief in these assessments will be as deep as any that the strictest scientific proofs inspire today.[51]

But on the other hand, he recognizes that scientific proof of moral principles may not be sufficient to inculcate them in social practice:

> But in developing the power of scientific proof to an extent hitherto impossible, positivism will avoid exaggerating its importance for moral education . . . However intellectually sound the study of morality as a science may be, *its viewpoint cannot be directly moral*, because scientific impartiality and clarity require it to analyze in terms of the conduct of everyone, not that of any particular student of the subject. That is, as a science it must always be objective, not subjective.[52]

It follows that if positivism is to be successfully propagated through society, Comte must rethink its structure so as to bring an internal, subjective moral sense within its purview. This will require him to take a new direction in his positivist theory, which he does in the *Politique positive*. In a dedication to the first volume of this treatise, he ascribes his new direction of thought to the influence of Clotilde de Vaux, a woman whom he idealized and with whom he shared 'an incomparable year of reciprocal virtuous tenderness'[53] before her untimely death. This new direction gives human feelings a primary role in the positivist scheme. Thus, he begins the *Politique positive* with the declaration:

> Positive philosophy intends as far as possible to systematize all human existence – individual and, above all, collective – taking into account together the three classes of phenomena that constitute it: thoughts, feelings and actions.[54]

This extends 'the structure of positivism, [which] without ceasing to be theoretical and practical, must also become moral, and draw upon human feelings for its true principle of universality'.[55] Corresponding to this, the twin pillars of order and progress (which respectively correspond to theory and practice) must also be extended. Comte adds *love* to these, and can now declare his final version of the fundamental ethos of positivism:

> Love as the principle, order as the foundation, and progress as the goal. This is ... to be the essential character of the positivist social order that will structure all human existence, individual and social, on the basis of a permanent and fixed combination of feelings, thoughts and actions.[56]

In summary, there are now three fundamental aspects of Comte's scheme, and three perspectives from which to view them. The pillars of positivism are: love, order and progress. The aspects of human existence that correspond to them are, respectively: feelings, thoughts (or the intellect) and actions. The structures of the positive social order that correspond to them are, respectively: morality, theory and practice.

We saw in the previous section that Comte demands a socially oriented morality. If love is now to be the underlying principle of morality – in Comte's words, 'positive morality's unique principle of universal love will bring it into its perfectly unified form'[57] – then love too must be socially oriented. In the positivist scheme, love will become socially oriented through education, which will draw humanity through 'the three essential successive modes of human existence, first personal, then familial, and finally social, representing the gradual education of fundamental human feelings'.[58]

Three major issues arise from the addition of 'love' to the positivist scheme. First, which individuals or classes are to ensure the propagation of love (or equivalently, morality) through society? Second, what is to be the status of love in relation to order and progress? Third, how are the objective and subjective aspects of morality to relate?

As to the first issue, in Section iii I discussed Comte's views on how best to propagate the plan for reorganization of society, seen then as based on the twofold pillars of order and progress. He now considers the issue of propagating love. In a discussion that plainly owes much to his idealization of de Vaux, he argues that this is to be the special province of women. He bases his argument on romanticized stereotypes of femininity and its traditional roles, and on what he perceives as the inherent affective morality of women.[59]

Comte's exposition of this aspect of his scheme needs no further elucidation here, except to note that the role that he prescribes for women does not entail any public activity or even presence. On the contrary, he stresses that under positivism women's role will increasingly be confined within the family.[60]

The second issue is what the status of love is to be in relation to order and progress. Put otherwise, this is the issue of how (social) feelings are to relate to thoughts (the intellect) and actions. Comte insists that 'thoughts are to be systematized before feelings, and feelings are to be systematized before actions'.[61] He requires thoughts to be systematized before anything else is done, because humanity is constrained by 'the unalterable reality of the world'.[62] It is the role of the intellect (thoughts) to discover this reality and systematize it. Plainly, only when this is achieved will it be possible to develop the moral sense through education, and thereafter to set up social practice.

But this represents the limit of the role of the intellect (thoughts) in the positivist scheme. Dismissing the idea of the primacy of the intellect with the statement that '[t]he intellect is destined not to rule but to serve',[63] Comte declares:

> The intellect . . . often fails to recognize that its necessary role is one of continuous service to social feelings . . . The universe is to be studied, not for its own sake but . . . for humanity. To study it with any other purpose would be deeply in conflict with reason as much

as with morality. Unless the intellect stays within this domain, *which is determined by social feelings*, our understanding will always be partial and futile.[64]

This accords with the second of Comte's five senses of 'positivism', as I discussed in Chapter 1, which demands that all intellectual activity be directed towards improving the human condition.

From this view of the intellect, together with his analysis of morality as the link between philosophy and politics, Comte derives an important new basic principle of positivism:

> From now on it is a fundamental philosophical and political doctrine of positivism that feelings have continuing primacy over the intellect (thoughts).[65]

In terms of structures of the positive social order, this demands that all human intellectual endeavours be directed towards establishing the appropriate moral order.

The third issue is how the objective and subjective aspects of morality are to relate. Under its objective aspect, positivist morality appears as a process of scientific reasoning. In Comte's hierarchy of the sciences, morality is at the summit, beyond sociology. Sociology, as a prescriptive scientific enterprise in Comte's scheme, is to determine what is good for human society. On the basis of these sociological determinations, morality as a science is then to determine what is right for human beings to do. *There is no other basis in Comte's scheme for scientifically determining a moral principle.* Expressed in terms familiar to modern moral philosophy, in positive *philosophy* 'the good' is prior to 'the right'.

It is a different matter when we turn to positivist morality in political practice. Comte's educational scheme requires that morality be primarily inculcated as feelings, rather than demonstrated as science. In consequence, people – including political decision-makers – will rely directly on their feelings in making moral determinations. They will not rework the scientific reasoning that led to the sociological principles that led to the moral principles that govern the situation at hand. Rather, they will *experience* positivist morality as subjective, as a kind of educated moral intuition. Expressed in terms familiar to modern moral philosophy, in positive *politics* 'the right' is prior to 'the good'.

Part II
The Development of Positivism through Mill and Littré

4
Comte and Mill

i. Harmony and discord

The English liberal philosopher John Stuart Mill was intimately concerned with Comte's development of positivism for much of his life. In his earlier years he had disliked Comte's ideas, but as his intellectual and political views developed he came to find them increasingly attractive.[1] Comte's *Philosophie positive* so impressed him that he promoted it as 'very nearly the grandest work of the age'.[2] In 1841, being already in his own assessment 'an ardent admirer of Comte's writings', he initiated a correspondence with Comte that lasted over five years.[3] He wrote approvingly of Comte in his *Logic*,[4] and felt that he had 'contributed more than any one else to make . . . [Comte's] speculations known in England, [so that] . . . he had readers and admirers [there] . . . at a time when his name had not yet in France emerged from obscurity'.[5] Although Mill rejected certain of Comte's later writings, he continued throughout his life largely to admire those aspects of Comte's work that he had admired in 1841.

There are striking similarities between the work of Comte in the *Philosophie positive* and that of Mill in the *Logic* and two other major works where he extensively reviews the *Philosophie positive*.[6] Where the two writers are similar it is generally Mill who follows Comte, often explicitly, although he sometimes has reservations. Mill follows Comte regarding the nature of the sciences and the broad reach of the scientific method, and also on some issues of social and political organization.

Mill has no reservations regarding Comte's surveys of the philosophies of the various sciences in the first several volumes of the *Philosophie positive*. He pays tribute to Comte's 'wonderful systematization of the philosophy of all the . . . sciences, from mathematics to physiology, which, if he had done nothing else, would have stamped him, in all minds competent to appreciate it, as one of the principal thinkers of the age'.[7] Mill also approves of Comte's hierarchical classification of the sciences and defends it against the attacks of other thinkers.[8] Here he does have some specific reservations, a typical example being that 'M. Comte should not have placed the laws of terrestrial gravity under Physics. They are part of the general theory of gravitation, and belong to astronomy'.[9] But the very specificity of such reservations only reinforces the sense of Mill's general acceptance of Comte's hierarchical structure. Moreover, Mill's reservations are really not a critique, since Comte had in any event acknowledged that his hierarchical structure would necessarily be imperfect.[10] Mill does not refer to this acknowledgement, and his tinkering with Comte's schema suggests an attempt to perfect it in which he seems more rigid in his positivism than Comte.

Mill also enthusiastically accepts Comte's general law of three stages, although he does have reservations: he is dubious about Comte's terminology; he substitutes his own account of the development of religious thought; and he feels that Comte has exaggerated the role of the metaphysical mode of thought.[11] Nevertheless, he believes that the law of three stages has 'that high degree of scientific evidence which is derived from the concurrence of the indications of history with the probabilities derived from the constitution of the human mind' and that it lets in a 'flood of light . . . upon the whole course of history'.[12]

But Mill found his greatest inspiration in Comte's contention that the methods of the physical sciences should be extended, first to history and then to the social and political areas of thought. This reinforced a view that he was already forming.[13] He regarded Comte as the first thinker to have 'penetrated to the philosophy of the matter, and placed the necessity of historical studies as the foundation of sociological speculation on the true footing'.[14] He added: 'Whoever disbelieves that the philosophy of history can be made a science, should suspend his judgment until he has read these volumes of M. Comte.'[15]

Mill shared Comte's view that the creation of sociology as a science was to be the ultimate extension of the methods of the physical sciences. He regarded Comte as having achieved a conception of the proper scientific method in sociology 'so much truer and more profound than that of any one who preceded him, as to constitute an era in its cultivation'. Mill's assessment was: 'If it cannot be said of him that he has created a science, it may be said truly that he has, for the first time, made the creation possible.'[16] He aspired to continue the development from Comte, and devoted the last book of his *Logic* to the principles and methods necessary for the future construction of the social sciences.[17]

Mill saw the time as ripe for this development. Comte's law of three stages, with the metaphysical stage as transitional, fitted his own growing sense of living in an era of transition. He stated that from Comte he 'obtained a clearer conception than ever before of the peculiarities of an era of transition in opinion, and ceased to mistake the moral and intellectual characteristics of such an era, for the normal attributes of humanity'.[18] Thus, he saw in his own era 'the anomalies and evils characteristic of the transition from a system of opinions which had worn out, to another only in process of being formed'.[19] He hoped that the failure to bring the social sciences to the positive (or scientific) stage of thought was merely a transitional matter, and foresaw the actual construction of these sciences as 'probably destined to be the great intellectual achievement of the next two or three generations of European thinkers'.[20]

Much now follows by an inexorable logic – for Mill just as for Comte – from the stipulation that the social sciences can be developed to an equally positive state as the physical sciences. Comte had held that it would be as unreasonable for anyone not an expert to reject the findings of these new sciences as to reject those of the physical sciences.[21] Mill likewise declared that 'the mass of mankind, including even their rulers in all the practical departments of life, must, from the necessity of the case, accept most of their opinions on political and social matters, *as they do on physical*, from the authority of those who have bestowed more study on those subjects than they generally have it in their power to do'.[22]

In an interesting application of this doctrine, Mill proposed in the context of the Reform Bill of 1859 that persons of 'proved superiority of education' should be given 'a plurality of votes' to cast in parliamentary elections. He favoured this 'as a means of reconciling the irresistible claim of every man or woman to be consulted, and to be allowed a voice, in the regulation of affairs which vitally concern them, with the superiority of weight justly due to opinions grounded on superiority of knowledge'. However, this proposal 'found favour with nobody', whereupon Mill demonstrated a remarkable positivist commitment:

> If [the proposal] . . . ever overcomes the strong feeling which exists
> against it, this will only be after the establishment of a systematic

National Education by which the various grades of politically valuable acquirement may be accurately defined and authenticated.[23]

The positivist commitment lies in the notion that it is indeed possible for a National Education to satisfy these criteria. This would require establishing the principles of such an education as authoritatively as the principles of the physical sciences, and the stipulation that this is possible is precisely the positivist commitment.

But although Mill is swept along by the logic of Comte's theories, he baulks at Comte's ideas for putting the principles of the new sciences into social practice. Recall that, as I discussed in Chapter 3, under Comte's political scheme an elite would develop a grand plan and harness all the forces of society to implement it, the entire life of the individual would be under public view and control, and the aspirations and imagination of the individual would be subordinated to social goals. Mill, on the contrary, valued individual liberty highly, and in fact he records that his correspondence with Comte was brought to an end over their differences regarding its importance.[24]

In taking up Comte's call to develop the new social sciences on the model of the physical sciences, Mill had quite different social and political expectations:

> I looked forward . . . to a future . . . [of] unchecked liberty of thought, unbounded freedom of individual action in all modes not hurtful to others; but also, convictions as to what is right and wrong, useful and pernicious, deeply graven on the feelings by early education and general unanimity of sentiment, and so firmly grounded in reason and the true exigencies of life, that they shall not, like all former and present creeds, religious, ethical, and political, require to be periodically thrown off and replaced by others.[25]

There is no need to wonder whether Comte would have found such a future appealing, since in any event he would have rejected it as impossible of realization. He had insisted that the collapse of religious illusions rendered close social control indispensable to compensate for the general lack of natural morality.[26] Thus, his relative pessimism contrasted sharply with Mill's relative optimism regarding the moral sentiments of the majority of people.

Notably, their differing on such a fundamental matter, *and finding no 'scientific' way to achieve unity on the correct view on the matter*, might itself have called into question the prospect of developing the social sciences on the model of the physical sciences. However, I am not aware that this point was ever made at the time, or indeed subsequently.[27]

It has often been suggested that this difference between Comte and Mill derived from the difference between Comte's Roman Catholic and Mill's Anglican Protestant mind-set. The nineteenth-century English scientist T. H. Huxley gibed that the all-embracing, tightly regulated social structure that Comte had proposed 'might be compendiously described as Catholicism minus Christianity'.[28] Such a rudimentary analysis might perhaps help in understanding the psychological differences that led to their philosophical differences. It is certainly arguable that their difference in religious backgrounds could engender differing views of how human beings would conduct themselves without close social control. However, it is not of much help in understanding the philosophical differences themselves.[29]

ii. Mill's empiricism

A better understanding of the differences between Comte and Mill derives from considering their respective epistemological frameworks. Here I use the term 'epistemology' in the sense of a set of views on the possibility, nature and scope of knowledge of the external world. Neither Comte nor Mill consistently maintained a coherent epistemology, but even the areas of incoherence in their respective epistemologies provide insight into the differences between them.

Mill is well known as an empiricist, in the sense that he holds 'that, of the outward world, we know and can know absolutely nothing, except the sensations which we experience from it'.[30] He considers under what circumstances our observation of events in the world may be relied on, and demands 'that what is supposed to have been observed shall really have been observed; that it be an observation, not an inference. For in almost every act of our perceiving faculties, observation and inference are intimately blended'. But this compels him to scepticism regarding any observation of the external world:

> I affirm, for example . . . that I saw my brother at a certain hour this morning. If any proposition concerning a matter of fact would commonly be said to be known by the direct testimony of the senses, this surely would be so. The truth, however, is far otherwise. I only saw a certain coloured surface; or rather I had the kind of visual sensations which are usually produced by a coloured surface; and from these as marks, known to be such by previous experience, I concluded

that I saw my brother . . . I might have been . . . in a nervous state of disorder, which brought his image before me in a waking hallucination . . . If [so] . . . the affirmation that I saw my brother would have been erroneous; but whatever was matter of direct perception, namely, the visual sensations, would have been real. The inference only would have been ill grounded; I should have ascribed those sensations to a wrong cause.[31]

In fact, Mill's premises imply a conclusion yet more radical than he acknowledges.[32] As he recognizes, within the epistemological framework that he posits he cannot conclude that he 'saw a certain coloured surface' because he can rely on no more than that he had visual sensations. This must be the case on every occasion – not only the present occasion – that he has visual sensations. Therefore, there could be no past occasion for which he could retrospectively conclude that his visual sensations were produced by a coloured surface. *A fortiori*, he cannot claim that certain visual sensations have *usually* been produced by a coloured surface. Consequently, he has no basis for regarding the visual sensations in question as 'the kind . . . usually produced by a coloured surface'.

A similar analysis applies to Mill's reference to the 'previous experience' that suggested that on the present occasion he saw his brother. Within his epistemological framework, 'previous experience' can amount to nothing more than experience of sensations.

It would of course be no answer to say that on previous occasions the presence of a coloured surface, or of his brother, was otherwise confirmed (by, for example, another person's statement), since any such supposed confirmation would itself appear as just another collection of sensations; and then the argument proceeds as before. In short, there is no way for the empiricism that Mill stipulates to break out of the realm of sense impressions. Nothing can ever provide any evidentiary support, however slight, for a conclusion that Mill saw his brother rather than suffered a hallucination. Indeed, in Mill's stipulated framework nothing can ever provide any evidentiary support, however slight, for any empirical assertion whatsoever. The very notion of evidence evanesces.

The problem with these conclusions is that one cannot live by them. Thus a sceptically empiricist philosopher may find himself driven to a sceptical position in his philosophical reflections that he cannot maintain in social and political life. But what epistemology will such a philosopher then maintain in social and political life? It is almost axiomatic that he will find no theoretically satisfactory epistemology, since if such an epistemology existed for him he need not have turned to sceptical empiricism in his philosophical reflections. It likely turns out that he flatly abandons the search for a theoretically satisfactory epistemology in his social and political life, and adopts there a naïve and wholly unreflecting realism.

This causes only limited difficulties for purely theoretical philosophers, who must merely cope with shifting between one epistemology for professional work and another for personal life. Although it is suspect to depend on such a distinction between professional work and personal life,[33] many theoretical philosophers seem to find the division viable. David Hume's charming confession that the warm pleasures of social life made him lose heart for his sceptical philosophical reflections is quite exceptional.[34]

However, there is more difficulty when the sceptically empirical philosopher is, like Mill, politically engaged as part of professional life. Sceptical empiricism bars political concern. Mill could not have maintained his concerns for social justice if he had acknowledged that what he perceived as instances of social injustice might equally well have been hallucinations. It is no answer that he might have gone on assuming that his perceptions corresponded to reality, on the ground that nothing would be lost if they were hallucinations. A great deal would be lost if, for example, the world were so constructed that all Mill's perceptions of situations of social injustice were hallucinatory distortions of underlying real-world situations of (according to Mill's criteria) social justice, and conversely. It is no answer that such a scenario is improbable, since sceptical empiricism provides no basis for assessing probability. A mere *feeling* that such a scenario is improbable is simply a further sense impression that, by hypothesis, is no evidence of reality.

Thus it should not be surprising that Mill paid little attention to sceptical empiricism beyond making the statement of it discussed above. Rather, he adopted, more or less implicitly, a sort of semi-empirical epistemology that must be gleaned from examination of his work. This epistemology stipulates two distinct levels of perception of reality. It appears plainly in Mill's analysis of the form of the traditional syllogism that has a general major premise (such as, 'All men are mortal'), a singular minor premise (such as, 'Lord Palmerston is a man'), and consequently a singular conclusion ('Lord Palmerston is mortal'). Mill begins: 'Suppose the syllogism to be, All cows ruminate; the animal which is before me is a cow; therefore it ruminates. The minor [premise], if true at all, is obviously so.' He dispenses rapidly with this supposedly obvious case, then turns to the following one:

But suppose the syllogism to be the following: – All arsenic is poisonous, the substance which is before me is arsenic, therefore it is poisonous. The truth of the minor [premise] may not here be obvious at first sight; it may not be intuitively evident, but may itself be known only by inference. It may be the conclusion of another argument, which, thrown into the syllogistic form, would stand thus: – Whatever when lighted produces a dark spot on a piece of white porcelain held in the flame, which spot is soluble in hypochloride of calcium, is arsenic; the substance before me conforms to this condition; therefore it is arsenic. To establish, therefore, the ultimate conclusion . . . requires . . . a Train of Reasoning.[35]

The problem here is that if we follow Mill's own analysis of seeing his brother, then there is nothing obvious about seeing a cow. Likewise, there is nothing obvious about the perceptions (the dark spot, the solubility in calcium hypochloride, and so forth) that he is ready to accept as a foundation for inferring the presence of arsenic. If Mill now finds these perceptions obvious he has simply abandoned the sceptical empiricism that he stipulated in his analysis of seeing his brother. Moreover, in now drawing a distinction between perceptions of reality that are obvious and perceptions of reality that depend on inference, he has implicitly resorted to a kind of two-level epistemology.

Epistemologies that stipulate two distinct levels of perception are found in a variety of guises. They have in common that they assert that there is a category of observations that require no theoretical underpinning. Such epistemologies are often, like Mill's, implicit, but where they are explicit they tend to describe this category of observations in such terms as 'direct', 'everyday', 'common-sense', 'basic' or 'low-level' observations. Unfortunately, epistemologies of this kind are generally naïve and do not withstand analysis of the distinction that they draw between categories of observations.[36] At the same time, they serve a practical need, since without them it is hard to see how to get started thinking or talking about anything.

The anthropologist and philosopher Robin Horton has attempted to put two-level epistemology on a sounder footing. I do not think that Horton's thesis succeeds in justifying two-level epistemology, but it does offer a clearer statement of such an epistemology than is generally found in the literature. His epistemology is similar in important respects to that which Mill, and also to an extent Comte, implicitly adopted. Consequently, it provides a useful template for discussing Mill's epistemology and the differences between him and Comte.

Horton introduces the notions of *primary theory* and *secondary theory*. Primary theory is to cover the supposed range of observations that require no theoretical underpinning, which he defines as follows:

> Primary theory gives the world a foreground filled with middle-sized (say between a hundred times as large and a hundred times as small as human beings), enduring, solid objects. These objects are interrelated, indeed interdefined, in terms of a 'push-pull' conception of causality, in which spatial and temporal contiguity are seen as crucial to the transmission of change.[37]

He claims that primary theory defined in this way is much the same among human beings everywhere, and so provides an overall framework of comprehension and communication. Whether or not this is true, Horton's primary theory fairly covers the kind of observation commonly accepted as 'direct'.

Horton then defines secondary theory indirectly, to cover epistemologically everything that primary theory does not. He explicates its development, and its relation to primary theory, as follows:

> [P]rimary theory . . . is an instrument associated with a limited, 'push-pull' causal vision, and as such leaves man with a wide range of events and contingencies for which he cannot account and which he therefore has no prospect of predicting or bringing under control . . . [S]econdary theory . . . postulat[es] a 'hidden' or 'underlying' realm of entities and processes of which the events of everyday experience, as described in primary-theory terms, are seen as surface manifestations. Once the causal regularities governing this hidden realm have been stated, their implications for the world as described in primary-theoretical terms are spelled out by a process akin to translation, guided by a 'dictionary' which correlates aspects of the 'hidden' world with aspects of the 'given'.[38]

Secondary theory, as Horton observes, varies in a 'startling' fashion between one worldview and another, giving rise to epistemological 'differences in kind'.[39] In effect, human beings through the ages have produced many quite different 'dictionaries' for correlating aspects of the 'hidden' world with aspects of the 'given'.

There is some correlation between Horton's concept of secondary theory with a 'dictionary' as guide to it and Thomas Kuhn's well-known concept of a *paradigm*. Kuhn defines this as the structurally coherent set of theoretical commitments that form the foundation of the worldview within any given societal context.[40] However, Kuhn does not present a two-level epistemology, and there is no explicit correlation between any aspect of Kuhn's approach and Horton's concept of primary theory. Nonetheless, both Kuhn and Horton provide frameworks suitable for considering the fact that a great variety of worldviews are be found, and I shall later find both of them helpful for illustration.

For ease of exposition, I shall from now on make statements such as 'Mill adopts primary theory', or 'Comte's dictionary from primary to secondary theory has such-and-such a property', or 'Mill's paradigm is such-and such'. Any such statement should be considered as an (obviously, retrospective) interpretation of the epistemological position at issue in terms of the conceptual framework of Horton or Kuhn, as appropriate.

iii. Mill's theory of induction

My discussion of Mill in the previous section shows that he adopts primary theory, with a category of direct observation that includes cows, dark spots and the process of dissolving. His analysis of the syllogism regarding arsenic suggests that his secondary theory is essentially that of nineteenth-century Western physical science, and this will become increasingly apparent in the course of the present discussion. He bases his secondary theory firmly on *induction*, which is the process of recognizing uniformities in entities and their behaviour, and framing general rules or laws expressing these uniformities. These rules or laws can then be applied to new instances involving similar entities.

Induction is the normal mode of reasoning from a range of specific observations to general conclusions, in daily life as much as in scientific work. Mill recognized that induction is also implicitly involved in the syllogistic deductive process that leads from a general to a specific conclusion. This is because in any syllogism the general premise (such as, 'All men are mortal') must itself have originally been obtained by induction from a range of observations (in this illustration, observations of the mortality of individuals).[41] Consequently, Mill recognized that it would not be possible to develop a general theory of logic without developing a general theory – indeed, he considered, a 'scientific theory' – of induction.[42] 'What Induction is . . . and what conditions render it legitimate, cannot but be deemed the main question of the science of logic – the question which includes all others.'[43]

Mill now considers the problem that we observe many examples of uniformity in the world around us, but some validly extend by induction to general conclusions and some do not. To adapt an example from Mill,[44] I might conclude by induction from my personal observations of individual men that no man wears his head underneath his shoulders and that no man is taller than two metres in height. Mill accepts the first conclusion as a valid induction, but the second conclusion clearly is not valid. In drawing the second conclusion I invalidly extrapolated from a limited sample to the entire world. Yet the two conclusions were based on the same observations. Mill's problem then is to develop a 'scientific theory' that will distinguish the valid from the invalid bases for induction.

Mill's solution in my example would be as follows. We know from experience that the general structure of human anatomy is fairly constant, so the fact that all the men I observed wear their heads on their shoulders makes the idea of men who wear their heads underneath their shoulders incredible. Consequently, my observations were sufficient to support the first induction, which therefore is reliable. However, we also know from experience that human height varies considerably, so the fact that all the men I observed were shorter than two metres does *not* make the idea of a man taller than two metres incredible. My observations may have accidentally been confined to an unrepresentative sample. Hence the second induction is not reliable.

Mill next considers how we get the experience that teaches us that the general structure of human anatomy is fairly constant. Such a general conclusion must itself be the result of induction from a range of individual observations. Mill acknowledges the circularity, that 'it is impossible to frame any scientific method of induction, or test of the correctness of inductions, unless on the hypothesis that some inductions deserving of reliance have been already made'.[45] This raises the question of how I can *ever* know that a case of uniformity that I observe is a reliable basis for induction, and not merely the result of my observations accidentally being confined to an unrepresentative sample. This is essentially the problem of *constant conjunction* to which David Hume had drawn attention.[46]

Many thinkers had finessed Hume's problem by simply positing that the course of nature is uniform and that coherent laws govern the universe. Mill agrees that this is a necessary foundation, and describes it as the fundamental principle of induction. But he denies that it can *explain* the inductive process. On the contrary, he insists that thinkers formulated this principle as a response to finding uniformity and coherent laws in a great variety of contexts. That is, this principle generalizes the uniformity and coherence found in various contexts to a universal uniformity and coherence. Put otherwise, this principle is itself the result of induction, and indeed the ultimate form of induction.[47]

Mill must now consider how we can escape from the circularity inherent in induction. That is, if every induction depends on a prior induction, how can we begin the process of reasoning by induction? He offers primary theory as the answer:

> Some facts are so perpetually and familiarly accompanied by certain others, that mankind learnt, as children learn, to expect the one where they found the other, long before they knew how to put their expectation into words by asserting, in a proposition, the existence of a connection between those phenomena. No science was needed to teach that food nourishes, that water drowns, or quenches thirst, that the sun gives light and heat, that bodies fall to the ground. The first scientific inquirers assumed these and the like as known truths, and set out from them to discover others which were unknown . . . subject, however, as they afterwards began to see, to an ulterior revision of these spontaneous generalisations themselves, when the progress of knowledge pointed out limits to them.[48]

This 'progress of knowledge' will be a development of secondary theory. Mill has already told us that progress in reasoning by induction depends on experience. How can we gain the necessary experience, and how do we judge whether our experience is reliable? According to Mill:

> [W]e make experience its own test. Experience testifies that among the uniformities which it exhibits or seems to exhibit, some are more to be relied on than others; and uniformity, therefore, may be presumed, from any given number of instances, with a greater degree of assurance, in proportion as the case belongs to a class in which the uniformities have hitherto been found more uniform.[49]

He nonetheless recognizes that, despite experience, it is possible to go astray with invalid induction. He considers this danger under the rubric 'Fallacies of Generalisation', where he states that 'the most fertile source of them is bad classification'. He defines this as 'bringing together in one group, and under one name, things which have no common properties, or none but such as are too unimportant to allow general propositions of any considerable value to be made respecting the class'.[50]

Mill's concept of bad classification derives from Bacon, as he acknowledges. He pays tribute to Bacon's analysis of the kind of faulty reasoning that can result, but then accuses Bacon of falling into the same trap himself in another context. Mill gives an analogy that is helpful for understanding the issue, stating that Bacon 'proceeds like one who, seeking for the cause of hardness, after examining that quality in iron, flint, and diamond, should expect to find that it is something which can be traced also in hard water, a hard knot, and a hard heart'. Mill applies this critique to a similar use of several terms in the works of the Greek philosophers of antiquity, particularly *kinesis*, 'which properly signified motion, [but] was taken to denote not only all motion, but even all change'. He declares that 'Aristotle and Plato laboured under a continual embarrassment from this misuse of terms'.[51]

A strong belief in progress pervades Mill's theory of induction. In his view, Aristotle and Plato were really rather bad at classifying, and Bacon made fair progress but still fell into error. However, we have now (in Mill's era) become quite good at classifying. We are able to avoid the 'Fallacies of Generalisation' of our predecessors because we have more and better experience, including more and better experience in the proper use of experience, than they had. Simply put, we have become better at recognizing good classifications and avoiding bad classifications than they were. And it follows from Mill's belief in the development of the science of sociology that we will certainly improve yet further.

However, Mill fails to recognize that such conclusions depend crucially on context, in two ways. First, even within the physical sciences from which he draws his illustrations of induction, a classification may be good in one context but less so in another. In Kuhn's terminology, Mill does not recognize that whether a classification is good or bad may depend on the paradigm within which it is viewed.

This becomes clear in comparing Mill's observations with Kuhn's on an example that they both use: the concept of air as an elastic fluid. Mill discusses this in connection with the development of the science of sound, which in his era had developed from a collection of isolated empirical facts to a substantial theoretical structure that explained these facts and others besides. In Mill's terminology, knowledge about sound had progressed from *experimental* to *deductive* science:

> [T]he science of sound, which previously stood in the lowest rank of merely experimental science, became deductive when it was proved by experiment that every variety of sound was consequent on, and

therefore a mark of, a distinct and definable variety of oscillatory motion among the particles of the transmitting medium . . . And thus many truths, not before suspected, concerning sound become deducible from the known laws of the propagation of motion through an elastic medium; while facts already empirically known respecting sound become an indication of corresponding properties of vibrating bodies, previously undiscovered.[52]

Compare this with Kuhn's view:

Perhaps it is not apparent that a paradigm is prerequisite to the discovery of laws like . . . [Boyle's Law relating gas pressure to volume]. We often hear that they are found by examining measurements undertaken for their own sake and without theoretical commitment. But . . . Boyle's experiments were not conceivable (and if conceived would have received another interpretation or none at all) until air was recognized as an elastic fluid to which all the elaborate concepts of hydrostatics could be applied.[53]

Mill finesses the stage in scientific development that for Kuhn is crucial. In Mill's view, experiment and deduction led inevitably to the recognition of air as an elastic fluid. Any notion of a paradigm shift appears alien to his thought. But in Kuhn's view, a paradigm shift was prerequisite to recognizing air as an elastic fluid. Moreover, Kuhn's view does not support the conclusion that this development was inevitable, since there is no reason to suppose that any particular paradigm shift is inevitable. Note also that Kuhn's arguments effectively deny the possibility of any universal theory of induction of the kind that Mill sought.

The second way in which Mill failed to take account of context is that as we shift context from the physical to the social sciences, classification criteria may also shift. Since Mill is committed to extending positivism to the social sciences his approach to classifications must hold there too. His example of classification schemes for 'hard' can illustrate the problem. Certainly, a materials scientist would reject a classification scheme that lumps together the hardness of iron, flint, diamond, water, knots and hearts. However, a sociologist might value such a scheme for the insight it gives into the worldview of speakers of English and other languages that use a similar scheme.[54] In Horton's terminology, different contexts may give rise to different secondary theories. Mill shows no awareness of this.

iv. Comte's epistemology

As with Mill, Comte's epistemology must be gleaned from examination of his work. However, Comte is unconcerned with the kind of empiricism that vexed Mill: that is, the view that we can know nothing of the external world except the sensations that we experience from it.[55] Rather, Comte takes a 'common sense' view that our perceptions correspond to reality. In fact he takes this so much for granted that he does not state it explicitly, but it is nonetheless clear from his texts. Thus, to give one of many possible examples, he states that 'the true philosophical spirit consists above all in systematically extending plain good sense to the whole range of genuinely accessible theoretical investigations'.[56]

Moreover, in considering the relation between human perceptive capacities and scientific achievements, he declares that 'a blind species, however intelligent it might be, could not develop astronomy'.[57] But if we now claim – as Comte certainly does – that humanity *has* developed astronomy, it follows that human sight perceptions of astronomical events have made this development possible. That is, human sight perceptions of astronomical events must correspond to the real events themselves. Plainly, Comte assumes that this is so. This in turn shows that he adopts a quite extensive primary theory, in the sense that I discussed in Section ii.

Comte sets out his secondary theory in a remarkable passage:

Since the time of Bacon, everyone of good sense has recited that the only real knowledge is that which is based on observed facts. This fundamental maxim is plainly indisputable as long as one applies it to its appropriate context, the mature state of our mental development. But when we turn to the early development of human knowledge, it is equally certain that the primitive mind neither could nor needed to think in this way. For if, on the one hand, every positive theory must be based on observations, it is equally plain that, on the other hand, our minds need some kind of theory in order to engage in observation. If when contemplating phenomena we did not immediately tie them to some principle, it would not only be impossible for us to put isolated observations together in any productive way, but we would even be wholly unable to hold them in our minds. We would remain largely unaware of facts that stare us in the face.[58]

Several points should be made. First, putting isolated observations together in a productive way entails observing uniformities and making classifications on the basis of them. In arguing that this depends on a prior sense of theory, Comte thus recognizes that, in Kuhn's terminology (see Section ii), whether a classification is good or bad may depend on the paradigm within which it is viewed. In this he differs sharply from Mill. It is also fair to say that he anticipates Kuhn's concept of a paradigm. I shall return to this in the next section.

Second, such a view was essential to Comte's thesis. For, if there could be observations prior to and independent of any theory, such observations would constitute ultimate facts incapable of analysis. Consequently, the mental processes that produced these observations would defy being structured as a positive science. Comte could not have accepted this limitation of his positivist programme.[59]

Third, Comte's argument raises the issue of how human thought first developed. His solution is that 'early humanity, caught between the need to observe in order to form a theory and the need to create a theory in order to observe, would have found itself trapped in a vicious circle had a natural exit route not fortunately opened, whereby humanity in its infancy spontaneously developed a theological mode of thought'.[60] It is hard to imagine that this purportedly historical conclusion derives from any positive investigation. I consider the vicious circle further in the next section. For the present, I note only that this supposed origin of human thought asserts the first stage of Comte's law of three stages, and so provides the foundation of all that will follow in his philosophical and political thesis.

Fourth, Comte should not be pressed too far on the need for theory prior to observation. Like Mill, Comte states a radical epistemological theory then mitigates it in practice. A variety of his texts show that in practice he accepts the basic phenomena of primary theory as being prior to attempts to fit them into a structured secondary theory.[61]

Fifth, Comte's position leads to epistemological relativism. He stresses that 'in our positive investigations . . . it is important to be aware that our observations are not in any way absolute, but are always relative to our structure and our situation'.[62] He then draws on the illustration that a blind species could not develop astronomy, and argues:

> If the loss of one important sense could completely conceal an entire order of natural phenomena from us, then, conversely, there is every reason to suppose that acquiring an additional sense would unveil

some class of facts of which we now have no notion. This is unless we believe that in the human organism every sense required to explore the outside world is developed to the highest possible degree. But such a presumption is unfounded, and indeed almost ridiculous.[63]

Note that this is epistemological and not ontological relativism. Comte's ontology – that is, his views on what there is in the world[64] – is naïve and absolute. He accepts unquestioningly that there is a fixed reality independent of our perception of it. Again, he takes this so much for granted that he does not state it explicitly, but it is nonetheless clear from a variety of statements that he makes in passing, at various points in his texts. To give four of many possible examples, he refers to 'the external world, the fixed foundation for all scientific study', to the goal of science in producing 'an exact description of the real world', to 'undeniable reality', and to 'the unalterable reality of the world'.[65]

Note also that Comte's epistemological relativism is not the kind that gained influence in the late twentieth century, in which all worldviews are deemed equally valid. On the contrary, Comte insists on the superiority of positivism over any other way of investigating the world. I shall return to this in the next section.

Finally, Comte's relativism requires that positivism be understood contextually in the various sciences. 'The positive method is not open to being studied apart from the research in which it is being applied. Anything one can say about it in the abstract reduces to generalities too vague to have any substantive intellectual influence, and gives far less clear knowledge of the method than would deeper study of a single positive science.'[66] Here again Comte differs from Mill and also anticipates twentieth-century developments, specifically regarding the heuristic nature of scientific reasoning. I shall return to this too in the next section.

v. Differences over induction

We have seen that Comte recognized, as Mill did not, the two important ways in which the reciprocal processes of making observations and forming theories may depend on context. First, they may depend on the paradigm within which the observations are made and the theories formed. Second, even within the positivist paradigm, observations and theories may depend on the particular scientific context. Moreover, induction entails deriving classifications of phenomena from observations and theories, so we can restate the positions of Comte and Mill as follows: Comte recognized, as Mill did not, that induction is contextually dependent in both of these ways. Consequently, Comte could form no general, context-independent theory of induction akin to Mill's. Any such theory would fundamentally conflict with Comte's context-sensitive epistemology, and so with his entire scheme.

Mill did not understand the depth of the difference between Comte and himself over induction. He notes that Comte had read his *Logic* and had 'expressed . . . his high approval . . . of the Inductive part'. But, he continues, 'we cannot discover that he was indebted to it for a single idea, or that it influenced, in the smallest particular, the course of his subsequent speculations'.[67] Moreover, he complains that Comte did not even attempt to create a general theory of induction.[68] This makes it clear that Mill failed to recognize that Comte, by virtue of his epistemology, *could* not have a general theory of induction of the kind that Mill would have approved.

It is less easy to determine whether Comte understood the depth of this difference between himself and Mill. His praise of Mill's work might indicate that he could not understand it or that he had not read it closely. On the other hand, the praise might merely have been courtesy to an admirer. But there is yet another possibility. As I interpret Comte's expression of praise it has a subtle sting in the tail, in the form of a veiled suggestion that Mill's theory of induction is admirable *within the limitations of Mill's point of view*.[69] This opens the possibility that Comte admired Mill's work for its thoroughness of analysis and exposition, and perhaps for its potential for application in any given specific context of positive science. Since Comte was not writing a treatise on any individual science, it would then be expected that Mill's ideas on induction would not influence his work. If this interpretation is correct, then Comte fully understood the difference between himself and Mill.

The difference between Comte and Mill over induction has important consequences for their respective socio-political positions. Let us follow this through in detail, beginning with the views of Mill and Comte regarding the early stages of human development. Mill states:

The simplest observation, without which the preservation of life would have been impossible, must have pointed out many uniformities in nature, many objects which, under given circumstances, acted exactly like one another: and whenever this was observed, men's natural and untutored faculties led them to form the similar objects into a class, and to think of them together.[70]

An obvious consequence of this (although Mill does not make it explicit) is that at these early stages everyone must have viewed the world in much the same way.

However, we have seen that Comte holds that in these early stages of development the formation of classifications begins from a theological mode of thought. But theology, according to Comte, has never been unitary. He refers to 'the varied pack of numerous independent deities that primitive humanity had imagined'.[71] An obvious consequence of having a varied pack of deities (although Comte does not make it explicit) is a correspondingly varied range of theologies. So under Comte's view it can hardly be expected that everyone would have viewed the world in the same way in the early stages of human development.

Turning now to humanity at its mature stage of development, we have seen that Mill and Comte share a commitment to progression to positive thought. However, they take different views of the path to that goal. Mill relies on 'early education and general unanimity of sentiment' to set people on the right path, and experience as a guide to maintain them on it. Since experience is generic rather than contextual in his epistemology, no further maintenance will be required. Humanity will inevitably progress to the positive state and maintain itself in this state, since these true convictions 'shall not . . . require to be periodically thrown off and replaced by others'.[72] In Horton's terminology, Mill envisages a straight, clear path from primary theory to the positivist secondary theory, with steady progress along that path guided by experience.

But Comte sees many paths leading from primary theory to a variety of secondary theories with diverse dictionaries. He believes that the social order will ultimately reach positivism as its secondary theory, but, as I discussed in Chapter 3, he fears that human opposition might disrupt progress towards this goal. He cannot rely on experience alone to ensure undisrupted progress, because in his epistemology experience is not generic but rather is informed by whatever secondary theory has been adopted.[73] Consequently, human beings need vigilant direction, to keep them on the right path so that they reach the positivist state and to maintain them permanently in that state.

Since Comte recognizes that there are many possible secondary theories, with each being justifiable on its own terms, we might ask how he justifies his preference for a positivist secondary theory. Put otherwise, since Comte recognizes that our observations and our theories are context-dependent, how can he suppose that there are to be only three stages of thought, with the positive stage being the ultimate one? Indeed, how does he avoid lapsing into a radical position that rejects the very notion of positive knowledge?

A number of thinkers have moved in such a radical direction, including Richard Rorty, whom several writers have compared with Comte. The interest that they find in the comparison is that Comte and Rorty share epistemological similarities while being socio-politically opposed. Thus, Hilary Putnam observes that 'what is common to Rorty and Comte is the idea that much of what we think we know cannot have the status it seems to have. For Richard Rorty the recommended response is to take a more "playful" attitude to what we think we know; and for Auguste Comte it is to sternly restrict ourselves to "positive knowledge".'[74]

The explanation for the difference is that Comte's goals differ from Rorty's. Comte is committed to reorganizing the entire social order for the benefit of humanity. Radical doubts do not build a social order, but, as Comte sees it, positivism does. From Comte's point of view, the twofold context-dependency of our observations and theories is both a challenge and a danger. It is a challenge in that it requires each positive science to develop its own methods of investigation and principles of induction. It is a danger in that it might lead to humanity straying away from positivism altogether. While positivism is only one of many goals that humanity *could* choose, it is definitely the only one that humanity *should* choose. From this perspective, taking a playful attitude is dangerously irresponsible.

Returning to Comte and Mill, we have seen that despite their sharing certain socio-political goals, differing epistemologies set them on diverging courses that lead them to widely different socio-political commitments. Comte's position leads inexorably to his commitment to a scheme of social organization that will constantly keep human beings firmly on the rails that guide towards positive thought. Nor is it surprising that he should ultimately have structured his proposed social order as a religion, the kind of social order historically so successful in maintaining constant guidance over human thought processes. However, Mill's epistemology allows him to afford 'unchecked liberty of thought, [and] unbounded freedom of individual action in all modes not hurtful to others',[75] and still look forward confidently to humanity's smooth accession to the positive state. He may require some level of social agreement on the form of early education, but this is far less social control than Comte proposed.

Mill did not acknowledge that the differences between Comte and himself regarding individual freedom had such deep roots. On the contrary, in describing the split between them he asserts: 'while as logicians we were nearly at one, as sociologists we could travel together no further'.[76] We have seen that the first part of this assertion is dubious. However, Mill's belief in it was crucial to his role in the development of positivism after Comte.

5
The Critic and the Disciple

i. Mill as critic

In Chapter 1 I noted that there was a longstanding controversy over whether it was possible to separate the philosophical and socio-political aspects of Comte's work, either conceptually or textually. In this chapter I consider the most influential attempts to achieve such a separation and their effect on positivist doctrine.

Mill was particularly influential in this regard. As I discussed in the previous chapter, he contrasted his concord with Comte in matters of logic with his discord in matters of sociology. He was less in agreement with Comte on matters of logic than he supposed, but his statement nonetheless showed his desire to separate the two aspects of Comte's work. He expressed this in strong terms shortly after his correspondence with Comte ended, writing about him to Émile Littré in 1848 as follows: 'I have a very high respect for his works in so far as concerns the theory of the positive method, but am far removed from his mode of applying this method to social questions. Most of his sociological views are diametrically opposed to mine.'[1]

Mill had obvious political reasons for insisting on this division between the two aspects of Comte's work. He observed that the 'better parts' of Comte's work were becoming well established. These were essentially the theory of the evolution of human knowledge to the positivist stage that I discussed in Chapters 1 and 2. However, he expressed concern that 'under cover of those better parts those of a worse character, greatly developed and added to in his later writings, had also made some way'. Here, Mill is referring essentially to Comte's scheme for social reorganization, as I discussed in Chapter 3. Consequently, he found it desirable to sift 'what is good from what is bad' in Comte's work, and felt that because he had greatly contributed to making Comte better known he was personally obliged to undertake this task.[2]

But the matter surely goes deeper. As I discussed in Chapter 4, Mill believed (albeit mistakenly) that he and Comte shared a common philosophy, but abhorred some major social and political consequences that, according to Comte, would inexorably follow from that common philosophy. In rescuing Comte's philosophy from Comte's politics, Mill was effectively rescuing his own philosophy and politics from Comte's politics. It is easy to see why he should wish to do so. Comte's most fundamental tenets – including those with which Mill wholeheartedly agreed – had received a good deal of public criticism that would only be strengthened if Comte's plan for social reorganization were seen as their inevitable consequence.

Recall in particular that Mill agreed with Comte that the positive method should be extended to matters of social organization and that, in consequence, the authority of experts on social, political and moral matters should be recognized. Nineteenth-century English novelists mercilessly attacked and satirized this kind of approach. Even in their early stage of development before Comte such ideas had suffered the incisive satire of Jane Austen,[3] and Charles Dickens mounted a savage contemporaneous assault on them.[4] While public criticism might not have shaken Mill's beliefs, he had seen that it could damage the prospects for implementing the positivist goals that he supported.[5] Moreover, he was aware that public opposition to positivism had driven people who had in fact adopted a positivist approach to deny any association with positivism.[6]

However, two obstacles stood between Mill and his goal of deflecting opposition to positivism by dividing Comte's philosophy from his politics. First, there was Comte's own statement rejecting any such division. In 1851, three years after Mill's letter to Littré quoted above, Comte issued his rejoinder. He opened the first volume of his massive new work, the *Politique positive*, with the ringing declaration: 'Positivism consists in its essence of a philosophy and a politics, inseparably combined, with the one forming the foundation and the other the goal of a single universal system.'[7] Mill did not really confront Comte on this issue, but rather avoided it by dismissing Comte's later work, as I discuss below.

The second obstacle was the set of substantive arguments that had led Comte from principles with which Mill agreed to consequences that Mill rejected. Mill could not draw on the epistemological differences between himself and Comte to deal with these arguments, because he did not recognize their epistemological differences. Surely then Mill should have produced substantive arguments in response to Comte's, and particularly to counter Comte's claim that tight and continuing social control over the individual would be needed to reach the positive state without unacceptable levels of social upheaval. Moreover, since Mill claimed to be committed to the development of sociology as a positive science, he should have produced such arguments within the positive framework. That is, he should have offered 'scientific' arguments to show that Comte's sociological reasoning was false, or at least not supported by evidence derived from 'scientific' observation.

But Mill did nothing of the kind. His only substantive response focused on Comte's view that scientific research should be directed to serve human wants, against which he retorted that 'those wants and interests are . . . extremely multifarious, and the order of preference among them . . . cannot be cast into precise general propositions'.[8] The problem with this rejoinder *from Mill's own acknowledged positivist perspective* is that it severely restricts the potential scope of the positive science of sociology that was supposedly to be developed. Human wants and interests would be among the chief subjects of investigation of such a science, and general propositions about them would be among the most important of its laws. It seems that Mill faltered in his commitment to positivism when faced with the consequences of his own positivist premises.

Confronted by Comte's own view that his work was indivisible, and lacking substantive arguments to the contrary, Mill resorted to other means of separating the philosophical from the socio-political aspects of Comte's work. In a work published a few years after Comte's death, he took two distinct approaches. In the first, he criticizes Comte for *not* faltering when faced with the consequences of his own positivist premises. In this regard, Mill lumps Comte together with Descartes and Leibnitz (whom Comte indeed had regarded as among his principal precursors) as 'of all great scientific thinkers, the most consistent, and for that reason often the most absurd, because they shrank from no consequences, however contrary to common sense, to which their premises appeared to lead'.[9]

Here Mill reflects the practical side of his thinking, of which he was proud, as well as contemporaneous public criticisms of systems that ignored 'common sense'.[10] But this is an unsatisfactory approach to the development of a positive science. If sociology is eventually to be as positive a science as physics (as Mill believed), we should surely proceed in sociology just as we do in physics when the consequences of a principle conflict with common sense. When this happens in physics we do not merely say that it is absurd to press a scientific principle to the point where it conflicts with common sense, and leave it at that. Rather, we re-examine the principle and the reasoning processes that led from it, and if they survive this scrutiny we may ultimately modify our common sense. This approach is widely applied. As Littré retorted against Mill on this matter: 'Following through to the consequences is the chief virtue of a philosopher; and without this, philosophizing is a wretched job.'[11]

Mill's second approach was to disparage Comte's later writings. Comte as a young man (a few years before writing the *Philosophie positive*) had suffered a mental breakdown, from which he recovered; but in the last year or two of his life his mental condition deteriorated. His writing became increasingly bizarre, showing a particular tendency to obsess about trivia. Thus, for example, he insisted that the basis of the number system must be a prime number, and proposed precise regulation of the number of chapters, parts, sections and sentences of every treatise that might be written on any subject. Mill comments:

> Others may laugh, but we could far rather weep at this melancholy decadence of a great intellect. M. Comte used to reproach his early English admirers with maintaining the 'conspiracy of silence' concerning his later performances. The reader can now judge whether such reticence is not more than sufficiently explained by tenderness for his fame, and a conscientious fear of bringing undeserved discredit on the noble speculations of his earlier career.[12]

But Mill is disingenuous here. The conspiracy of silence to which he refers did not relate merely to the curious ideas of Comte's last year or so but at least from the appearance of the first volume of the *Politique positive* several years before.[13] This volume could hardly be dismissed as the product of mental deterioration, and I am not aware of any critic seriously attempting to do so at the time.[14] But Mill's retrospective manoeuvre enables him to lump the *Politique positive* together with Comte's bizarre last pieces, as equally calling for silence out of 'tenderness for his fame'. In this way Mill can dismiss the *Politique positive* and other later works out of hand. Thus, whereas in the *Philosophie positive* he finds 'an essentially sound view of philosophy', he deems all the later works 'in their general character . . . false and misleading'.[15]

There are two difficulties in this approach. First, the tenor of Comte's future thought is already apparent in the final volume of the *Philosophie positive*, which appeared in 1842. Mill considers this point, and declares that he finds in this volume 'the germ of the perversion of

[Comte's] . . . philosophy which marked his later years'.[16] Since Mill had earlier praised and publicized the whole of the *Philosophie positive*, one might then ask why did he not focus on this 'germ' at the time. Mill anticipates this, and his answer is that Comte was then 'so unknown and unappreciated . . . that to criticise his weak points might well appear superfluous, while it was a duty to give as much publicity as one could to the important contributions he had made to philosophic thought'.[17]

The second difficulty is that, as I discussed in Chapters 1 and 3, Comte had outlined his entire scheme for social reorganization in a very early work (the *Plan*). This already prefigured much of the content of the *Politique positive*. Some admirers of the *Philosophie positive* may not have known this early work, but Comte republished it (with minor revisions) in 1854, at the end of the *Politique positive*, declaring that he did so 'above all to demonstrate the perfect harmony between the efforts of my youth and the accomplishments of my mature years'.[18] Comte overstates in claiming *perfect* harmony, but there is certainly considerable harmony between the *Plan* and the *Politique positive*.

Plainly then, any division between the philosophical and sociopolitical aspects of Comte's work does not strongly correlate with a division between Comte's early work in his prime and his later work in his dotage or as presentiment of his mental deterioration. Moreover, Mill was surely sufficiently familiar with the corpus of Comte's works to have known this.

It is fair to say that Mill was not concerned with arguing against Comte's socio-political ideas. He just wanted to guard against their being put into practice. To this end he did his best to ensure that, at least in England, the general 'conspiracy of silence' would continue regarding all of Comte's work outside the acceptable parts of the *Philosophie positive*.

In conclusion, note that there is nothing to suggest that Mill's views on the acceptable parts of the *Philosophie positive* changed as a result of his rejection of the *Politique positive*. In particular, as I discussed in Chapter 4, Mill continued to regard the creation of the science of sociology as the great task in the future development of positivism. He acknowledged that Comte had made a substantial contribution to this task in the *Philosophie positive*, but felt that much remained to be done by future generations. The publication of the *Politique positive* and Comte's other later works might be missteps on the path towards the ultimate goal, but they could not change the fundamental nature of the goal: the creation by experts of a science of sociology with the authority and predictive capacity of the physical sciences.

ii. Littré as disciple

Émile Littré, student of mathematics, brilliant linguist and translator, widely respected medical scientist and historian, and creator of the monumental dictionary of the French language that bears his name, encountered Comte's *Philosophie positive* in 1840, at the age of thirty-nine.[19] A quarter of a century later he wrote of that experience:

> His book enthralled me. My mind became conflicted between my old opinions and the new ones to which I was now exposed. The latter triumphed, especially in that they demonstrated to me that my past was merely a preliminary stage. As a result, they produced not disruption and contradiction but growth and development. From that point on, I became a disciple of positive philosophy. I have remained one ever since.[20]

From the 1840s until shortly before his death in 1881 Littré was an important and influential expositor of positivism. His views came to diverge from Comte's, and in due course he broke entirely from him. Littré and a number of other positivists in general agreement with him (a fairly incohesive group sometimes referred to as the Littréists) rejected the idea that Comte's work, including the religion of humanity, constituted the final exposition of an all-embracing positivist way of life. Rather, they regarded Comte's achievement as a philosophical and socio-political work in progress, for his successors to continue. Indeed, they regarded the continuing incompleteness of positivism as a virtue, demonstrating its capacity for development and progress. Thus, comparing positivism with the major religions of the world, Littré wrote:

> These theologies have . . . an . . . irreparable defect that makes them entirely unfit to serve the needs of the international state of the world: they are static. No movement, no development, no progress, is possible for them . . . One needs something with the capacity for life and growth that the positivist spirit possesses.[21]

This of course conflicted with Comte's view that he had brought positive philosophy close to completion and readiness for social implementation. But how could Littré claim to be a disciple of positive philosophy while conflicting with its creator on a basic positivist issue? He called on positivism itself as justification:

> M. Comte, in founding the positive philosophy and extending the
> positive method to the entire range of human knowledge, has placed
> in the public domain a powerful instrument of which he is certainly
> the creator, but which does not belong to him exclusively. This
> method rules him as much as everyone else . . . Once Newton and
> Leibnitz had set up the differential calculus they themselves imme-
> diately became subject to it . . . Likewise here the positive method is
> an impersonal judge, bound to deliver judgement on everything that
> has been done by the master, on everything that will be done by the
> disciples.[22]

The comparison here with a physical or mathematical science is of
course a characteristic positivist move.

It was Comte's *Politique positive* that first drove Littré to call on positivism itself against Comte. He recalled what he had expected from
hearing Comte read the first few chapters of this work to the *Société
positiviste* in Paris before publication:

> This work . . . made its appearance shortly after the Paris revolution
> of 1848 and while the threat of violence was still present. It promised
> to be decisive for both the present and the future. There was never
> a more ready listener than I. Needless to say, I was expecting some-
> thing as new and enlightening for politics as positive philosophy had
> given me ten years before.[23]

He was disappointed. Recall that, as I discussed in Chapter 3, in the
Politique positive Comte introduces the 'subjective' principle into positivism. This is the principle prioritizing feelings over the intellect,
whereby positivism would achieve its synthesis of love, order and
progress. Littré found this wholly unacceptable:

> In the subjective method, the starting point is a mental state that
> produces *a priori* a certain metaphysical principle, and from this it
> proceeds to make deductions . . . The results are as metaphysical as
> the starting point . . . They do not get nor even seek for the *a
> posteriori* confirmation of experience.[24]

He pursued the association between the subjective principle and metaphysics, dismissing them together as 'the same thing', and declared that
'M. Comte, . . . in bringing back the subjective method, which has no
place in the sciences, . . . has himself ruined that which brought him
philosophical fame and authority'.[25]

Recalling my discussion in the previous section, we see that both Littré and Mill largely accepted positivism as Comte had presented it in the *Philosophie positive*, but felt that he had gone badly astray in much of the *Politique positive*. This might suggest that they took a similar approach to Comte's work. However, this is not the case. Mill simply excised the *Politique positive* and Comte's other later works from the positivist canon. This allowed him to remain committed to the goals of the *Philosophie positive*, in particular the creation by experts of a science of sociology with the authority and predictive capacity of the physical sciences.

Littré did not simply reject and forget the *Politique positive*. He went on to consider why Comte had introduced the subjective principle and what its rejection would entail for positivism. He argued as follows. Comte had introduced the subjective principle because the objective positive method alone, as set out in the *Philosophie positive*, could not support his scheme. But 'one of the most secure principles of positive philosophy, one of those that M. Comte has stated most firmly and that gives him the highest honour, is that the higher a science is in the hierarchy [of the sciences], the lower the deductive power is within it'.[26] Consequently, in the sciences of humanity, at the pinnacle of the hierarchy, the deductive power would be far lower than in the physical sciences, at the base of the hierarchy. But this would severely limit the predictive power of the sciences of humanity and thereby undermine Comte's scheme. Littré concluded that Comte was led astray to introduce the subjective principle in order to avoid this limitation:

> The subjective method, which is not submitted to experimental verification but only to verification in terms of coherence between premises and conclusions, has an unlimited field open to it. Nothing stops it, nothing limits it . . . On the other hand, the deductive method offered only a slow, obstacle-strewn course . . . Closed in by this dilemma, M. Comte slid away along the path of premises and conclusions, a deceptive path in the higher sciences and particularly in sociology, the highest of them all.[27]

But if Littré recognized that the objective principle alone would not yield predictive power in the human sciences, and refused to tolerate the introduction of the subjective principle for this purpose, then how was positivism to achieve predictive power in the human sciences? The point is that Littré had ceased to believe that this was possible by any means at all. At one time he had strongly shared Comte's belief that positivism could achieve predictive power in the human sciences, especially after Comte had successfully predicted the 1848 revolution. Littré himself then made various predictions of social and political events, publishing them in the first edition of his book *Conservation, Révolution et Positivisme* in 1852.

The problem was that most of these predictions proved wrong. In the second edition of *Conservation, Révolution et Positivisme*, published in 1879, Littré criticized and retracted a range of views that he had expressed in the first edition and that had led him to try to predict the future.[28] He had already expressed his disenchantment with Comte's capacity to predict the future in terms that showed that this was a general disenchantment. Referring to Comte's prediction of the 1848 revolution, he stated:

> I would not want to draw too strong a conclusion from this prediction, because the selfsame M. Comte predicted that the republic would not be destroyed in France and that the great war would not break out in Europe. The failure of such predictions shows . . . that *it is impossible for us to press the deductive process very far in political and social matters.*[29]

This was an extraordinary concession. The entire goal of positivism in Comte's scheme had been 'to regulate the present in accordance with the desired future as deduced from the past'.[30] This goal, which Comte had declared in the *Philosophie positive*, wholly depended on achieving predictive power in the human sciences. Consequently, it might now seem that in accepting that this was impossible Littré had abandoned positivism altogether. This would then contrast with Mill's apparent fidelity to the principles of the *Philosophie positive*.

But this would be a misleading perspective. Mill's fidelity was conditional. If he had been compelled to accept that the human sciences would not achieve predictive power he would surely have abandoned positivism altogether, because for him the entire future promise of positivism would thereby have been lost. However, Littré's commitment to the core of positivism was absolute, akin to a religious commitment. As he succinctly expressed the distinction: 'I am a disciple of positive philosophy; M. Mill is a critic of it'.[31] This explains how he proceeded. Rather than abandoning his faith in positivism, he purified it by unceremoniously tossing aside the unsupportable burden of achieving predictive power.

What then does positivism now consist of, according to Littré? Again disagreeing with Mill, he shifts the focus of positivism away from the creation of sociology, declaring that 'setting up sociology was only a step towards a goal for M. Comte, not a goal itself; the goal was positive philosophy'.[32] And in his view Comte had already achieved this goal in the *Philosophie positive*.[33] What he had achieved was to create an all-important *method*. Drawing on a statement of Comte's in the *Philosophie positive* for authority, Littré insisted that this general method was more important than the particular doctrine of any area of investigation.[34] We know from the *Philosophie positive* that this method is the scientific method based on deduction and induction, and that each science will develop its own approach within this framework, with its own epistemology, according to its needs.

But even if setting up sociology had been for Comte merely a step towards the goal of positive philosophy, we still need to know what it means to set up sociology, now that it is no longer to be a predictive science. Littré explained that 'sociology is set up [as a science] when one has grasped the law whereby the social order passes down its [social and cultural] heritage through the ages.'[35] More specifically, sociology as a science will enable us to draw a key distinction:

> The deductive method in sociology . . . distinguishes among past events those that belong to the regular process of development from those that belong to the category of disruptions . . . and thereby establishes the philosophy of history and determines its laws. It does likewise for future events . . . But future events have not yet happened, and, because of the complexity of sociology, it cannot predict them except within the narrowest limits. Consequently, it must wait until they occur.[36]

Expressing this in the terms of positivism that I discussed in Chapter 2, sociology is to *explain* past events in terms of laws that specify what the regular process of development is. But recall that Comte's scheme insisted that explanation and prediction were merely two aspects of the same process: making connections between phenomena. Thus, in a sharp departure from Comte, Littré separated explanation from prediction, retaining the former as fundamental to the human sciences while discarding the latter as unachievable.

This raises the question of how we are to determine when an explanation according to Littré's requirements is satisfactory. After all, anyone can make any number of statements about how the social order passes down its social and cultural heritage through the ages, and about which past events are part of the steady process of development and which are disruptions. What criteria are we supposed to apply to tell us whether any such statement is valid? There is no apparent way within Littré's schema, since he has abandoned predictive power as the test of scientific validity and offered no alternative. Littré gave no direct answer to this question.

However, we have a kind of answer in the fact that each science must determine its own epistemology, according to its needs. This means that each science must determine its own tests of validity internally. Moreover, since knowledge of any given scientific discipline is largely confined to the experts who work in it, an internal decision is necessarily to a great extent an autonomous decision. Put otherwise, each science must largely decide for itself what is to count as a valid explanation of events that concern it.

The remaining question is what is to be the role of sociology in the social and political sphere in Littré's scheme, given that it cannot predict future events except within the narrowest limits. Littré defined it as follows:

> Its function – and it is one of supreme importance that it alone can carry out – thus consists in showing governments and peoples which social and political developments should be promoted and which, rather, should be snuffed out at birth.[37]

Although this gave sociology a weaker role than Comte's scheme had done, it remained a substantial role. Sociology would still be charged with determining what would be beneficial for human society. This now became a guiding role, whereas under Comte's scheme it had been a detailed planning role. Nonetheless, it remained a prescriptive role, so Littré effectively maintained the status of sociology as a prescriptive science.

Littré's development of positivism also affected the role of morality. Recall that, as I discussed in Chapter 3, Comte's introduction of the subjective principle dealt with the problem that the development of morality into a positive science would not in itself make human beings moral. With the subjective principle, morality acquired a twofold aspect, as both an objective moral science and a subjective moral sense. As a science, morality stood at the summit of the hierarchy of the sciences and would derive its laws from the conclusions of sociology regarding the benefit of humanity. As a subjective sense, socially inculcated morality would form the foundation of positivist social practice. Morality would thus form the link between theory and practice in the positivist scheme.

Littré's rejection of the subjective principle broke this link. The conclusions of sociology could now offer only broad guidance in social organization, and on the basis of broad guidance moral science could do no more than develop fairly general principles of conduct. These would be insufficient to support an inculcated subjective morality that, in the terminology of modern moral philosophy, would constitute a comprehensive sense of 'the right' as prior to 'the good', as Comte had intended. In any event, without the subjective principle positivism would have no process for inculcating the conclusions of sociology as a moral sense. Consequently, positivist moral principles would now exist only as scientific conclusions, to be ultimately justified by reference to the benefit of humanity. Thus, under Littré's development of positivism 'the good' is prior to 'the right', both philosophically and politically.

Littré's shift of the positivist analysis was a remarkable move. Some of the ideas he expressed may already have been current in and beyond his circle, but he seems to have been the first to set them out coherently. Their influence spread far beyond the circle of committed adherents of positivism, although it is impossible to determine to what extent this resulted from Littré's exposition. I discuss the influence of these ideas in the next chapter.

6
The Structure of the Legacy of Positivism

i. Positivism as creed: diversions from the legacy

In this chapter I shall identify some pervasive aspects of modern thought that, I argue, ultimately derive from positivism as Comte enunciated it and from the developments in positivism that Littré set down. These are what I define collectively as the legacy of positivism. I do not claim that the aspects of thought that I identify are the only long-term influences of positivism on modern thought, but I draw attention to those influences that are crucial to present-day philosophical and political debates. This will be the subject of the next and subsequent sections.

In the present section I consider some viewpoints that have become associated with positivism, but that I do not include within the legacy of positivism. It is nonetheless important to consider them, because they have come to define the attitudes of many people towards positivism, and as a result can divert attention from its legacy in modern thought. These viewpoints largely arise from conscious attempts to evaluate Comte's works as he in fact intended them to be evaluated: as a creed or manifesto for organizing ideas about society and for social reorganization itself. A few of these attempts have concluded in trying to adopt some adapted version of Comte's scheme for social reorganization. Others have concluded in rejecting his scheme in favour of some other scheme or no particular scheme at all. However, the outcome in every case has been to establish a particular view of positivism in some socio-political context.

The attempts to adopt a variant of Comte's scheme are of historical interest, and of course they may have significant present-day consequences – as may any notable historical events or processes. Although

I briefly discuss the most widely influential of these attempts below, the inevitable consequences of these and other such historical events are not my main subject. They do not fall within what I define as the legacy of positivism in modern thought. This legacy is not a consequence, direct or indirect, of consciously adopting positivism as a way of organizing thoughts or life. Rather, it is the substance of certain positivist ideas as they have become pervasively woven into modern thought, whether we are mindful of them or not.

As I have indicated, the attitudes towards positivism that I review in this section are generally concerned exclusively with Comte's work, although in some cases they have referred also to Mill. They largely reject positivism as they perceive it, and indeed generally express antipathy against it. Admittedly, once one fully comprehends Comte's scheme for social reorganization, as I discussed it in Chapter 3, there is certainly good reason for antipathy against many aspects of it. Mill's concern to maintain a 'conspiracy of silence' regarding Comte's socio-political scheme in order to protect positivism as a philosophy was, as I discussed in Chapter 5, politically astute in this regard. But ironically, as I discuss below, in some cases antipathy against Comte's scheme has in fact stemmed from failure to comprehend it fully.

However, it will in any event become clear that there is only a limited intersection between the aspects of Comte's scheme that have evoked antipathy and what I shall define as the legacy of positivism. Consequently, existing critiques of Comte's scheme and established attitudes towards positivism largely turn out to be irrelevant to the legacy of positivism in modern thought.

Moreover, some of the most important facets of the legacy of positivism derive not directly from Comte's work but through the ideas that Littré set down. I am not aware that any attention has been focused on the influence of these ideas. Consequently, the modes of thought to which they have given rise have largely remained unexamined. As I discuss in later sections, these modes of thought and some associated views on social organization are problematic in a number of ways, and call for further critique.

Adverse attitudes to Comte's positivism have a long history. Recall Mill's observation that many people whose mode of thought could fairly be described as positivist preferred not to be so described.[1] In Mill's time and through to around the end of the nineteenth century, we can roughly distinguish three kinds of reasons for this attitude: philosophical, political and religious. The philosophical reasons largely focused on Comte's obsession with systematization, which, as I discussed in

Chapter 5, many thinkers even in that era regarded as excessive. Indeed, Mill himself, asserting a stalwart English practicality despite his own considerable tendencies to systematize, criticizes Comte for 'the extraordinary height to which he carries the mania for regulation by which Frenchmen are distinguished among Europeans, and M. Comte among Frenchmen'.[2]

This view of positivism as obsessed with systematization has come through to the present day. Closely connected with it is a sense of positivism as being obsessed with certainty and precision. Thus, for example, Karl Popper has declared that the demand for criteria for the application of concepts seems 'to express the very heart of positivistic tendencies'.[3] This view in fact represents the area where the common critiques of positivism do intersect with the legacy of positivism. As I show in the following sections, to some extent Comte's view that a single method, with epistemological variations, could extend from the physical to the human sciences has become part of the legacy of positivism in modern thought. In so far as this is the case, the kind of focus on certainty and precision within a systematized conceptual structure that characterizes the physical sciences tends to extend to other disciplines.

It is convenient to consider here another widely held view of positivism: that it asserts that it is possible to observe phenomena in a 'neutral' and 'objective' manner. As a rough definition of these terms, observations are neutral and objective if they do not in any way depend on the worldview of the observer – that is, if they are plain observations of what there is, uncoloured by any theory.[4] Since a number of political conservatives express the belief that their own observations are uncoloured by theory, positivism has consequently been generally associated with political conservatism. However, recall that Comte insisted that every observation always depends on a prior theory,[5] which declares the very opposite of a belief in neutral and objective observation.

Admittedly, once Comte becomes involved in developing his theory he quickly becomes oblivious to any worldview other than the positivist. He then fails to question consistently the validity of his own observations, and thus treats them in practice as if they were indeed uncoloured by any theory. But in these respects he hardly differs from many other thinkers, as I discussed in Chapter 4. Consequently, in so far as a belief in neutral and objective observation has entered modern thought, Comte and his development of positivism cannot be considered a primary source. For this reason, I do not include such a belief within the legacy of positivism in modern thought. I discuss this further in Section iii.

I now consider the main political critiques of positivism in the nineteenth century, which derived from adverse reaction to Comte's scheme of social reorganization. I discussed this in Chapter 5 under the rubric of Mill's criticisms of Comte. In particular, the rigid organization of Comte's social scheme and the intensity of his aversion to revolution further conveyed a sense of strong political conservatism as a general theme in his work, notwithstanding his insistence on progress. His views on the sovereignty of the people, freedom of conscience and the role of women further confirmed this impression.

However, it does not seem that these aspects of Comte's scheme have had any traceable influence on modern thought. Although some of the more objectionable views on social organization that he expressed are still to be found today, people who hold them do not appear to hold them by virtue of the influence, direct or indirect, of Comte and positivism. If they seek authority for their views they find other sources than Comte or positivism to serve their purpose. Thus, Comte's views on such matters as freedom of conscience and the role of women are essentially irrelevant to the legacy of positivism. Admittedly, it may gall to acknowledge that Comte, given that he held such views, has strongly influenced modern thought in any context. Nevertheless, galling or not, I shall show in the following sections that such is the case.

What I call the religious reason for an adverse attitude to positivism in the nineteenth century derived from rejection of Comte's positivist religion of humanity. This was a particular issue in England, where the religious positivists were relatively prominent. Shortly after Comte's death in 1857 they began to set up positivist churches that practised the liturgy that Comte had designed, and promised a synthesis of religion and science.[6] There was a period of some success. A contemporary was to observe many years later: 'There is a long article in the "Spectator" at the beginning of 1882 on "the ever-increasing wonder" of that strange faith, "Positivism". It is difficult for the present generation to realize how large a space in the minds of the young men of the eighties was occupied by the religion invented by Auguste Comte.'[7]

In this context, it is fair to say that anyone who 'gave his assent to Positivism did so in awareness of the existence of a Positivist Church'.[8] Consequently, as increasingly many people came to find the religion unappealing, adverse attitudes to positivism were bound to gain hold. However, the religion of humanity is now almost entirely of historical interest only,[9] and it seems to have left no traceable influence in modern thought. Thus it is essentially irrelevant to the legacy of positivism.

I now turn to adverse attitudes to positivism that stem from particular historical developments. Again, there are philosophical and political reasons. The philosophical reason stems from rejection of the now generally disregarded movement of logical positivism.[10] This is in fact a poor reason because, as is well known, Comte's positivism and logical positivism have little in common beyond the fact that both insist on statements being verifiable and consequently reject metaphysics. Even on these issues the approaches are quite different: logical positivism stipulates that statements that are not verifiable are cognitively vacuous, whereas for Comte they are simply of no value to humanity as subjects of investigation. There are many other differences. Logical positivism is deeply concerned with formal language structures, of which Comte is oblivious. Logical positivism seeks a universal scientific epistemology, whereas Comte recognizes variance in epistemology from one science to another. Perhaps most crucially, logical positivism insists that statements of value cannot be verifiable, whereas Comte's goal is the development of sciences of humanity in which the whole point is to derive statements of value as scientific laws. In sum, there was never any close connection between Comte's positivism and logical positivism, and consequently logical positivism is essentially irrelevant to the legacy of positivism in modern thought.

The political reasons stem from two separate historical developments that, once again, identify positivism with strong political conservatism. However, the identification in these cases is more specific than the general sense, discussed above, of conservative attitudes running through Comte's scheme. In particular, these historical developments focus on the locus and exercise of political power in society, whereas the critiques discussed above are more broadly concerned with the nature of the social order and its impact on the individual.

One of these historical developments can be traced back to the comparisons that were commonly drawn between Comte and G. W. F. Hegel in the context of philosophical and political thought through much of the nineteenth century. On a general level, it is easy to compare Comte, particularly in the *Philosophie positive*, with Hegel, particularly in his *Philosophie der Geschichte* (*Philosophy of History*). Both sought a rational synthesis of the gamut of human knowledge; both recognized that human thought is conditioned by context; both sought a rational process of development in human history; and both were broadly concerned with the relationship between individual freedom and social structure.[11]

Awareness of these comparisons led Karl Marx to read parts of Comte's *Philosophie positive.* In 1866 he expressed his views to Friedrich Engels:

> Incidentally, I am also studying Comte now because the English and French go on so much about the fellow. The encyclopaedic aspect, the 'synthesis,' is what appeals to them. But this is pitiful compared to Hegel . . . And this positivist shit appeared [as recently as] 1832![12]

A number of writers have gone far beyond this simple dismissal and interpreted Comte as directly oppositional to the kind of social change that Marx and his followers sought. Thus, for example, one scholar asserts that (1) 'the very purpose and result of [Comte's] extending the positive scientific method to human and social phenomena are to secure in the public at large the acceptance of the existing order and its predominant forces'. She then claims that (2) Comte is dedicated to establishing social control under the aegis of scientific and industrial forces, and derives from this that (3) he is 'the theoretical exponent *par excellence* of modern capitalism'. She concludes that (4) Comte and Marx are intellectually representative of 'the two major antagonistic forces' in nineteenth-century European social philosophy.[13]

These four statements are quite typical of the genre. If they were a fair assessment of Comte's thesis, one could well understand the association between positivism and political conservatism in the context of the locus of political power in society. But they are not. Rather, this is a case where, as I mentioned above, antipathy against Comte's scheme stems from failure to comprehend it fully. First, my discussion in Chapter 3 makes it plain that Comte did not propose 'to secure in the public at large the acceptance of the existing order'. To find such a goal in his thesis would require positing and justifying a subtext in his works that promulgated the exact opposite of his explicit statements; no one has done so. Second, the conflation of scientific with industrial forces has insufficient support in Comte's texts. Comte did in fact give industrial forces a role in the *practice* of social reorganization, but he gave them no role at all in framing the *theoretical plan* for social reorganization.[14] Unless, again, we interpret Comte as promulgating the opposite of what he stated, we must acknowledge that the distinction between theory and practice was crucial in his thesis, and that the former was far more important.

Third, Comte insisted that property was social in nature and must be socially regulated.[15] This of course followed from his requirement that all aspects of human existence must be regulated for the benefit of humanity as a whole, as I discussed in Chapter 3. It is therefore hardly appropriate to regard him as 'the theoretical exponent *par excellence* of modern capitalism'. This dismisses the third point, and thereby removes any support for the fourth point.[16] In sum, the comparisons between Comte and Marx add nothing to my assessment, above, of the effect of his general conservatism on the legacy of positivism. That is, they are essentially irrelevant.

The other historical development that I consider derives from Latin American political thought. This stems from serious and concerted nineteenth-century attempts to implement positivism directly as a socio-political system in various degrees in many countries of that region. These attempts were largely driven by the desire of political theorists, leaders and activists to break free of forces that they saw as having stifled societal development since national independence, and to create a progressive social order. At the same time, they wished to avoid the slaughter and turmoil that in so much of Latin America had characterized attempts at societal restructuring. It was understandable that they should turn to Comte's schema, and particularly to its theme of harmonizing order and progress.

Those who introduced positivism in this way certainly did not see it as politically conservative. The positivist movement inspired various reforms, especially in the administrative and educational arenas.[17] However, in the later years of the nineteenth century and in the early twentieth century these positivist reforms became associated with rigid and repressive regimes in several countries, and to an extent were considered responsible for them. This has given positivism the retrospective reputation among some Latin American thinkers of having been the source of many ills throughout the continent and led to its association with strong political conservatism.[18] But it does not appear that these attempts to implement positivism as a political system in Latin America have left any traceable influence in the modes of modern thought that I discuss in the following sections, so this history also turns out to be essentially irrelevant to the legacy of positivism.[19]

ii. The received view of the legacy

Delivering the first Auguste Comte Memorial Trust Lecture at the London School of Economics in 1953, Isaiah Berlin stated:

> Comte's views have affected the categories of our thought more deeply than is commonly supposed . . . He understood the role of

natural science and the true reasons for its prestige better than most contemporary thinkers . . . He believed in the application of scientific . . . canons of explanation in all fields: and saw no reason why they should not apply to relations of human beings as well as relations of things.[20]

This states what has now become very much the accepted view of the influence of Comte. It recognizes that Comte's influence has often gone unrecognized, and acknowledges that influence within certain parameters. Let us consider more closely what these parameters are.

As Berlin says, Comte's view of the role of the physical (natural) sciences and the reasons for their prestige has deeply affected the categories of our thought. We expect the physical sciences to investigate phenomena in such a way as to derive general laws, and we regard those laws as providing certain and accurate knowledge of the relations between phenomena. These were the views that Comte set down.

It would be disingenuous to deny that we live our lives in accordance with these views. Among myriad possible illustrations of this, let me give one that recalls my discussion in Chapter 4 of the empiricism of Mill and Hume. When we press a light switch, we may be vaguely aware of depending on a technological complex that in turn relies on the certainty and accuracy of scientifically derived laws of electricity. If on occasion we press the light switch and nothing happens, we do not suppose for a moment that these laws of electricity have gone into abeyance. Rather, we seek a reason for the failure in terms of the technological complex that relies on those laws – we might check the light bulb or the switch or the circuit breaker, or look around to see if there has been a power cut. In any event, the very reason that we seek for the failure of illumination will itself presume the continuing reliability of the scientific laws of electricity. Their certainty and accuracy go unchallenged. It is this kind of mental process that, as Berlin claims, forms part of the legacy of Comte's thought in ours.

This positivist view of the physical sciences very much stems from nineteenth-century science. Scientists of that era generally presumed that the principles they derived were certain and permanently settled. However, in due course relativity theory unsettled the previously most settled of all scientific principles, Newton's law of universal gravitation. This disabused scientists of their illusions of permanence. Nineteenth-century scientists also generally took external reality for granted, but in due course quantum theory compelled scientists to recognize the fragility of even that notion. Nevertheless, the positivist, nineteenth-century view of science is not seriously questioned as a day-to-day matter except in the most rarefied of scholarly circles. Otherwise, the positivist idea that physical science – even as it extends to new frontiers – provides answers that are accurate, settled, and verified beyond the point where discussion would be useful, remains entrenched throughout society.

This view of the physical sciences also encompasses Comte's insistence on investigating verifiable, positive laws as relations between phenomena rather than troubling with metaphysical notions of causes of phenomena. It further entails Comte's linkage between explanatory and predictive power in the physical sciences, as being two aspects of the process of making connections between phenomena. These too are embedded in the categories of our thought.

As Berlin observes, Comte's demand for the application of scientific canons of explanation in all fields, including what were to become the human sciences, has also deeply affected the categories of our thought. Although we might not quite believe in Comte's law of three stages in the form that he presented it, yet the esteem in which the sciences are held has encouraged various humanities disciplines to aspire to or claim scientific status.

We can see this in action particularly easily in history and anthropology, since in each of these fields some good scholars have made a study of method and explicitly set out the claims of the field to scientific status. Their insights into method will in fact provide helpful illustrations of the legacy of positivism throughout this chapter.

Thus, E. H. Carr, arguing in support of 'the claim of history to be included among the sciences', considers how to counter those who would deny this claim:

> One remedy I would suggest is to improve the standard of our history, to make it – if I may dare to say so – more scientific, to make our demands on those who pursue it more rigorous . . . [H]istory is a far more difficult subject than classics, and quite as serious as any science . . . Some historians – and more of those who write about history without being historians . . . are so busy telling us that history is not a science, and explaining what it cannot and should not be or do, that they have no time for its achievements and its potentialities.[21]

We see here a respect for the sciences as serious, difficult and rigorous, coupled with a sense of aspiration that history, if it takes the appropriate measures, can aspire to scientific status.

Just as we might not quite believe in Comte's law of three stages, we also might not quite believe in his hierarchy of the sciences in the form that he presented it. Yet we do generally accept that there is a weaker, more loosely hierarchical set of inter-scientific relationships, so that, for example, the study of biology depends to some extent on knowledge of chemistry, and the study of chemistry depends to some extent on knowledge of physics. This does in fact correspond roughly to Comte's hierarchy, at least within the physical sciences.

This is essentially as far as Berlin goes in his assessment of Comte's influence on the categories of our thought. It encompasses a range of aspects of Comte's thesis that I discussed in Chapter 1 and Chapter 2, Section iii. Berlin's assessment in effect amounts to a claim that Mill's view of what was valuable in Comte's work has come down to us, but without touching upon the issue of predictive power in the human sciences. This assessment is unexceptionable as far as it goes, but it does not go nearly far enough.

iii. The legacy in method

Other aspects of Comte's work have also deeply affected the categories of our thought. These encompass matters that I discussed in previous chapters. It is convenient to begin the discussion of these various influences with another, but in this case rather misleading statement by Berlin:

> Comte . . . did not say that history was, or was reducible to, a kind of physics; but his conception of sociology pointed in that direction – of one complete and all-embracing pyramid of scientific knowledge; one method; one truth; one scale of rational, 'scientific' values. This naïve craving for unity and symmetry at the expense of experience is with us still.[22]

This statement will not detain us long, as it has little to do with what Comte actually said. However, it is a fair statement of what Mill, and others such as Russell who continued in his tradition, hoped for,[23] and before putting it aside we should recognize that this Millian view has also affected the categories of our thought. Its influence appears in various forms. It supports the belief, in so far as it still persists, that the human sciences can be reduced to formulation in terms of mathematics or the physical sciences, with the same epistemology serving for all.

Furthermore, by thus making context irrelevant to observation, analysis and formulation of scientific laws, this Millian viewpoint supports a belief in the idea of neutral and objective science, in the human sciences as well as in the physical sciences. I discussed this in Section i, and noted there that this directly conflicts with Comte's insight that every observation rests on a prior theory. Consequently, I do not regard such a belief as deriving from positivism and so do not include it within the legacy of positivism in modern thought.

The influence of Comte in this area is quite different, and exists alongside and largely in opposition to that of Mill. In assessing this influence, note first that Comte in fact *did* say that all the human sciences could be regarded as a kind of physics – his 'social physics', the term he used before he introduced 'sociology'.[24] But, as I discussed in Chapter 2, he expressly denied that any of the human sciences could feasibly be *reduced* to anything akin to the physical science of physics. On the contrary, each science would develop its own epistemology that could not be reduced to that of other sciences. This, I now argue, is part of the legacy of Comte's thought in ours.

It is convenient to illustrate this together with a closely linked aspect of Comte's legacy in our thought: his views on method. Their influence consists in our awareness that a single method *cannot* serve for all areas of investigation. Admittedly, in a sense Comte said the contrary: that the positive method should be used in all the sciences, human as well as physical. But, as I discussed in Chapter 4, this was only in the most general sense. For any practical investigation, he insisted that the positive method could not be understood in the abstract but only contextually in each of the various sciences. From this comes our awareness that a mode of investigation and proof that is appropriate in one area might not be so in another.

Let me give an example from anthropology that explicitly insists on the need for different modes in different scientific disciplines. Clifford Geertz writes:

The besetting sin of interpretive approaches to anything – literature, dreams, symptoms, culture – is that they tend to resist, or to be permitted to resist, conceptual articulation and thus to escape systematic modes of assessment . . . For a field of study which, however timidly (though I, myself, am not timid about the matter at all) asserts itself to be a science, this just will not do. There is no reason why the conceptual structure of a cultural interpretation should be any less formulable, and thus less susceptible to explicit canons of appraisal, than that of, say, a biological observation or a physical experiment – no reason except that the terms in which such formulations can be cast are, if not wholly nonexistent, very nearly so. We are reduced to insinuating theories because we lack the power to state them . . . [T]here is no serious attempt here to apply the concepts and theories of biology, psychology, or even sociology to the analysis of culture (and, of course, not even a suggestion of the reverse exchange) but merely a placing of supposed facts from the cultural and subcultural levels side by side so as to induce a vague sense that some kind of relationship between them – an obscure sort of 'tailoring' – obtains.[25]

Another closely linked influence that is part of Comte's legacy in our thought is the awareness that our observations of the world are not somehow neutral, but depend on a prior sense of theory. Consequently, we are aware that our sense of the world is not absolute but relative to our worldview. Again, I give an example from anthropology:

Because, theory, scientific or otherwise, moves mainly by analogy, . . . when its course shifts, the conceits in which it expresses itself shift with it. In the earlier stages of the natural sciences . . . it has been the world of the crafts and, later, of industry that have for the most part provided the well-understood realities . . . with which the ill-understood ones . . . could be brought into the circle of the known. Science owes more to the steam engine than the steam engine owes to science; without the dyer's art there would be no chemistry; metallurgy is mining theorized. In the social sciences, or at least in those that have abandoned a reductionist conception of what they are about, the analogies are coming more and more from the contrivances of cultural performance than from those of physical manipulation – from theater, painting, grammar, literature, law, play. What the lever did for physics, the chess move promises to do for sociology.[26]

This awareness that our sense of the world is relative to our worldview is an uneasy one, because it threatens to trap us in the vicious circle to which Comte drew attention, 'caught between the need to observe in order to form a theory and the need to create a theory in order to observe'. Since we do not quite believe in his law of three stages, we lack his solution to the problem: that humanity had the natural exit route of spontaneously developing a theological mode of thought.[27] To a great extent we finesse the problem regarding the physical sciences (recall the example of the light switch, above); but as the above illustration from anthropology shows, we are keenly aware of it in the human sciences.

iv. The legacy in structured explanation

From this point on, the aspects of the legacy of positivism in our thought that I discuss do not derive directly from Comte. Rather, they have come to us via the development of the positivist structure that Littré set out, and that I discussed in the previous chapter.

Recall that Littré departed from Comte's scheme by separating explanation from prediction in the human sciences. He considered the capacity to explain as fundamental to the human sciences. However, he regarded the capacity to predict as limited to distinguishing events in the regular course of development from disruptions. I now argue that this structure is part of modern thought.

My illustration again comes from Carr in the context of history. Carr approaches the idea of explanation in history by relating it to explanation in everyday life. He argues that in everyday life, when a habitually conventional acquaintance suddenly behaves in an unprecedented way we expect there to be an *explanation*, generally in terms of some causative event. In effect, he extrapolates to routine human affairs the point I made in my light-switch illustration in Section ii. He continues:

> Now let us look at the historian. Like the ordinary man, he believes that human actions have causes which are in principle ascertainable. History, like everyday life, would be impossible if this assumption were not made. It is the special function of the historian to investigate these causes.[28]

Note here that Carr does not mean 'causes' in the sense of primary or ultimate causes, which of course Comte rejected as the subject of scientific investigation. Rather, his sense of 'causes' is of prior events that relate to the event at issue and so explain it. This is the kind of subject of scientific investigation that Comte considered appropriate, as I discussed in Chapter 2.

Now Carr asserts a role for prediction in history very similar to Littré's:

> The historian . . . is bound to generalize; and, in so doing, he provides general guides for future action which, though not specific predictions, are both valid and useful. But he cannot predict specific

events, because the specific is unique and because the element of accident enters into it.[29]

Thus he asserts a distinction between explanation and prediction, and a limited capacity for prediction, that reflects exactly the ideas we find in Littré's work and represents an aspect of the legacy of positivism in modern thought.

Moreover, note Carr's argument that 'the element of accident' prevents history from predicting specific events in the future. But if this is the case, how is it that the selfsame element of accident does not prevent history from explaining specific events in the past? The only possible answer is that history is capable of distinguishing past accidents from past events that, in some sense, are not mere accidents. This in essence is a restatement of Littré's distinction between 'disruptions' and 'events in the regular process of development'.[30]

But this raises the question of how one might test the validity of such a distinction between accidents or disruptions and regular events. More generally, it raises the question of how one might test the validity of any explanation that the science puts forward. As I indicated in Chapter 5, the only possible answer under the legacy of positivism is that each science must determine its own validity tests internally. As I discuss further in the next and subsequent sections, this gives rise to significant problems.

Lest it be thought that Carr's work reflects a now dated approach – his book was published in 1961 – I conclude this section with an illustration from 2005:

> Comparison and analysis, properly conceived, are the lifeblood of historical analysis . . . Taken in the right spirit, therefore, history can provide its own unique kind of help to understand the present. As a discipline it is neither predictive, nor a practical guide to action: its lessons are not so specific. Yet it remains an essential tool for scrutinising the easy moralising, the ideological certainties and the expansive claims that batter our ears. It can serve as a politician's cheerleader, but it can also weigh policy assumptions and contexts.[31]

v. The legacy in scientific autonomy

Littré's abandonment of the goal of predictive power in the human sciences has consequences in modern thought for the relationships between the various human sciences. To see this, first consider the relationship between historical and sociological investigations that would have obtained under Comte's scheme. Comte did not classify history as a separate science, so that he necessarily incorporated historical investigations within the broad scope of sociology. It is nevertheless convenient for purposes of exposition to draw a rough distinction between history and sociology here, and since Comte recognized that his divisions between the sciences were essentially artificial it is quite appropriate to do so.[32]

Taking this approach, the relationship between historical and sociological investigations under Comte's scheme is clear from my discussion in Chapters 2 and 3. Historical investigations would establish laws allowing prediction of consequences in the future starting from any given set of circumstances in the present. Sociological investigations would determine what kind of future society was desired. A process of reasoning would then enable sociology, armed with the laws of history, to determine how to organize society in the present so that the desired consequences would ensue in the future. We might say that history would provide input to sociology, in much the same way as what modern writers call the 'auxiliary sciences' of history provide history with input.[33] Moreover, history would have a social responsibility to provide sociology with input, as part of its role in constructing Comte's theoretical plan for the reorganization of society.

When we abandon the goal of predictive power, this entire scheme collapses. Sociology might still declare what kind of future society is desired, but now history can offer it no laws that would enable it to organize present-day society accordingly. In effect, the separation between history and sociology that I posited for purposes of exposition becomes a substantive separation. But any separation between the sciences threatens Comte's plan, as he was keenly aware. He focused attention on this issue in regard to the tendency, apparent even in his day, towards narrow scientific specialization. While he acknowledged that specialization was necessary for advancing the sciences, he recognized that it could not develop the expertise needed to fashion a unified plan for the reorganization of society.[34] His proposed solution was as follows:

> Let there be a new class of experts, prepared by a suitable education, who will not commit themselves to the development of any particular branch of science. Rather, they will take the various sciences as they are, and engage entirely in precisely determining the essence of each of them and discovering the relations and connections between

them . . . In so doing they will at all times comply with the fundamental principles of the positive method.[35]

But such generalist experts cannot bridge the substantive separation
between the sciences that appears when we abandon the goal of predictive power. No experts can discover connections between the sciences sufficient to unify them into Comte's plan for the reorganization
of society, because now there will be no such connections to discover.
This devastates Comte's scheme. His goal of constructing a complete
theoretical plan for the reorganization of society must be abandoned.
Moreover, there is no basis – or at most, a much-diminished basis – for
imposing on history any social responsibility to provide input for sociology; indeed, we must recognize that except to a very limited degree
it cannot do so. A similar conclusion applies throughout the range of
the human sciences.

Consequently, each human science is able to assert a high degree of
independence of the others. Moreover, as I discussed in Section iii,
Comte's stipulation that different sciences use different variants of scientific method has become part of the legacy of positivism in modern
thought, and this encourages separatist tendencies among the human
sciences. Recall my illustration in Section iii of anthropology insisting
on its separateness from biology, psychology and sociology. These assertions of independence and separateness are in effect claims of autonomy, and in this way the principle that each human science may
claim a degree of autonomy has become part of the legacy of positivism
in modern thought.

There is no obligation to claim scientific autonomy, so that, at least
in theory, it is open to anyone working in any of the human sciences
to seek parallels and linkages with any of the others. But in practice,
given the usual academic rivalries, any inter-scientific overture of this
kind may suffer scornful rejection from the other disciplines. We have
seen an illustration of this in Carr's defence of the scientific status
of history against 'those who write about history without being
historians'.

Each relatively autonomous human science thus provides its own
context and its own methods. In Kuhn's terminology, as I discussed in
Chapter 4, it provides its own specific paradigm. The more insightful
practitioners of the science will be aware that they are working within
a paradigm that validates their conclusions within the internal structure of their science only. This restriction is the price that each human
science pays for its autonomy; as noted above, there are now no experts

to validate inter-scientific claims in the human sciences. However, on a day-to-day basis even the more insightful practitioners can easily be unconscious of this restriction and regard themselves as engaging in universally valid scientific investigations. The less insightful practitioners might take this view at all times. This can be problematic, as I discuss in the following sections.

To conclude this section, I note that in some disciplines a claim to autonomy has been used to avoid difficulties that might undermine the discipline. An example from sociology illustrates this tendency:

> [T]he sociology of knowledge, like all empirical disciplines that accumulate evidence concerning the relativity and determination of human thought, leads toward epistemological questions concerning sociology itself as well as any other scientific body of knowledge . . . How can I be sure, say, of my sociological analysis of American middle-class mores in view of the fact that . . . I am myself a member of the American middle class? . . . [S]uch questions . . . are not themselves part of the empirical discipline of sociology. They properly belong to the methodology of the social sciences, an enterprise that belongs to philosophy and is by definition other than sociology, which is indeed an object of its inquiries. The sociology of knowledge . . . will 'feed' problems to this methodological inquiry. It cannot solve these problems within its own proper frame of reference.[36]

This kind of approach really constitutes an abuse of autonomy claims. It allows a discipline to maintain its sense that it is producing valid conclusions, because any issue that threatens this sense may be conveniently shunted off for another discipline to worry about. A discipline that indulges itself in this way is building castles in the air, or on sand.

vi. The legacy regarding benefit to humanity

Recall that, as I discussed in Chapter 1, Comte insisted that all scientific investigation should be devoted to the benefit of humanity rather than to the satisfaction of academic curiosity. I now argue that this view has to a considerable extent, even if not entirely, entered modern thought as part of the legacy of positivism. It is less generally held in the sciences at the base of Comte's hierarchy – mathematics, astronomy and theoretical physics – which may profess to value knowledge for its own sake. However, in the human sciences at the head of the hierarchy it is quite widely accepted that the aim of furthering the benefit of humanity must always be held in view.

This aspect of the legacy of positivism links with the autonomy claims that I discussed in the previous section. The net result is that each science claims an entitlement to make its own 'scientific' determination of what constitutes the benefit of humanity. I shall take up the issue of how it does this in the next section.

It is not fatal to my argument that there is no overall consensus on what constitutes the benefit of humanity and, moreover, that any consensus that is reached may prove temporary. Consider the following statement by Carr:

> Scientists, social scientists, and historians are all engaged in different branches of the same study: the study of man and his environment, of the effects of man on his environment and of the environment on man. The object of the study is the same: to increase man's understanding of, and mastery over, his environment.[37]

The mood has changed since this was first published in 1961, and there is now some discomfort with declaring a goal of increasing mastery over the environment. However, at that time increasing mastery over the environment was seen as equivalent to acting for the benefit of humanity, and it is fair to say that the latter was the main goal. The view of what constitutes the benefit of humanity may have changed, but the view that science should pursue the benefit of humanity remains unchanged.

Four points should be noted. First, the fact that science engages in investigations that may have harmful effects, such as weapons research, does not contradict the main point of this section. In such cases it is generally considered necessary to justify the investigations by asserting that their beneficial effects will outweigh the detriment. Thus, it may be claimed that weapons research will ultimately strengthen world peace, and so forth. Any arguments on the matter are likely to focus on whether the justification is adequate. Again, this reflects possible disagreement on what constitutes the benefit of humanity, not on whether science should pursue the benefit of humanity.

Second, the concept of 'humanity' is often applied rather narrowly in this context, and may in particular be constrained by nationality. Thus, for example, weapons research may be justified on the ground of benefiting the nation pursuing it.

Third, I have claimed only that the view that science should pursue the benefit of humanity is widely held, not that it is universally held. Some people would surely favour a different goal, such as environmental conservation. One might counter that such people see the ultimate human benefit in environmental conservation, but this would unduly strain to make the argument.

Fourth, some people explicitly reject the goal of the benefit of humanity, and insist that science must be pursued for its own sake. Thus, for example, Serge Sur, retorting to a suggestion that international lawyers should pursue the benefit of humanity in the same way as doctors (physicians), declared:

> I in no way feel . . . like a doctor . . . I feel more like a *biologist*, and it seems to me that the biologist does not choose between the microbes and the patient. The doctor's mission is to cure; he is concerned with eliminating the microbes. But the biologist studies the microbes' conditions of existence, and properly speaking, there is no professional ethic that brings him to a choice between microbe and patient.[38]

However, although this view exists, I suspect that most people would utterly reject it, tending to confirm my main point.

vii. The legacy in prescriptive human science

Recall that, as I discussed in Chapter 5, Littré retained a prescriptive role for the human sciences. Under his development of positivism, their function was to determine what would be beneficial for humanity, so that they could then 'show[ ] governments and peoples which social and political developments should be promoted and which, rather, should be snuffed out at birth'.[39] As I noted, this is a guiding rather than a planning role, but it remains nonetheless a prescriptive role. I argue in this section that this function of the human sciences has entered modern thought as part of the legacy of positivism.

This can on occasion be a socially beneficial role. However, I also argue in this section that it can give rise to problems in social organization. This is particularly the case when the several aspects of the legacy of positivism that derive from the ideas that Littré set down are combined. That is, when the authority of an autonomous human science is used to explain 'scientifically' not only what constitutes the benefit of humanity but also what social actions will further that benefit, and then to propose as prescriptive guidance for society that it should take those social actions.

Of course modern society is under no compulsion to accept any prescriptive guidance that the human sciences offer. Whether it does so may depend on the level of authority that the human sciences enjoy in the society, on how uncontroversial the 'scientific' determination of what constitutes the benefit of humanity is, and on other such factors. Nonetheless, my illustrations will suggest that it would be socially beneficial to apply further critique to the aspects of the legacy of positivism that derive from the ideas that Littré set down.

An immediate question is what qualifies the human sciences to offer prescriptive guidance to society. In Littré's development of Comte's positivism, the expertise of the human sciences lies in their capacity to explain events. But determining what constitutes the benefit of humanity calls for a normative conclusion. How can an expertise in explaining events engender, as a 'scientific' matter, an expertise in deriving normative conclusions about events? What, for example, justifies Carr's declaration that the conclusions of history serve 'both as a guide to action and a key to our understanding of how things happen'?[40] This of course introduces an aspect of Hume's problem regarding how it is possible to move from 'is' to 'ought'. An illustration from anthropology will show how the human sciences deal with this issue in practice, and will also demonstrate the kind of problems to which this role gives rise.

My illustration comes from the role that the American Anthropological Association (AAA) has asserted in regard to human rights. I am concerned with its 1947 Statement and its 1999 Declaration on this subject. The 1999 Declaration is posted on the website of the AAA and represents its current official position. The 1947 Statement was a protest to the United Nations Commission on Human Rights against the adoption of what was to become the Universal Declaration of Human Rights.[41] The AAA has changed its substantive position regarding the Universal Declaration, but I nonetheless draw on the 1947 Statement because its approach is similar to that of the 1999 Declaration on the matters that concern me here. In the terminology of Comte and Littré, the AAA changed its doctrine between 1947 and 1999, but its method remained unchanged. I shall first consider its method, and in doing so I can therefore treat the 1947 Statement and the 1999 Declaration together. When I turn to the doctrine the differences between these two documents will become significant.

The Preamble to the 1999 Declaration begins by asserting that '[t]he capacity for culture is tantamount to the capacity for humanity'.[42] The

Declaration in due course uses this assertion to justify a slide from pursuing the benefit of humanity to pursuing the benefit of cultural groups. However, before it can do so the assertion itself must be justified. The justification is more fully expressed in the 1947 Statement, which begins its argument in support of an essentially equivalent assertion by stating that 'it will be necessary for us to outline some of the findings of the sciences that deal with the study of human culture'. It then explains that an individual's acculturation shapes every aspect of his being, and declares: 'The process by means of which this is accomplished is so subtle, and its effects are so far-reaching, that only after considerable training are we conscious of it.'[43]

By means of this argument the AAA stakes an exclusive claim, declaring in effect that acculturation is a subject that requires scientific investigation and that the only scientists qualified to investigate it are trained anthropologists. As a consequence of this, its statement that '[t]he capacity for culture is tantamount to the capacity for humanity' now gains the status of a scientific fact that it would be absurd for anyone not a trained anthropologist to dispute. Note that this reflects precisely the joint view of Comte and Mill,[44] and moreover nothing in Littré's development of positivism suggests that he held a different view.

On this basis the 1999 Declaration can make the move from explanation to normative conclusion. It declares that 'the AAA founds its approach [to human rights issues] on anthropological principles of respect for concrete human differences, both collective and individual'. This bald statement must be explicated to see how its underlying argument avoids Hume's problem.

First, the reference to the human differences to be taken into account describes them as 'concrete'; that is, they are asserted as facts. We have already been warned that such facts are so subtle that only trained anthropologists can perceive them. Moreover, the reference to 'collective' human differences brings in the idea of culture, since cultures are precisely the entities that anthropology identifies as monads and recognizes as displaying collective human differences.[45] Next, the statement implicitly relies on what the AAA has previously stipulated: the 'scientific fact' of the equivalence between the idea of culture and the idea of humanity.

Next, the requirement of 'respect' is introduced as resting on 'anthropological principles'; that is, this too is presented as 'scientifically' justified. Thus, the underlying argument essentially asserts, as a 'scientific fact', that respect for human differences is equivalent to respect for cultures, and that this in turn is equivalent to the benefit of humanity. The final step in the underlying argument now relies, again implicitly, on the accepted normative obligation to further the benefit of humanity. This gives the desired normative conclusion.

The 1999 Declaration does not leave this normative conclusion as a mere statement of principle. It continues that it is 'incumbent on anthropologists to be involved in the debate on enlarging our understanding of human rights on the basis of anthropological knowledge and research'. This stakes a claim, again based on the scientific status of anthropology, to offer society guidance in determining the substantive content of human rights principles.

This scheme of argument is quite typical of how the human sciences offer guidance to society. First comes a general assertion of exclusive qualification to stipulate 'scientific' facts and forms of argument regarding the subject matter at issue. Relying on this assertion, there is next a stipulation of particular 'scientific' facts and arguments that equate the normative conclusion that is to be offered as guidance with a normative statement that is so universally accepted that it brooks no disagreement. The assertion of exclusivity is then used a second time to establish a privileged role in determining the substantive reach of that normative conclusion in society. The result is to implement Littré's view of the role of the human sciences in the social order. It shows the full operation of aspects of the legacy of positivism that have come to us through the ideas that he set down.

The problem with this scheme of argument is that it presents facts and forms of argument as universally valid even though they have been validated only within the paradigm of the specific science concerned. This problem may not be considered serious if the science in question has consistently offered guidance of established social value. Note that this is really the only basis for credence in the determinations of a science that makes autonomy claims, because such claims shield the internal validation processes of the science from external appraisal. This is the case with the AAA statements under discussion. To illustrate the problems that can arise from this aspect of the legacy of positivism, I now turn to the doctrines that these statements espoused.

The doctrinal change from 1947 to 1999 was dramatic. In the 1947 Statement, the AAA mounted a sustained attack on the proposed Universal Declaration of Human Rights on the basis of a doctrine of cultural relativism, and concluded:

> Only when a statement of the right of men to live in terms of their own traditions is incorporated into the proposed [Universal] Decla-

ration [of Human Rights], then, can the next step of defining the rights and duties of human groups as regards each other be set upon the firm foundation of the present-day scientific knowledge of Man.[46]

However, the guidance of the AAA was rejected, and no 'statement of the right of men to live in terms of their own traditions' was incorporated into the Universal Declaration of Human Rights. Consequently, the Universal Declaration of Human Rights as the General Assembly of the United Nations adopted it in 1948 was, according to the AAA, in sharp conflict with scientifically established facts.

Yet in the 1999 Declaration, the AAA, continuing a text that I quoted above, was able to declare:

> [T]he AAA founds its approach [to human rights issues] on anthropological principles of respect for concrete human differences, both collective and individual . . . In practical terms, however, its working definition builds on the Universal Declaration of Human Rights . . . and other treaties which bring basic human rights within the parameters of the international written and customary law and practice. The AAA definition thus reflects a commitment to human rights consistent with international principles but not limited by them.

Certainly, this is an improved political position from its 1947 predecessor. However, the improvement in political position does not validate the method of argument that the AAA used to assert both this new position and its 1947 predecessor as scientifically valid. Note that there was no change in pertinent facts between 1947 and 1999 that could explain the radical doctrinal shift from one position to the other; the Universal Declaration of Human Rights was not amended, and the importance of culture to human wellbeing presumably neither diminished nor increased appreciably. It seems that the AAA simply changed its corporate mind on some aspect of its argument. Yet it presented its argument as scientifically valid in every one of its aspects, in both the 1947 Statement and the 1999 Declaration.

The AAA asserted scientific autonomy claims in both of these documents, and it is therefore appropriate to assume that the arguments in both were adequately validated within the paradigm of the science of anthropology. However, the unexplained radical doctrinal shift from one to the other undermines any claim of either doctrine to universal validity as a scientific pronouncement. In sum, this illustration shows the danger in accepting the policy pronouncements of a human science on matters of social organization, when that science makes autonomy claims that shield its validation processes from external assessment. My analysis of it constitutes an overall critique of the aspects of the legacy of positivism that derive from Comte's scheme through the ideas that Littré set down. Further critique is called for.

viii. The legacy in moral non-science

Recall that, as I discussed in Chapter 1, many of Comte's predecessors had hoped that the use of reason would guide humanity not only to a correct view of the physical world but also to right moral action. As I discussed in Chapter 3, Comte claimed that his scheme would achieve this as part of a comprehensive scientific structure. In this structure, the science of sociology would determine the good of humanity. The science of morality would determine the structured morality to be inculcated in order to achieve this good. This morality would then be inculcated as a subjective sense of what was right for people to do. Thus, in Comte's scheme society would progress morally, just as it would progress physically and socially, to the ultimate positivist stage of development.[47]

However, as I discussed in Chapter 5, the development of positivism that Littré set down narrowed the prospective scope of any science of morality that might be developed along the lines that Comte had intended. The conclusions of sociology would now be able to offer only broad guidance in social organization, and on such a basis a science of morality would be able to develop only fairly general principles of conduct. Moreover, the rejection of Comte's subjective principle entailed abandoning the idea of inculcating a structured morality as a subjective sense in harmony with the good of humanity. Consequently, investigations into what would constitute a proper morality and how it should be developed would largely lack any authoritative, scientific foundation in Littré's development of positivism.

Littré of course focused specifically on Comte's scheme. However, the arguments that he set down have become widely (even if not universally) accepted with regard to any attempt to construct morality scientifically by the kind of route that Comte proposed. This has had correspondingly broad consequences, because Comte had proposed a way to realize a dream that many shared – even if his proposed realization of the dream was nightmarish. Critiques of the kind that Littré set down devastated this crucial aspect of Comte's scheme and undermined confidence in anything that might resemble it. I shall now argue that this development has influenced modern thought. I shall identify two kinds of influences, and although their relationship to positivism is plainly indirect, I shall for consistency of presentation nonetheless describe them as aspects of the legacy of positivism in modern thought.

First, it is widely accepted that it will not be possible in any way to develop a science of sociology to a level where it can serve as foundation for a science of morality. Modern social sciences such as sociology and anthropology reflect this view. These sciences are largely unconcerned with deriving conclusions to serve as the foundation for moral principles. In so far as they seek to influence society they tend to focus exclusively on what they consider to be 'good' for humanity, individually or socially. They may offer guidance as to how to achieve this good, as I discussed in the previous section, and this might include suggesting how people need to act if they are to achieve it. However, these sciences do not generally accept that their claimed knowledge of 'the good' entails a social responsibility to promote 'the right'. Consequently, they are relatively unlikely to suggest how society needs to train people in what is 'right' for them to feel or think, with a view to steering them towards acting to achieve the good in question.[48]

Second, the process of reasoning entailed in justifying moral principles or in attaining progress in developing a structure of morality – that is, what is generally described as 'moral reasoning' – has become detached from the modern idea of science. In this respect morality plainly differs from the physical sciences. It also differs from the human sciences such as sociology, in so far as justification of principles and attaining progress are linked in them with the modern idea of science. In sum, in any substantive sense morality has been taken out of what is normally viewed as the scientific structure.

To understand how moral reasoning is generally detached from modern scientific reasoning, let us look again at a statement of Bacon's that I discussed in Chapter 1:

> There are – and can only be – two ways to investigate and discover truth. The one leaps from particular sense experiences to the most general statements, which it then treats as inviolable axioms and the source of any intermediate assertions . . . The other elicits basic principles from particular sense experiences, and generalizes from them steadily and step by step, reaching the most general principles only at the culmination of the process.[49]

The second method that Bacon describes has developed into the modern scientific method. The first method that he describes in fact constitutes a fair description of a great range of moral reasoning, from ancient times to our own day. It encompasses attempts to identify an inviolable general substantive principle as a universal ground for moral judgement, whether that principle is, for example, theological, metaphysical or utilitarian.[50]

Moreover, an important aspect of justification of principles and attaining progress in modern science entails testing ideas by observation and experiment, and discarding those that fail the test. No substantive principle, however venerable, can be exempt. Moral reasoning sometimes uses the terminology of scientific experiment, but does not in fact apply the experimental method. Consider, for example, the following statement by Herbert Hart:

> In moral relationships with others the individual sees questions of conduct from an impersonal point of view and applies general rules impartially to himself and to others; he is made aware of and takes account of the wants, expectations, and reactions of others; he exerts self-discipline and control in adapting his conduct to a system of reciprocal claims . . . We have only to conduct the Hobbesian experiment of imagining these virtues totally absent to see that they are vital for the conduct of any cooperative form of human life and any successful personal life.[51]

I have no quarrel with Hart's moral sentiments here. However, what he describes as an experiment is by no means an experiment in modern scientific terms. When a scientist imagines that the absence of certain phenomena will have certain effects, in scientific terms she has merely formed a hypothesis, as I discussed in Chapter 2. If she wishes to reach a scientific conclusion she must devise a way to test her hypothesis by observation or experiment. That is, she must devise a way to determine whether what she has imagined is what in fact occurs. Except perhaps in rarefied fields of quantum theory, an act of imagining does not itself constitute a scientific experiment.[52] In sum, however persuasive Hart's moral reasoning here might be, it is quite different from scientific reasoning.[53]

Note that I am not claiming that it would in some fashion be 'better' if moral reasoning followed the methods of modern science, although it must be admitted that the lack of scientific method in moral reasoning adds a ground for scepticism regarding any moral principle *that is promoted on the basis of specific benefits predicted to flow from its adoption.* In any such case, the predicted benefits remain hypothetical until persuasive verification is forthcoming. But notwithstanding such scepticism, we have in any event no reason to suppose that it would be possible to develop a science of morality that proceeded steadily and step by step, testing its conclusions by observations and experiment at every step, and reaching the most general principles only at the culmination of the process. Indeed, the very fact that we have no reason to suppose that this would be possible derives, I argue, from the indirect influence of the legacy of positivism in modern thought, as I have defined it in this section.

Part III
The Legacy of Positivism in Law

7
The Legacy of Positivism in the Autonomy of Law

i. Introduction to Part III

As I discussed in Chapter 2, some of the ideas of science that Comte developed into the positivist scheme ultimately derived from the context of juridical laws. But it has generally been supposed that once positivism derived its ideas from juridical laws, it developed them in the context of the human sciences without much relevance to the juridical context. Specifically, it has been supposed that the development of positivism by Comte, and later through such figures as Littré and Mill, had relatively little influence on thought concerning juridical laws – that is, on legal reasoning, legal philosophy or jurisprudence. Some connection has been acknowledged between positivism and the doctrines known as legal positivism, but only as a tenuous association of general ideas.[1]

I shall argue in this part of the book that the legacy of positivism, as I discussed it in Chapter 6, has influenced not only reasoning and analysis within the juridical context but also modern thought about how the juridical process operates within society. Although the aspects of the legacy of positivism that have had this influence are among those that I have already discussed in Chapter 6, there are two reasons why the juridical context requires the separate treatment that I provide in this part.

The first reason concerns my *analysis* of the legacy of positivism. The application of the analysis in Chapter 6 to the juridical context is not obvious and requires separate explication. Admittedly, it is obvious that since the legacy of positivism has come to pervade modern thought it must equally pervade the thought of those, such as judges, who work with laws in society. However, the application of the analysis in Chapter

6 to the juridical context goes beyond this. It requires explication in so far as it involves issues that are generally more familiar to trained lawyers. It also requires explication in so far as it concerns law as a functional and institutional juridical system, because this view of law has become so embedded in modern socio-political thought that it is easy to overlook that, as I shall argue, its present form is in part due to the influence of the legacy of positivism.

The second reason concerns my *critique* of the legacy of positivism. My critique in Chapter 6 in the context of the human sciences takes a somewhat different form in the juridical context. This is because in present-day societies juridical conclusions take a different form from conclusions of the human sciences. Conclusions of the human sciences can take the form of guidance to society, but society is free to consider that guidance at its leisure, and accept or reject it. However, juridical conclusions take the form of decisions in law cases with immediate and substantial – and often irreversible – effects on individuals and society. Consequently, it is more troubling when judges rather than sociologists or anthropologists overreach as a consequence of the influence of the legacy of positivism. Critique is correspondingly more urgent and has a different focus.

In the next section of this chapter, I describe Comte's view of the role of law in his positivist scheme. I show that Comte largely thought in terms of law as a collection of rules. Although he saw lawyers somewhat as a breed apart, he had at most a weak sense of law as a functionally and institutionally distinct juridical system. He regarded lawyers as potentially disruptive of his plan to reorganize society, and so insisted on confining their role to practice only. This required him to adopt a view of the application of rules of law that derived in part from Immanuel Kant's work. Any issues that we might now think of as belonging to legal theory would be absorbed into the human sciences in Comte's scheme.

In the final section of this chapter, I first note that Comte's view of the role of law in the social order became untenable under Littré's development of positivism. In fact, Littré's development could not readily encompass law in any way within the positivist structure. However, I next argue that a new prospect opened: that law itself could claim to be a science in the institutional and functional sense that the legacy of positivism now permitted. In Comte's scheme this would have been a preposterous claim. There was no place for law as a science in Comte's scientific hierarchy, and moreover law in his scheme was what the human sciences instructed lawyers to write, not a socio-political entity in itself. But under the legacy of positivism, the hierarchy of the sciences had become a tenuous concept. Consequently, it was possible to argue that a discipline should be regarded as a science by virtue of its internal structure only, without reference to how it fitted into any external structure. From a purely internal point of view the claim of law to be a science could be tolerably well sustained.

This permitted law to make institutional and functional claims as an autonomous juridical system. Of course, to some extent law had previously enjoyed a degree of autonomy, but now the influence of the legacy of positivism enabled law to enhance its earlier claims to autonomy in a new functional and institutional context.

In the first two sections of Chapter 8, I discuss the influence of the legacy of positivism on the modern doctrines of legal positivism. Modern legal positivism is so fragmented that I can consider only a limited range of views within it. In the first section I focus on the faction that John Gardner represents. Although the terminology of science is now infrequently used in relation to law, I show that this faction nonetheless claims for law – in the sense of the juridical or legal system – an internal structure analogous to that of a science under the legacy of positivism. In particular, it asserts a virtually absolute autonomy for the juridical system in terms of the sources it draws on and its modes of interpreting those sources. By virtue of its claim to the structure of a science, this autonomy claim can by analogy be seen as equivalent to an assertion of epistemological autonomy.

I show that this assertion demonstrates together the influence of the legacy of positivism in method and the legacy of positivism in scientific autonomy, as I discussed in Chapter 6. This faction in legal positivism also asserts the autonomy of the juridical system in assessing the needs of society in relation to law, without external check, and then constructing its own epistemology in accordance with that assessment. I show that this demonstrates the influence of the legacy of positivism regarding benefit to humanity.

In my critique I argue that these claims of epistemological autonomy for the juridical system threaten to impose burdens on society that the juridical system itself may not be best placed to assess. I call for further critique of the legal positivist structure from this perspective.

In the second section of Chapter 8, I consider the influence of the legacy of positivism on the position of legal positivism regarding adjudication. Legal positivism acknowledges that the legal system is obliged to decide all cases that come before it. However, the epistemological autonomy that it claims for the legal system leads to legal reasoning being indeterminate and incomplete, and thus unable to decide all cases. Legal positivism resolves this tension by admitting moral considerations into adjudication, but I argue that this resolution is effective only if moral reasoning is determinate and complete. Consequently, legal positivism becomes incoherent unless it accepts that legal reasoning and moral reasoning are fundamentally different. This fits with my discussion of moral reasoning in Chapter 6, where I discussed the difference between moral and scientific reasoning.

I then argue that, although I did not claim in Chapter 6 that there is no other form of reasoning than these, in practice the legacy of positivism is so pervasive that no other mode of thought is sufficiently developed to serve the needs of a societal institution. Consequently, legal positivism either becomes incoherent or is inexorably pressed to fit the legal system into the mould of the reasoning structure of an autonomous science. However, my earlier discussions show that this too will result in tension with the societal role of the legal system. I note that this may explain the continuing controversy within legal positivism over the relationship between law and morality in adjudication.

In the final section of Chapter 8, I discuss an aspect of the influence of the legacy of positivism that is not confined to legal positivist theory, but appears in practice in juridical systems. It is particularly apparent in the US judicial system, as a result of the influence of the American Legal Realist school. Although Realist doctrine generally opposes legal positivism, the result of Realist influence has nonetheless been to open the US legal adjudicative process to the influence of the legacy of positivism. This occurs when a court applies the doctrine of judicial notice of legislative facts to adopt a conclusion of the human sciences as a rule of decision in a case. I argue that this shows a double influence of the legacy of positivism: in terms of an implicit assertion of epistemological autonomy on the part of the court, and in terms of the role ascribed to the relevant conclusion of the human sciences.

In critique, I recall my observations on the legal positivist claim of epistemological autonomy and join this with my observations in Chapter 6 on the conclusions of the human sciences as guidance for society. This double critique leads me to call for greater caution in the use of the conclusions of the human sciences in judicial proceedings. Finally, I note that it would be mistaken to suppose that such a more cautious approach would serve or disserve any particular socio-political goals.

ii. Law in Comte's positivism

Present-day societies rely greatly on law – in the sense of a legal or juridical system – to maintain themselves and develop. But as I discussed in Chapter 3, Comte's scheme relied heavily on the action of continuous, pervasive social pressure and the inculcation of moral sentiments for these functions. This suggests that Comte wishes to shift emphasis away from central authoritative structures such as government and law in favour of local and internal modes of control. To some extent this is the case, but it is no more than a shift in emphasis and not a complete abandonment of central authoritative structures. Comte does not suppose that even the combination of moral inculcation and social pressure could maintain a society. He stipulates that governmental authority would also be needed, because:

> [T]he instincts that drive us into isolation or conflict are of their nature more powerful than those that incline us to agreement and unity. And this determines the overall purpose of the force of social cohesion that is everywhere called *government*, the task of which is at one and the same time to control and to direct.[2]

Thus he can conclude that 'a society without a government is no more possible than a government without a society'.[3]

But if a government is to control and direct, it must ensure that people understand what is expected of them so that they can tailor their actions accordingly. Consequently, it must convey its directions to the populace. Comte considers the legal profession well qualified for this task because 'lawyers . . . are the only people who really understand working with rules, which is one of the most needed capabilities in the formation of the new social system'.[4] Thus, he in effect recognizes that the government must promulgate rules of law.

Before proceeding, I note that Comte's reference to 'rules' for prescriptive edicts raises the issues of terminological confusion that I discussed in Chapter 2, Section i regarding juridical and scientific laws. In particular, many writers in jurisprudence use the term 'rule' only for a narrow, specific edict. For such writers, the term 'law' may cover somewhat less specific edicts. However, it would not be appropriate to read any such limitation into Comte's terminology. He was not writing in a tradition that used this terminology to express this distinction, and he does not introduce it in his writings. Consequently, it would be unsound to derive any substantive conclusion from his use of 'rule' rather than 'law'.

Whether we describe the edicts of a government as rules or laws, if the government is to contribute to maintaining the tightly structured and harmonious social order that Comte intends, it must surely promulgate those edicts in a coherent and organized fashion. That is, to some extent it must have a code or other systematic presentation of its edicts, as well as a coherent process for applying them. We might now wish simply to state that it must have some kind of a legal or juridical *system*. However, Comte did not present the idea of law in such terms. His works offer little if any sense of 'the law' as a system in society, but rather present 'laws' as merely individual laws without any sense of structure or system.

The notion of law as a system was certainly current in Comte's era. Indeed, there were several concepts of law as a system from which to choose. Thus, for example, Comte's English near-contemporary John Austin regarded law as the commands of a lawgiver, and in the opening lectures to his course on jurisprudence, as later published, he referred to English law 'as a system or organic whole'.[5] But, as another example, Friedrich von Savigny had taken a quite different view, regarding German law as a system that had grown organically out of the spirit and customs of the German people.[6]

At the same time, the notion of law as a system was not then as robust nor as developed as it is now. In our era the general mode of thought consistently views law as constituting a functional and institutional social structure, but in the early nineteenth century even the basic notion of 'the law' as a system could still prove fragile in practice. Thus, for example, in Austin's lectures on jurisprudence the sense of law as a system does not survive beyond the opening lectures as quoted above. Throughout the main lectures, Austin views 'the law' merely as the aggregate of individual laws, with no sense of a legal system or structure.[7]

In any event, even if Comte was familiar with notions of law as a juridical system, his positivist scheme effectively rejected any such idea. We saw above that the positivist social order will need lawyers because they alone understand working with rules. Comte states that this capability 'will be put into play as soon as the purely theoretical part of the general work of reorganization is finished, or at least sufficiently advanced'.[8] Note that it will not be put into play *before* this point is reached. Indeed, Comte specifically excludes lawyers from the development of the theoretical structure of the positivist social order, declaring them to be wholly unsuited for this work. 'They make a profession out of knowing how to make any opinion whatsoever convincing. As practice increases their skill in this kind of work, so they become less fit to structure a theory according to its true principles.' They are 'strangers to any positive, theoretical idea'.[9] Thus, the role of lawyers in working with rules of law is to be entirely part of practice rather than theory in Comte's scheme.

Let us consider how Comte expected this view of the development of law to work in the positivist social order. As I discussed in Chapter 3, the social and moral scientists, drawing as necessary on the work of the various other positive scientists, were to create the theoretical plan for the reorganization of society in full detail. Issues that we might consider part of legal theory would necessarily be settled – scientifically – within the theoretical plan. This would include issues of justice or lawfulness, and also of authority, government, and such like. Consequently, experts in the positive sciences rather than law would be investigating and settling these issues. *There is no other context in Comte's scheme for dealing with these and other such issues.*

In the course of developing the theoretical plan for the reorganization of society, the positive sciences would have to establish the roles of the three societal means of maintaining order: the application of social pressure in the community, the inculcation of subjective morality, and the laws. As one aspect of this, they would need to decide whether the laws should in some fashion incorporate the values that the science of morality had determined to be right. This would be decided *in the course of development of the plan*; Comte's scheme does not impose any prior restriction on the conclusions that the scientific experts might reach regarding this. In particular, there is no doctrine in Comte's positivist scheme requiring or even suggesting any separation between law and morality. This is noteworthy in regard to the relationship between law and morality under legal positivism, one aspect of which I discuss in the next chapter.

Once the theoretical plan was completed, the practice stage of social reorganization would be undertaken. Any task requiring strong exercise of the intellect would have been included in the theory stage of the plan, so that it is fair to say that the practice stage would consist of routine processes only.[10] Consider how this applies to those parts of the plan that require rules of law to ensure their proper implementation, and that, according to Comte, fall within practice under the positivist scheme. He recognizes that working with rules of law calls for the skills of lawyers. Nonetheless, he implicitly assumes that this requires no interpretive process, because the notion of interpretation presupposes the exercise of intellectual judgement, and so could not be part of practice.

Comte sees this as possible because he regards working with rules of law as a routine process. This is further apparent from his statement that the lawyers who most fully understand working with rules are 'those who have thoroughly studied positive law'.[11] He introduces the expression 'positive law' here as a familiar notion requiring no explanation, and he does not relate it in any way to positive science. This is consistent with my earlier discussion of juridical law as positive law in Chapter 2, and makes it clear that Comte is thinking in terms of certain and precise rules of law. He recognizes no other kind of juridical law.

However, this might at first seem to conflict with his own positivist scheme. To see why this might be so, let us look again at a statement of Comte's that I discussed in Chapter 4:

> [O]ur minds need some kind of theory in order to engage in observation. If when contemplating phenomena we did not immediately tie them to some principle, it would not only be impossible for us to put isolated observations together in any productive way, but we would even be wholly unable to hold them in our minds. We would remain largely unaware of facts that stare us in the face.[12]

This principle is foundational for Comte's entire structure of a hierarchy of sciences in which each develops its own epistemological variant of the positive method.

From this principle we can at once derive an obvious but important consequence: *If we need a theory to be able to perceive facts, then we equally need a theory to be able to apply a law to fact situations.* An easy way to see this is to restate Comte's principle in the context of application of laws: 'Without some kind of theory, a given law and a given fact situation would be no more than an isolated idea and an isolated observation. We would remain unaware of connections between them that stare us in the face.' Thus, it follows directly from Comte's own positivist principles that the process of applying laws to fact situations cannot be free of theory.

This analysis has made no assumption regarding the context in which the law operates. It therefore applies equally whether the law is scientific or juridical. Comte could hardly have failed to see this. In fact, he essentially sees it in the juridical context itself when he notes the capacity of lawyers to 'make any opinion whatsoever convincing'.[13] After all, convincing someone of a particular opinion regarding a given situation is tantamount to persuading her that one theory rather than another best covers the situation. Indeed, much of the work of lawyers consists of constructing theories under which one law rather than another applies in a given fact situation.

Moreover, Comte was familiar with the work of Kant, who had already pointed out that applying laws to facts was far from being a routine process. Rather, it required a *capacity for judgement (Urteilskraft)*, and this was the case regardless of the context in which the law operated. Kant had specifically included juridical laws, along with rules for the practice of medicine and the conduct of politics, as examples.[14] Consequently, we must ask how Comte can regard the application of rules of juridical law – which is one aspect of 'working with rules' of law – as a routine matter that can be confined to practice.

The point is that an analysis such as Kant's would, if pressed to its limits, eliminate the category of practice entirely. Even the most trivial deduction in a straightforward practical situation can entail applying a rule to a fact situation. A need for theory in such situations would suggest that everything must belong to theory, with nothing left for practice. But the key to avoiding this conclusion, which would devastate Comte's scheme, is also in Kant's analysis. Kant had observed that the reason why a person can formally understand a law and yet be unable to apply it is 'either because he lacks any natural capacity for judgement . . . or because he has not been adequately trained by means of examples and in actual practice to exercise judgement in the situation in question'.[15]

Thus, the characteristic quality of an activity or process that can be constituted as practice is not that it is routine in some inherent sense, but that by training and exercise it can be made routine. Put otherwise, the process of applying the underlying theory can be made routine by training and exercise. Comte is not directly concerned with how this is to be achieved for any given area of practice, so he does not follow Kant in trying to develop a theory of judgement. This would have to be worked out in the course of development of the positivist plan.

Consequently, in Comte's scheme expert theoreticians would predetermine the underlying theory needed to constitute any given area of practice – that is, they would predetermine its epistemology. This epistemology would then be inculcated by training into persons who would thereby become practitioners in the activity in question. They then would not perceive the foundations of their activity as theory, but rather as professional judgement, skill and so forth. In any particular case, they would not regard themselves as interpreting the appropriate rules of their activity, but as simply applying them in direct reliance on their skills. We have seen an analogous structure in the relationship in Comte's scheme between morality as a science and morality as an inculcated subjective sense, as I discussed in Chapter 3.

This would be the process used to constitute the practice of law. The positive sciences would determine what laws were best suited to the society. They would also determine the interpretive principles that would make the application of the laws routine.[16] Note that the subjective moral sense would harmonize perfectly with the processes of practice in this context. In any particular case, a law practitioner (advocate, judge or any other) could apply her inculcated professional training and her inculcated moral sentiments in a single seamless process, while perceiving herself throughout as simply making a routine determination. This is clearly the kind of process that Comte intended in his unified scheme.

iii. The claim of law as a science

Recall that, as I discussed in Chapter 5, under Littré's development of positivism the human sciences would not form a cohesive, hierarchical structure to produce the positivist plan for the reorganization of society, but would be restricted to offering guidance to society. The society could then assess that guidance and determine whether to accept or reject it. But 'society' is not itself an entity with a mind, so in practice some socio-political process would be needed to make such assessments and act accordingly. Positivism now had nothing to say about what process would be appropriate for doing this. Under Littré's development, any such process would fall outside the positivist scheme.

In discussing law and society in relation to developments in positivism, the focus is necessarily on those societies in which positivism has been influential and in which there is law. This includes a broad range of Western or Western-influenced state societies, as appears from my discussion of the influence of positivism in Chapter 6, Section i. In any such society there is a lawmaking body, and in general this body has the primary responsibility for assessing any guidance that the human sciences might offer and determining whether to accept it and enact law accordingly, or to reject it. These of course are political bodies, and the ultimate choice of which policies they implement into laws generally results from a political victory of one faction over another or from political compromise, not from any kind of scientific analysis. All this was as true in Comte's day as it is in our own.

For Comte of course the political process of lawmaking was abhorrent, and others too have protested that a more 'scientific' process would yield better law. In the 1960s and 1970s the Yale policy-science school proposed this view with particular regard to the normative structure of the international system, but its arguments apply more generally.[17] Nonetheless, the political lawmaking process is widely considered to be the best available, at least in its more democratic manifestations, although it is recognized that the squeamish should best avoid close acquaintance with it.[18] In any event, this process was and remains well established in all the jurisdictions relevant to any discussion of Comte's positivism, the development of positivism under the ideas that Littré set down, or the legacy of positivism. Consequently, any analysis must presume the continuing presence of a political, determinedly non-positivist lawmaking body.

We can conveniently think of the human sciences under Littré's development of positivism as offering guidance that flows 'downstream' within society, but out of the positivist structure, to reach the political lawmaking body. Then from the lawmaking body laws flow further 'downstream' into the process that society sets up for applying the laws. Thus, under Littré's development there was no place for law within what remained as the positivist part of the social order.

The question of what kind of process society should set up for applying laws has given rise to various questions, particularly with regard to the degree of institutional and functional autonomy that this process should enjoy. Of course, to some extent the realities of the practice of law have long ensured law some degree of autonomy. Once courts began to sit permanently in fixed locations, and societies of lawyers formed about them, it was inevitable that the process of applying laws would become esoteric; this in turn provided a degree of autonomy in practice. In England, this development dates from as early as the fourteenth century, when the royal courts were already sitting permanently at Westminster and the Temple was becoming the home of a society of lawyers.

In addition, by the nineteenth century the political doctrines of separation of powers were providing theoretical support for autonomy claims for law. Various forms of these doctrines had been developed over several centuries. After the appearance of Montesquieu's *De l'Esprit des Loix* in 1748, separation of powers doctrines were generally presented and analyzed in terms of his familiar tripartite division into executive, legislative and judicial functions of government – the last of these of course representing the process of applying laws. However, the fact that a doctrine was presented in terms of Montesquieu's tripartite division did not necessarily mean that it favoured institutional separateness or autonomy for any of the respective governmental functions. Sometimes the contrary might be the case.[19] Consequently, it could hardly be supposed that separation-of-powers doctrines would consistently support a high degree of functional and institutional autonomy for law.

A particular issue regarding autonomy for law concerned how the interpretive principles for the application of laws would be determined. Recall that in Comte's scheme the positive sciences would predetermine these principles, but this prospect vanished with the demise of his plan for the reorganization of society. There was no guarantee that separation-of-powers doctrines would support autonomy for law in this respect. Indeed, Montesquieu had insisted on very narrow interpretive principles in the judicial function.[20]

Thus, not only was there no place for law within what remained as the positivist part of the social order under Littré's development, but it was not clear what the place of law was to be outside the positivist part of the social order. However, a new prospect opened, and I argue that this was the result of the development of the legacy of positivism. Recall that under the legacy of positivism each of the human sciences claims a degree of autonomy, and the notion of an overall hierarchy of the sciences becomes a more tenuous concept. Moreover, as is apparent from my analysis in Chapter 6 of the various aspects of the legacy of positivism, the defining qualities of a science are found largely in its internal structure, and only to a very limited extent in its relationship to society and other sciences.

In this context in the second half of the nineteenth century a number of legal scholars began to assert that law should be considered a science. They were not the first persons to associate law with science. The earlier associations had been largely of two kinds. First, legal decision-making had been compared with decision-making in the physical sciences on the ground of tantalizing similarities perceived in the use of deduction and induction in the two contexts.[21] Second, until the eighteenth century the term 'science' (and its equivalents in other European languages) had been used to signify any organized body of knowledge. In this sense law and the physical sciences were all equally sciences. This sense even persisted into the nineteenth century, so that Austin can use 'scientific' generically to mean 'systematic', while recognizing the existence of a specific category of 'sciences which rest upon observation and induction'.[22]

It was the latter sense of science that the new claims in the second half of the nineteenth century had in mind. These claims encompassed not only the intellectual character but also issues of the institutional structure, the social role and, especially, the prestige of law as a discipline. Regarding prestige, some legal scholars were concerned that if their discipline could not aspire to be a science at a time when a great range of humanities disciplines were successfully claiming that status, its position in a respectable university would be tenuous.

Thus, Christopher Columbus Langdell, appointed the first dean of Harvard Law School in 1870, argued: 'If law be not a science, a university will best consult its own dignity in declining to teach it. If it be not a science, it is a species of handicraft, and may best be learned by serving an apprenticeship to one who practices it.'[23] He described this science as follows:

> [L]aw is a science . . . [and] all the available materials of that science are contained in printed books . . . [T]he library is the proper workshop of professors and students alike . . . it is to us all that the laboratories of the university are to the chemists and physicists, all that the museum of natural history is to the zoologists, all that the botanical garden is to the botanists.[24]

In a manner that recalls Carr's argument that the difficulty of history justifies its scientific status, Langdell declares of law that 'it will scarcely be disputed that it is one of the greatest and most difficult of sciences'.[25]

Langdell's claim would have been preposterous in Comte's scheme. Comte regarded his scientific hierarchy as complete, beginning with the physical sciences and concluding with the science of morality, which would lead directly to the area of practice. There was no place for law as a science in this hierarchy. Moreover, as I discussed in the previous section, the process of applying laws (which is plainly the subject matter of Langdell's science) was in fact to be constituted as an area of practice in Comte's scheme.

However, under the legacy of positivism, as I noted above, the defining qualities of a science are found in its internal structure. And in terms of law's internal structure, Langdell's claim is not preposterous. In particular, the idea of a science whose materials are contained in printed books is not inherently unreasonable. It all depends on the use to which those materials are put. To understand this, it is helpful first to recognize certain uses for materials contained in printed books that certainly do *not* fit with the idea of science. A leading critic of Langdell, Roscoe Pound, regarded such schemes as Langdell's as positing nothing but 'a rigid scheme of deductions from *a priori* conceptions', and rejected this as presenting an obsolete view of science.[26]

In effect, Pound was echoing Bacon's criticisms of the science of his day that I discussed in Chapter 1. Under such a view of science one might, for example, take as an *a priori* conception (which one could find in a number of printed books) that a perfect deity created the universe, and ultimately deduce from it that the orbits of the planets are circles around the earth as centre. Thus, under the approach that Bacon condemned, a discipline would rely on specific texts *as the source of dogmas for determining the structure of the material universe beyond the texts*. This indeed would be unacceptable under the legacy of positivism.

But this is quite different from the approach of a discipline that draws on specific texts *as its universe of materials to be investigated and interpreted*. This approach is wholly compatible with the idea of science under the legacy of positivism. Such quite respected disciplines as philology and various subdisciplines of archaeology are among many examples of disciplines that concern themselves with texts and their interpretation, and this has not prevented their being regarded as sciences under the legacy of positivism.

The question now is whether Langdell's supposed science of law uses the texts in its library as the source of dogmas or as its universe of materials to be investigated and interpreted. Frederick Pollock, a contemporary supporter of Langdell, implicitly answered this:

> The ultimate object of natural science is to predict events – to say with approximate accuracy what will happen under given conditions. Every special department of science occupies itself with predicting events of a particular kind . . . The object of legal science . . . is likewise to predict events. The particular kind of events it seeks to predict are the decisions of courts of justice.[27]

It is clear from this that the science of law is to use the texts in its library as its universe of materials to be investigated and interpreted, and not as the source of dogmas.

In this way, Langdell and his supporters were able to assert an autonomy claim with functional and institutional ramifications for their structure of law as a science. This claim relied on the growing concept of scientific autonomy that, as I argued in Chapter 6, was an aspect of the influence of the legacy of positivism. Admittedly, it was an unsophisticated claim that relied on a rudimentary notion of a science. In particular, Langdell and his supporters did not discuss how their science was to develop its interpretive principles, and were indeed justifiably criticized for assuming that it could derive all its conclusions by the application of pure logic alone. Nonetheless, this claim was a noteworthy stage in the development under the influence of the legacy of positivism of the sense of law as an autonomous societal entity characterized in terms of its internal structure.

8
Aspects of the Legacy of Positivism in Law

i. From the legacy of positivism to legal positivism

The doctrines now known as legal positivism underwent their first substantial development in the work of Jeremy Bentham and John Austin in the late eighteenth and early nineteenth centuries, although their roots can already be seen in the work of Thomas Hobbes and David Hume. Indeed, debates on some of the major themes that became prominent in legal positivism go back to antiquity. Some ideas that began to appear quite early in these debates are akin to ideas that, as I discussed in Chapter 6, arose in regard to the human sciences as aspects of the influence of the legacy of positivism. Thus, as I indicated in Chapter 7, in the juridical field these ideas developed to some extent independently of the influence of the legacy of positivism. However, I argue in the present chapter that more recently they have further developed and been shaped under the influence of the legacy of positivism.

A continuing major issue in legal positivist debates has been how to determine what is law in society. Bentham and Austin focused on this issue in the particular context of reorganizing English law, with codification along the lines of European systems being their ultimate aim. In their view, the lack of codification in the English common-law tradition enabled judges to make decisions, and commentators to exercise influence, on the basis of confusion between the actual law and what these judges and commentators thought ought to be the law. Consequently, Bentham and Austin insisted that these notions must be scrupulously distinguished. Thus, Austin famously declared:

> The existence of law is one thing; its merit or demerit is another. Whether it be or be not is one enquiry; whether it be or be not con-

formable to an assumed standard, is a different enquiry. A law, which actually exists, is a law, though we happen to dislike it, or though it vary from the text, by which we regulate our approbation and disapprobation.[1]

The distinction that Austin drew is commonly expressed as being between 'what the law is' and 'what the law ought to be'. The stipulation that this distinction is to be taken as expressing a social fact about law became a tenet of the doctrines of legal positivism.

However, a problem in discussing the development of legal positivism is that the mass of self-described legal positivists today agree on very little else beyond Austin's statement. The field of legal positivism has long been fragmented, and in recent years has been marked by acerbic factional disputes. In fact, the situation here is remarkably similar to that regarding positivism around the third quarter of the nineteenth century. Positivism then was split into numerous factions, each insisting that its positivism was the one true positivism, and with endless and often acrimonious rivalries between them. At the same time, a number of opponents of positivism attempted to define and denigrate positivism, and were countered by positivists insisting that they had fundamentally misunderstood positivism. Different factions within positivism presented different explanations for this misunderstanding on the part of the opponents of positivism.[2] In every respect, this equally well describes the situation in modern legal positivism.

This factionalism makes it impossible to craft a clear definition of legal positivism as a whole in doctrinal terms. Consequently, it is not feasible to trace the influence of the legacy of positivism on the doctrinal development of legal positivism as a whole, because to trace the development of a doctrine one needs to begin with a clear sense of what that doctrine is.[3] The best that one can do is to trace the influence of the legacy of positivism on the development of the doctrines of particular factions or on the development of particular doctrinal issues within legal positivism.

In the present book, in which the influence of the legacy of positivism on legal positivism is but one aspect of a much greater whole, I have space to consider only a limited range of views regarding each of two themes that have been of the greatest importance in legal positivism. The first of these themes concerns Austin's statement itself, and considers how the influence of the legacy of positivism has led to this statement being reinterpreted in modern legal positivism. In the remainder of this section I consider this development in regard to the doctrine that the legal positivist John Gardner espouses. There are parallels to Gardner's views in the works of other legal positivist writers, but I do not explore this here. The second of these themes concerns the influence of the legacy of positivism on the development of the relationship between law and morality in the doctrines of legal positivists. I consider this in the next section in the context of adjudication.

In a recent paper, Gardner introduces the following proposition as, he claims, the defining tenet of legal positivism:

> In any legal system, whether a given norm is legally valid, and hence whether it forms part of the law of that system, depends on its sources, not its merits.

Specifically, he 'designate[s] as "legal positivists" all and only those who advance or endorse this proposition'.[4] Thus, he asserts that agreement with this proposition is both a necessary and a sufficient condition for someone to be describable as a legal positivist. The great majority of self-described legal positivists probably agree with Gardner's proposition and with his assertion that to be a legal positivist it is necessary to agree with his proposition. It is less clear that the great majority of self-described legal positivists agree with Gardner's assertion that to be a legal positivist it is *sufficient* to agree with his proposition.[5] However, since in this section my focus is on Gardner and the doctrinal faction within legal positivism that he represents, it is not strictly relevant that others may disagree on this issue of sufficiency.

Gardner then further asserts that 'subject to some differences of interpretation' all the dominant historical figures in legal positivism would likewise have agreed on this proposition. He includes Austin in his list of dominant historical figures, referring in this connection to Austin's statement that I quoted above.[6] Essentially, Gardner's claim is that his proposition and Austin's statement are, 'subject to some differences of interpretation', equivalent assertions.

However, these differences of interpretation are crucial, since Gardner's interpretation of his proposition leads him to doctrines of legal positivism that, in my view, Austin would not have accepted. I argue that the interpretive shift from Austin's thought to Gardner's shows the pervasive influence of the legacy of positivism, and most pervasively the legacy of positivism in scientific autonomy, as I discussed in Chapter 6, Section v.

Note first that Gardner stresses the notion of law as a legal *system*. As I discussed in Chapter 7, although Austin acknowledged the structure of law as a system it was not a sufficiently robust notion in his works to serve as the foundation for analysis. However, Gardner's analysis relies on a strong functional and institutional sense of law as a system. To see this, consider his doctrines regarding the sources on which the legal system draws and the interpretive principles that it applies to those sources.

The question of the sources on which the legal system draws raises two kinds of issues, both of which have been controversial. First, it raises the issue of whether judges are limited to applying existing law in the process of adjudication, or whether they may make new law. Second, it raises the issue of whether judges may apply provisions of morality in the adjudicative process. Gardner states his position regarding both of these issues together as follows:

> [I]n a case which cannot be decided by applying only existing legal norms it is possible to use legal reasoning to arrive at a new norm that enables (or constitutes) a decision in the case, and this norm is validated as a new legal norm in the process. Obviously, legal reasoning, in this sense, is not simply reasoning about what legal norms already apply to the case. It is reasoning that has already-valid legal norms among its major or operative premises, but combines them nonredundantly in the same argument with moral or other merit-based premises.[7]

This analysis effectively subsumes the determination of sources for the legal system under the legal reasoning process. Put otherwise, under Gardner's doctrine of legal positivism, the determination of sources for the legal system becomes part of the judicial interpretive process of laws.

This is an important analytical development, because Gardner goes on to stipulate a high degree of autonomy for the legal system in determining its principles of interpretation of laws. Note in this connection that many jurists insist that the role of the legal system in relation to the political lawmaking body substantially restricts the judiciary in its choice of interpretive principles.[8] Gardner rejects this. The only substantial restriction he admits is that judges 'have a professional obligation to reach their decisions by legal reasoning'.[9] Beyond this, he insists that legal positivism imposes no substantive constraints on the interpretive role of judges.

There is, he argues, simply no point in any such constraint because a 'feedback loop' between lawmakers and adjudicators makes it unnecessary. 'So long as the local norms of interpretation can be grasped by the lawmakers . . . the laws can be intentionally shaped by anticipating how they will be interpreted by others [the adjudicative legal system] and drafting them accordingly.'[10] As illustration, he suggests that if lawmakers find that judges 'are perverse types who will always read "cat" to mean "dog"', they 'can make . . . dog-regulating laws . . . by passing a Cat Regulation Act'.[11]

But there is no other societal institution that the legal system could feasibly need to take into account in determining its principles of interpretation. Consequently, the only realistic possibility under Gardner's legal positivism is that the legal system will determine its own interpretive principles without any external substantive constraint. Since under his doctrine the determination of sources for the legal system is part of the interpretive process, it follows that the legal system will also determine its own sources.

Gardner does recognize that the legal system has a responsibility to society as a whole, and in fulfilment of this declares that 'the achievement of all-round better judicial decision . . . is the proper basis for selecting (and legally validating) norms of interpretation'.[12] He does not give criteria for better judicial decision-making. Indeed, the foregoing analysis of legal positivism plainly leaves the legal system itself as the only body in society qualified to devise such criteria. Presumably, the criteria for better judicial decision-making would take into account the role of the legal system in satisfying the needs of society, but if so the foregoing analysis of legal positivism also leaves the legal system itself as the only body qualified to assess the needs of society in this respect. Consequently, there would be no external check on the adequacy of this assessment.

Under Gardner's doctrines the legal system acquires a dual nature. Viewed externally, it is a functional and institutional social structure downstream of the political lawmaking body with substantial social responsibilities. But viewed internally, it is an autonomous structure that determines its own sources and principles of interpretation. Gardner offers the analogy that from the internal viewpoint legal positivism 'does not distinguish law from a game', although of course from the external viewpoint law is not a game at all.[13] Austin, who saw each individual law as integrated into the social order in the form of the command of a sovereign addressed to the citizenry, could not have comprehended either the idea of a dual nature of the legal system or the idea of the legal system viewed as a game.

But there is another and arguably better analogy than that between the legal system, viewed internally, and a game. Gardner's autonomy claims for the legal system are structurally similar to Langdell's claim that law is a science, as I discussed in Chapter 7. Gardner, like Langdell, abstracts the legal system from its societal role and views it exclusively in terms of its internal structure. The autonomy that Gardner grants to the legal system in terms of sources corresponds to the autonomous realm of Langdell's law library. In both schemes, the process of legal reasoning is internal and autonomous. However, Gardner's scheme is a more sophisticated development of Langdell's, especially in that Gardner admits a greater range of sources and acknowledges the possibility of a range of interpretive principles from which law could choose.

The terminology of science is sometimes used in modern legal positivism, but it is no longer common. In general I do not need to introduce it here. However, one terminological analogy will be helpful. The choice of the sources and modes of interpretation of a science constitute its epistemology, and I shall refer by analogy to the epistemology of a legal system, viewed internally as discussed above, as constituted by its sources and modes of interpretation. With this terminology, my assessment above is that the shift in mode of thought from Austin to Gardner's legal positivism may be summarized as follows. Under Gardner's legal positivism, but not under Austin's view, the legal system asserts a degree of functional and institutional autonomy sufficient to allow it to assess the needs of society in relation to law, without external check on that assessment, and then to construct its own epistemology in accordance with that assessment.

The conceptual structure here is that of the legacy of positivism, as I discussed it in Chapter 6. Most obviously, the influence of the legacy of positivism in scientific autonomy, as I discussed in Chapter 6, Section v, pervades this conceptual structure. Other aspects of the legacy of positivism are also apparent. Thus, the influence of the legacy of positivism in method, as I discussed in Chapter 6, Section iii, has underpinned the development of the idea that a legal system would require modes of interpretation peculiar to itself. The legacy of positivism regarding benefit to humanity, as I discussed in Chapter 6, Section vi, has underpinned the idea that a legal system fulfils its role in society by focusing on making better judicial decisions, based on its own assessment of the needs of society in relation to law. In this way we see the epistemological connection between the legacy of positivism and modern legal positivism in Gardner's version.

I turn now to critique. As in Chapter 6, my concern is with the sociopolitical effects of the influence of the legacy of positivism, and the immediate question is whether Gardner's doctrines are properly subject to critique of this kind. He insists that his basic proposition, quoted above, 'is itself normatively inert. It does not provide any guidance at all on what anyone should do about anything on any occasion.'[14] The feedback-loop structure that he describes, with its attendant autonomy claims, is not normatively inert if it is taken as a proposal for socio-political implementation. However, I do not think that Gardner intends it as such a proposal. Rather, his goal is to show that, consistently with legal positivism, a legal system *could* employ such a feedback-loop structure. He does not claim that it would be a desirable legal system. Consequently, my critique should be read as applying to any proposal to implement a system such as Gardner describes, without regarding him as a proponent of it.

In Chapter 6, I developed an overall critique of the aspects of the legacy of positivism that derive from the ideas that Littré set down. I argued that it is dangerous to accept the policy pronouncements of a human science on matters of social organization, when that science makes autonomy claims that shield its validation processes from external assessment. In so far as Gardner's legal positivism claims for the legal system a structure analogous to that of a science (even if his claim does not use the terminology of science), my critique in Chapter 6 applies to it equally. Moreover, as I pointed out in Chapter 7, when a human science that makes autonomy claims offers policy pronouncements, the political lawmaking body can accept or reject them as it pleases. But the pronouncements of the legal system can have immediate impact as effective law, so my critique applies here with additional force.

In this regard, the autonomy claims that Gardner's system makes for principles of interpretation are strong enough to be troubling. Consider first what substantive problems might arise with the 'feedback loop' between the political lawmaking body and the legal system. As Gardner puts it, for the feedback loop to function, 'legislators and other lawmakers . . . [would have to] work out, backwards, how they should speak or behave in order to be held to have made the law that they are trying to make'.[15] The problem is that they might find it burdensome to do so. Moreover, members of the general public would also have to work out, backwards, how they should speak or behave in order to avoid falling foul of the laws that the lawmakers had enacted. Since, unlike lawmakers, members of the general public are not usually in continuing interaction with the legal system, they might find the feedback-loop structure very burdensome. In particular, to take up Gardner's illustration, above, it would be risky to keep either a cat or a dog without consulting an experienced lawyer as to the governing regulations.[16]

The point here is not that the feedback-loop structure imposes burdens. After all, any process of social organization imposes burdens, and the crucial societal question is whether the benefits that the process brings outweigh the burdens. Rather, the point here concerns which body in society is to make this determination. As I discussed above, the unavoidable implication of the legal positivist system that Gardner describes is that the legal system alone is to make this determination, since it alone is to determine what constitutes better decision-making from the perspective of society as a whole. Yet it is questionable whether the kind of autonomous legal system that legal positivism proposes is well placed in society to determine such matters as this. Further critique of the influence of the legacy of positivism in the legal positivist structure in this regard is called for.

ii. Law and morality in adjudication under legal positivism

In the previous section I referred to the introduction of moral provisions into the process of adjudication. This in fact is a very controversial subject within legal positivism, as well as between legal positivism and its opponents. On this subject it is hard to find any two legal positivists in complete agreement. However, I do not wish to enter the debate on the role of moral considerations in the process of adjudication but merely to indicate an aspect of the role of the influence of the legacy of positivism in setting the terms of this debate.[17]

Specifically, I argue that the influence of the legacy of positivism presses legal positivism to choose between two doctrinal positions, of which one is incoherent and the other ascribes to law the reasoning structure of an autonomous science, with the attendant problems that I discussed in the previous section and in Chapter 7. To understand this choice requires analysis of the view of legal positivism regarding the process of adjudication. My analysis proceeds in four stages.

The first stage deals with legal positivism's treatment of a tension between two of its concerns. On the one hand, legal positivism acknowledges that in the legal systems under consideration a judge is obliged to decide every case that comes before him. But on the other hand, legal positivism insists that the judge must apply only the law as it is, not the law as it ought to be. This insistence, as I discussed in the previous section, is bound up with the legal positivist claim of epistemological autonomy for the legal system. The tension now arises because there might be no law covering the case. Indeed, it is a tenet of modern legal positivism that, as Hart expresses it, 'in any legal system there will always be . . . cases in which on some point no decision either way is dictated by the law and the law is accordingly partly indeterminate or incomplete'.[18] He regards this as entailed by the 'vagueness or open character' of language itself.[19] He concludes that 'in such cases . . . [the judge] must . . . *make* law for the case instead of merely applying already pre-existing settled law'.[20]

This tenet derives from the work of Austin, who regarded law as essentially incomplete in a similar sense, and yet also insisted that a judge is obliged to decide every case that comes before him. He presented the straightforward solution that the judge should *legislate* in the case.[21] A broader acceptance of separation of powers since Austin's era has led modern legal positivism to reject the term 'legislate' in the context of judicial lawmaking, and insist that while judges must and do make law, they have only 'interstitial' powers to do so.[22] That is, in stepping outside existing law to make new law, judges must nevertheless base their reasoning closely on existing law.[23]

The question now is on what sources and processes of reasoning the judge draws when exercising these interstitial lawmaking powers. Since by definition the judge steps outside existing law in exercising these powers, she cannot draw on legal sources and legal processes of reasoning. The only possibility that legal positivism recognizes is that for sources she must draw on social aims and, since she is to determine what *ought* to be the outcome, for processes of reasoning she must apply moral reasoning.[24]

A different and potentially less autonomous view of legal epistemology would avoid this conclusion. In particular, Ronald Dworkin argues that if law were defined to incorporate the relevant social and moral considerations, then it would be seen as determinate and complete. With this approach, a judge would not need to step outside the law to seek sources in social aims and principles of interpretation in moral reasoning. By definition, all this would already be within the law. He further argues that this view better represents real-life legal systems, so that it *should* be adopted, and the legal positivist view of law should consequently be abandoned.[25]

Essentially, legal positivism accepts the presence of moral reasoning within the adjudicative process as a cost of maintaining the epistemological autonomy of legal reasoning. But this autonomy would be undermined if the two processes of reasoning were confused. Consequently, legal positivism insists that jurisprudential analysis of the adjudicative process should as far as possible regard legal reasoning and moral reasoning as distinct processes in the decision of a case – even though, of course, courts in practice do not divide their opinions in any such way.[26] This is the legal positivist resolution of the tension at the first stage of my analysis.

The second stage of my analysis introduces the concern that this means of resolution might in fact be ineffective. As we have seen, legal positivism stipulates that law is indeterminate and incomplete and therefore must draw on morality to achieve determinacy and completeness. But this solves the problem only if morality itself is determinate and complete. If morality were indeterminate or incomplete, the introduction of moral reasoning into adjudication might *mitigate* the problem of the indeterminacy and incompleteness of law in so far as morality resolved cases that law did not. However, there would still be cases that morality did not resolve, and these might be cases that law also did not resolve. Consequently, the introduction of moral reasoning into adjudication would not *solve* the problem of the indeterminacy and incompleteness of law.

Note that if legal positivism fails to deal with this problem, the epistemological autonomy of the legal system (which admits moral reasoning to resolve cases that legal reasoning cannot resolve) would fall into conflict with its functional role (which requires it to resolve every case that comes before it). This would undermine the claim of epistemological autonomy, and with it the foundations of legal positivism.

The third stage of my analysis considers how legal positivism can deal with this concern. I am aware of only one serious attempt, by Joseph Raz, to find a solution that preserves the structure of legal positivism while allowing for morality to be indeterminate or incomplete. However, I do not find his attempt persuasive.[27] Indeed, I cannot see that a solution along these lines would be possible within the confines of legal positivism.

Consequently, legal positivism cannot doctrinally accept that moral reasoning is indeterminate or incomplete. But from this it follows that legal positivism becomes incoherent unless it accepts that legal reasoning and moral reasoning are fundamentally different. In particular, since legal positivism derives the indeterminacy and incompleteness of law from the vagueness or open character of language, it becomes incoherent unless it concludes that moral reasoning is at least in part not contingent on expression in language. This in fact fits with my comments on moral reasoning in my discussion of the legacy of positivism in moral non-science, in Chapter 6, Section viii.

It is questionable how far legal positivists recognize this conclusion. Raz in fact appears to deny it, claiming that 'legal reasoning is an instance of moral reasoning'.[28] However, he seems to mean no more than that the legal principles that courts apply should be regarded as morally acceptable.[29] But it is possible to apply morally acceptable principles without engaging in moral reasoning, as follows from my discussion in Chapter 6. Other positivist writers seem to suggest that legal reasoning is technical or purely deductive, which *a fortiori* would imply that it is unlike moral reasoning.[30] But in general, legal positivists seem disinclined to define clearly or analyze their notion of moral reasoning in this context.

The final stage of my analysis concerns what kind of reasoning legal reasoning is under legal positivism, if, as I have argued, it is fundamentally different from moral reasoning. Here the influence of the legacy of positivism again appears. I argued in Chapter 6 that moral reasoning differs from scientific reasoning. I did not claim that there is no other form of reasoning than these, but I now argue that in practice the legacy of positivism is so pervasive that no other mode of thought is sufficiently developed to serve the needs of a social institution. That is, in my view once legal positivism claims epistemological autonomy for law, and stipulates the epistemological indeterminacy and incompleteness of legal reasoning, the influence of the legacy of positivism presses it inexorably to fit the legal system into the mould of the reasoning structure of an autonomous science, with the characteristics that I discussed in Chapters 2 and 4.

However, as I discussed in the previous section and in Chapter 7, this structure is also in tension with the functional and institutional role of the legal system in society. It appears therefore that, under the influence of the legacy of positivism, whatever position legal positivism takes regarding the relationship between law and morality in adjudication will be in tension with the societal role of the legal system. In my view, this in part explains the continuing controversy within legal positivism on this subject.

iii. The human sciences in law

In the societies that the legacy of positivism has influenced, as I discussed in Chapter 7, the political lawmaking body separates the legal system downstream of it from the human sciences upstream of it. But separation is not necessarily isolation. Consequently, the question arises whether the lawmaking body is to be the only institutional source of substantive conclusions (in the form of statutes and so forth) to serve as 'raw materials' for the legal system to interpret and develop, or whether the human sciences could also provide such a source. I argue in this section that for the legal system to draw on the human sciences in this way shows a double influence of the legacy of positivism.

The relevant issues are most readily explored in the jurisprudence of the United States, where the influence of one branch of the American Legal Realist school has resulted in a considerable history of courts explicitly taking findings of the human sciences into account.[31] The fundamental Realist doctrine was that law had lost touch with life and should be brought back in touch with life. As I mentioned in the previous section, one branch of the Realists focused on bringing moral and other formerly extrinsic considerations into the conceptual structure of law. However, protagonists of a second branch held that '[t]he task of bringing law back in touch with life meant that law needed to become a mirror of social relations. Since their goal was to develop a method that permitted the legal system to receive undistorted messages from reality, they turned to the social sciences to learn what that reality was.'[32]

Thus, almost a century ago the US Supreme Court in *Muller* v. *Oregon*[33] considered sociological findings in deciding that women's physical nature and appropriate social role justified, against constitutional challenge, a statute that limited the hours of labour of women employed in laundries to ten hours daily. A brief submitted to the court contained 'extracts from over ninety reports of committees, bureaus of statistics, commissioners of hygiene, inspectors of factories . . . to the effect that long hours of labor are dangerous for women, primarily because of their special physical organization'.[34] The court summed up these reports in the words of one of the inspectors:

> The reasons for the reduction of the working day to ten hours – (a) the physical organization of women, (b) her maternal functions, (c) the rearing and education of the children, (d) the maintenance of the home – are all so important and so far reaching that the need for such reduction need hardly be discussed.[35]

The court treated these findings as facts of general knowledge, and declared: 'We take judicial cognizance of all matters of general knowledge.'[36]

It is not unusual for US courts to treat sociological findings in this way, as scientifically determined facts of which the court takes 'judicial cognizance' or, in the more usual modern terminology, judicial notice. Jack Friedenthal and I have previously commented on this process,[37] particularly in regard to the holding of the US Supreme Court in *Brown v. Board of Education* that racial segregation in schools run by the public authorities violates constitutional equal-protection provisions.[38] The court relied on sociological findings, which it cited, to conclude that 'to separate . . . [children] from others of similar age and qualifications solely because of their race generates a feeling of inferiority as to their status in the community that may affect their hearts and minds in a way unlikely ever to be undone'.[39]

The way in which sociological findings are treated in these cases is part of the broader process known as *judicial notice of legislative facts*, in which the court relies on what it declares (or tacitly considers) to be generally accepted facts, particularly with regard to human nature and society. This process is commonly used in justifying a determination of a policy for the application of a law. Because it is regarded as 'woven into the very texture of the judicial function',[40] it is subject to no control external to the legal system itself. Within the US judicial system, judicial notice of legislative facts may be taken at the trial or any appellate level, and notice taken at one level is subject to review at any higher level. Thus, the judges who ultimately take judicial notice of some legislative fact may be far removed from the social setting on the nature of which they conclusively pronounce.[41] However, as I mentioned above, the Realist doctrine encourages judges to rely on conclusions of sociology and other human sciences to substitute for their lack of direct social knowledge.

I now argue that this shows a double influence of the legacy of positivism. The first form of influence appears in the fact that the conclusions of the human sciences are deemed to be authoritative. This influence is just as I discussed in Chapter 6.

To see the second form of influence, observe that the doctrine of judicial notice of legislative facts constitutes an implicit assertion of epistemological autonomy on the part of the courts, in that the legal system thereby determines for itself what its sources are to be and how it will interpret them. Note that in making this assessment I am rejecting the Realist view that admission of the conclusions of the human sciences *'challenged* the assertion of the autonomy of law' that was particularly to be found in legal positivism.[42] Rather, I characterize a decision to draw on certain sources as and when one pleases (the Realist proposals for the legal system did not seriously contemplate external compulsion) as an assertion, not a renunciation, of autonomy.

Of course, as I discussed in Chapter 7, the law has long made autonomy claims, and the basic doctrine of judicial notice of legislative facts, in which judges rely on their own supposed social knowledge, falls within the traditional scope of the epistemological autonomy of the law. Certainly, the basic doctrine well predates the development of the legacy of positivism. However, it is in the unilateral judicial extension of the basic doctrine to allow the adoption of conclusions of the human sciences that I find the influence of the legacy of positivism. This extension transforms the basic doctrine into an extraordinarily broad epistemological autonomy claim. In my view, it is akin to those claims that, as I argued in Chapter 7 and in Section i of the present chapter, show the influence of the legacy of positivism.

In sum, the first form of influence of the legacy of positivism appears in the human sciences making an authoritative *offer* of guidance to society, and the second form of influence appears in the judicial *acceptance* of the offer and implementation of the guidance as law.

I now turn to critique. I argued in Chapter 6 that it is dangerous to accept the conclusions of the human sciences in so far as these sciences make autonomy claims that shield their validation processes from external assessment. To a great extent the political lawmaking body rather than the legal system has the responsibility for avoiding this danger in society, while making the best use of the guidance that the human sciences offer. Part of the role of the political lawmaking body in this regard is to determine when that guidance is to be accepted into the social system and when it is to be rejected. Moreover, since it is a *political* body it is not obliged to develop any general principle governing the treatment of conclusions of the human sciences, but rather is free to decide on purely policy grounds on a case-by-case basis.

However, in the legal systems under consideration here it is generally expected that judges will reach their decisions primarily by legal reasoning, as I discussed in the previous section. Consequently, they are subject to pressure to develop principles governing the treatment of conclusions of the human sciences. My arguments in Chapter 6 lead me to conclude here that these should be cautious principles that entail careful probing in every case of the validation processes of the human sciences in question. Without such probing, it cannot be presumed that either the methods or the conclusions of the human sciences are dependable enough to serve as the foundation of adjudication.[43] Further critique is called for to establish appropriate principles.

Finally, note that a cautious approach to the methods and conclusions of the human sciences in the context of the legal system does not in itself serve any particular socio-political goals at the expense of others. A cautious approach is neither 'progressive' nor 'conservative';

it is neither 'radical' nor 'reactionary'. My discussion of the shift in the views of the American Anthropological Association regarding human rights in Chapter 6 shows that a human science can apply the same methods to the same facts and yet reach dramatically different conclusions, with dramatically different potential socio-political consequences, at different times. A comparison of *Muller* v. *Oregon* with *Brown* v. *Board of Education* shows a similar phenomenon in relation to a shift in sociological views on traditional stereotypes. While these specific shifts in anthropology and sociology are to be welcomed, there is no reason to suppose that the more recent views will endure as the socio-political attitudes of these sciences. In sum, reliance on conclusions of the human sciences cannot be expected to work consistently to the benefit or detriment of any given socio-political goal.

Notes and References

1 The Philosophy of Positivism

1. This was Comte, *Plan*.
2. For an account see the introduction by Frederic Harrison to Martineau, *Positive Philosophy of Auguste Comte*, pp. 13–14.
3. See e.g. Berlin, 'Historical Inevitability', p. 42 ('grotesque pedantry . . . unreadable dullness'); Grange, *La philosophie d'Auguste Comte*, p. 22 ('Comte . . . fears neither redundancy nor repetition' – 'Comte . . . ne craint ni la redondance ni la répétition'); T.H. Huxley, quoted Congreve, *Essays*, vol. I, p. 262 ('dreary and verbose'); Pickering, *Auguste Comte*, p. 587 ('atrocious style . . . almost unreadable').
4. For this view, see Grange, Introduction, in Comte, *Leçons*, p. 20.
5. I note shifts in Comte's viewpoint, shifts in emphasis, and the use of synonyms at various points in the text and notes. Grange, *Le vocabulaire de Comte*, p. 4, and Kolakowski, *Positivist Philosophy*, p. 61, overstate the level of consistency of Comte's works.
6. A translation that is also a condensation is obviously even more problematic. Some scholars have nevertheless relied on Harriet Martineau's well-known translation and condensation of the *Philosophie positive*, on the ground that Comte enthusiastically approved it. However, Comte read only the preface, table of contents and a few chapters that he considered crucial. See letter dated 29 December 1853, in 'Lettres à Miss Henriette [sic] Martineau', in Littré, *Auguste Comte et la Philosophie Positive*, p. 647; letter to Eugène Deullin, 30 December 1853, in *Correspondance inédite d'Auguste Comte*. His approval focused less on the work's fidelity to his own than on the potential of such a readily accessible condensation to promote the spread of positivist doctrine, and in any event he acknowledged that his original text would remain necessary for genuine scholars. See letter to Eugène Deullin, *ibid*.

   Frederic Harrison, a committed follower of Comte's doctrines and one of the translators into English of the *Politique positive*, observes in his introduction to the 1896 edition of Martineau's work that she wholly suppressed the 'crucial' concluding ten pages of the *Philosophie positive*, which 'contain the entire scheme of Comte's future philosophical labours as he designed them' (Martineau, *Positive Philosophy of Auguste Comte*, vol. I., p. 16). He further notes that 'there are points, and even points of great importance, in which the translator failed to grasp the author's meaning', and insists that the French original remains essential for serious study or criticism (*ibid.*, p. 17). In my view, the latter comment applies also to the *Politique positive*, in regard to Harrison's translation.
7. For this view, see Grange, *La philosophie d'Auguste Comte*, p. 22.
8. However, I do not join a number of recent writers in exploring whether selected (and sometimes hitherto neglected) aspects of Comte's scheme

might be resurrected to yield promising ideas for present-day philosophical or social development. See e.g. Scharff, *Comte after Positivism*, p. 176; Grange, *Auguste Comte: La Politique et la Science*, p. 83; Wernick, *Auguste Comte and the Religion of Humanity*, p. 9.

9. For consideration of how far Comte's ideas were original within his own social and cultural context rather than derived from those of his near-contemporaries, see Gouhier, *La jeunesse d'Auguste Comte*.

10. 'Il arrivera donc, ce moment où le soleil n'éclairera plus sur la terre que des hommes libres, ne reconnaissant d'autre maître que leur raison; où les tyrans et les esclaves ... n'existeront plus que dans l'histoire et sur les théâtres.' Condorcet, *Esquisse*, Dixième Époque, *Des progrès futurs de l'esprit humain*, p. 210. Comte recognized the influence of Condorcet on his thought; see *Philosophie positive*, vol. IV, leçon 47, p. 253.

11. There is a considerable literature on Bacon's contribution to the development of science. The various assessments cover the full spectrum from viewing him as innovative, important and shamefully underrated to viewing him as derivative, insignificant and shamefully overrated. For a discussion with review and critique of the literature, see Wheeler, 'The Invention of Modern Empiricism'.

    Comte recognizes Bacon, along with René Descartes and Galileo Galilei, as the founders of the positivist mode of thought. He declares that each of them was aware of the true character of positivism and the conditions necessary to put it into practice, as well as of its ultimate ascendancy, but sharply criticizes all three for the limitations of their respective approaches and levels of understanding. *Philosophie positive*, vol. VI, leçon 56, pp. 301–8. Elsewhere, Comte also acknowledges Johannes Kepler as foundational, *Esprit positif*, p. 48.

12. '... experimentorum longe major est subtilitas quam sensus ipsius ... (de iis loquimur experimentis, quae ad intentionem ejus quod quaeritur perite et secundum artem excogitata et apposita sunt). Itaque perceptioni sensus immediatae ac propriae non multum tribuimus: sed eo rem deducimus, ut sensus tantum de experimento, experimentum de re judicet.' Bacon, *Novum Organum: Instauratio Magna*, p. 138.

13. 'Duae viae sunt, atque esse possunt, ad inquirendam et inveniendam veritatem. Altera a sensu et particularibus advolat ad axiomata maxime generalia, atque ex iis principiis eorumque immota veritate judicat et invenit axiomata media; atque haec via in usu est: altera a sensu et particularibus excitat axiomata, ascendendo continenter et gradatim, ut ultimo loco perveniatur ad maxime generalia; quae via vera est, sed intentata.' Bacon, *Novum Organum*, Bk I, Aphorism XIX. On the same issues, see also *ibid.*, Aphorisms XX and XXII.

14. 'In ... philosophia [experimentali] propositiones deducuntur ex phænomenis, et redduntur generales per inductionem.' Newton, *Principia Mathematica*, vol. II, p. 764 (Bk III, Scholium Generale, §530). My use of the term 'sciences' in translation is admittedly potentially controversial.

15. '... nos âmes se sont corrompues à mesure que nos Sciences et nos Arts se sont avancés à la perfection'. Rousseau, *Discours sur les sciences et les arts* (Première Partie), p. 13.

16. '. . . nous trouverons . . . dans l'observation des progrès que les sciences . . . ont faits jusqu'ici . . . les motifs les plus forts de croire que la nature n'a mis aucun terme à nos espérances'. Condorcet, *Esquisse*, p. 205.

    This difference between Rousseau and Condorcet in views on progress was closely associated with an aspect of the well-known *querelle des anciens et des modernes* that raged in France in the eighteenth century and that reflected similar developments elsewhere, including in England.

17. See Comte, *Plan*, p. 73. The term *positif* had long encompassed this sense in relation to juridical law, as I discuss in Chapter 2.

18. '[L]e mot *positif* désigne le réel, par opposition au chimérique: sous ce rapport, il convient pleinement au nouvel esprit philosophique, ainsi caractérisé d'après sa constante consécration aux recherches vraiment accessibles à notre intelligence, à l'exclusion permanente des impénétrables mystères dont s'occupait surtout son enfance.' Comte, *Esprit positif*, p. 41.

19. '[L]e mot *positif* . . . indique le contraste de l'utile à l'oiseux: alors il rappelle, en philosophie, la destination nécessaire de toutes nos saines spéculations pour l'amélioration continue de notre vraie condition, individuelle et collective, au lieu de la vaine satisfaction d'une stérile curiosité.' *Ibid.*, p. 41.

    The terms *spéculation* and *spéculatif* occur frequently in Comte's works and convey a sense of intellectually committed theorizing. The modern, somewhat pejorative sense of unfocused hypothesizing and surmise is largely absent from French usage of the period, as is similarly the case with the English *speculation* and *speculative*. In French usage of the period there can occasionally be a pejorative sense, but it is of a different kind. A robustly pragmatic writer may contrast *spéculation* with *pratique*, to the detriment of the former, or a religious writer may oppose *vaines spéculations de la science* to simple faith, again to the detriment of the former. See Littré, *Dictionnaire*, Tome 7, pp. 418–20. Some modern writing on Comte ignores the shades of meaning in these terms, resulting in confusion.

    Laudan, 'Reassessment of Comte's "Méthode Positive"', 36, gives a wholly misleading assessment of Comte's view of the useful and the futile.

20. '[L]e mot *positif* . . . est fréquemment employé [*sic*] à qualifier l'opposition entre la certitude et l'indécision . . . [*et*] indique ainsi l'aptitude caractéristique d'une telle philosophie à constituer spontanément l'harmonie logique dans l'individu et la communion spirituelle dans l'espèce entière, au lieu de ces doutes indéfinis et de ces débats interminables que devait susciter l'antique régime mental.' Comte, *Esprit positif*, pp. 41–2.

21. '[L]e mot *positif* . . . oppose[ ] le précis au vague: ce sens rappelle la tendance constante du véritable esprit philosophique à obtenir partout le degré de précision compatible avec la nature des phénomènes et conforme à l'exigence de nos vrais besoins; tandis que l'ancienne manière de philosopher conduisait nécessairement à des opinions vagues, ne comportant une indispensable discipline que d'après une compression permanente, appuyée sur une autorité surnaturelle.' *Ibid.*

22. '[L]e mot *positif* . . . [est] le contraire de *négatif*. Sous cet aspect, il indique l'une des plus éminentes propriétés de la vraie philosophie moderne, en la montrant destinée surtout, par sa nature, non à détruire, mais à organiser.' *Ibid.*, p. 42 (emphasis in original).

23. 'En étudiant . . . le développement total de l'intelligence humaine dans ses diverses sphères d'activité, depuis son premier essor le plus simple jusqu'à nos jours, je crois avoir découvert une grande loi fondamentale . . . Cette loi consiste en ce que chacune de nos conceptions principales, chaque branche de nos connaissances, passe successivement par trois états théoriques différents: l'état théologique, ou fictif; l'état métaphysique, ou abstrait; l'état scientifique, ou positif.' Comte, *Philosophie positive*, vol. I, leçon 1 (Exposition), p. 3.

    In the English literature on Comte, both 'stage' and 'state' are found as translations of Comte's *état* in this context, with some writers using both terms within a single work, often indiscriminately. My sense is that 'stage' is more widely used than 'state' in the literature, so I shall follow this usage to minimize confusion. There is no other reason. Scharff has argued that *état* expresses a developing rather than static condition and that 'stage' conveys this in English better than 'state'. Scharff, *Comte after Positivism*, p. 74. However, this is too much to hang on the term *état*, which in Comte's time largely conveyed a static sense (as it still does). See Littré, *Dictionnaire*, Tome 3, pp. 1097–102.

24. '. . . la grande conception de Dieu'. Comte, *Esprit positif*, p. 25.

25. 'Dans l'état théologique, l'esprit humain dirigeant essentiellement ses recherches . . . vers les connaissances absolues, se représente les phénomènes comme produits par l'action directe et continue d'agents surnaturels plus ou moins nombreux, dont l'intervention arbitraire explique toutes les anomalies apparentes de l'univers.' Comte, *Philosophie positive*, vol. I, leçon 1 (Exposition), p. 4.

26. '. . . la vague pensée de la Nature'. Comte, *Esprit positif*, p. 25.

27. 'Dans l'état métaphysique, qui n'est au fond qu'une simple modification générale du premier, les agents surnaturels sont remplacés par des . . . abstractions personnifiées . . . conçues comme capables d'engendrer par elles-mêmes tous les phénomènes observés, dont l'explication consiste alors à assigner pour chacun l'entité correspondante.' Comte, *Philosophie positive*, vol. I, leçon 1 (Exposition), p. 4.

28. '. . . la notion prépondérante de l'Humanité doit nécessairement constituer, dans l'état positif, une pleine systématisation mentale'. Comte, *Esprit positif*, p. 25.

29. 'Enfin, dans l'état positif, l'esprit humain reconnaissant l'impossibilité d'obtenir des notions absolues, renonce à chercher l'origine et la destination de l'univers . . . pour s'attacher uniquement à découvrir, par l'usage bien combiné du raisonnement et de l'observation, leurs lois effectives.' Comte, *Philosophie positive*, vol. I, leçon 1 (Exposition), pp. 4–5.

30. '[L]'esprit positif . . . n'a plus laissé possible d'autre unité mentale que celle qui résulterait de son propre ascendant universel, chaque nouveau domaine successivement acquis par lui ne pouvant plus jamais retourner à la théologie ni à la métaphysique, en vertu de la consécration définitive que ces acquisitions croissantes trouvaient de plus en plus dans la raison vulgaire.' Comte, *Esprit positif*, p. 48.

31. '. . . trois sortes de philosophies . . . qui s'excluent mutuellement: la première est le point de départ nécessaire de l'intelligence humaine; la troisième, son

état fixe et définitif; la seconde est uniquement destinée à servir de transition'. Comte, *Philosophie positive*, vol. I, leçon 1 (Exposition), pp. 3–4.

32. '[N]otre entendement, contraint à ne marcher que par degrés presque insensibles, ne pouvait passer brusquement, et sans intermédiaires, de la philosophie théologique à la philosophie positive. La théologie et la physique sont si profondément incompatibles, leurs conceptions ont un caractère si radicalement opposé, qu'avant de renoncer aux unes pour employer exclusivement les autres, l'intelligence humaine a dû se servir de conceptions intermédiaires, d'un caractère bâtard, propres, par cela même, à opérer graduellement la transition.' *Ibid.*, p. 13.

33. '... l'incompatibilité finale des conceptions positives avec toutes les opinions théologiques quelconques... l'impossibilité d'aucune conciliation durable entre les deux philosophies, soit quant à la méthode, ou à la doctrine; en sorte que toute incertitude à ce sujet peut être ici facilement dissipée'. Comte, *Esprit positif*, p. 33.

34. Scharff, *Comte after Positivism*, p. 5, states that Comte argues that '[s]cience ... transforms rather than supersedes theology and metaphysics'. As a statement of Comte's views this is clearly erroneous (Scharff provides no citation to Comte's texts in support). However, at other points in his text Scharff presents Comte's view on this accurately, see *ibid.*, p. 8, p. 53.

35. '[L]'athéisme ... tend à prolonger indéfiniment l'état métaphysique en poursuivant sans cesse de nouvelles solutions des problèmes théologiques, au lieu d'écarter comme radicalement vaines toutes les recherches inaccessibles. Le véritable esprit positif ... est ... incompatible avec les orgueilleuses rêveries d'un ténébreux athéisme sur la formation de l'univers, l'origine des animaux, etc.' Comte, *Politique positive*, vol. I, pp. 46–7.

36. With this view of atheism, Comte himself then lapses briefly into metaphysics, declaring that '[a]lthough the natural world may be very imperfect in every respect, it is considerably more compatible with the presumption of an intelligent will than with that of a blind mechanism'. ('Quoique l'ordre naturel soit, à tous égards, très-imparfait, sa production se concilierait beaucoup mieux avec la supposition d'une volonté intelligente qu'avec celle d'un aveugle mécanisme.') *Ibid.*, p. 48.

37. 'Loin de compter sur l'appui des athées actuels, le positivisme doit donc y trouver des adversaires naturels.' *Ibid.*, p. 49.

38. '... ne combattre les croyances arriérées que d'après son aptitude générale à mieux satisfaire tous les besoins moraux et sociaux'. *Ibid.*, p. 49.

39. 'Personne, sans doute, n'a jamais démontré logiquement la non-existence d'Apollon, de Minerve, etc.... ce qui n'a nullement empêché l'esprit humain d'abandonner irrévocablement les dogmes antiques, quand ils ont enfin cessé de convenir à l'ensemble de sa situation.' Comte, *Esprit positif*, p. 43.

Comte may have been premature in supposing that the ancient Greek deities had been irrevocably abandoned. A small organization, Hellenion, now describes itself as 'a US-based religious organization dedicated to the revival and practice of Hellenic polytheism'. See http://www.hellenion.org (visited 9 January 2005).

40. '... la haine aveugle qu'il inspire envers l'ensemble du passé'. Comte, *Politique positive*, vol. I, p. 48.

41. '[L]a nature absolue des anciennes doctrines, soit théologiques, soit métaphysiques, déterminait nécessairement chacune d'elles à devenir négative envers toutes les autres ... C'est, au contraire, en vertu de son génie relatif que la nouvelle philosophie peut toujours apprécier la valeur propre des théories qui lui sont le plus opposées, sans toutefois aboutir jamais à aucune vaine concession, susceptible d'altérer la netteté de ses vues ou la fermeté de ses décisions.' Comte, *Esprit positif*, p. 44.

42. Thus, for example, regarding the separation of theory and practice in his socio-political scheme, which I discuss in Chapter 3, Comte states: 'With the complete establishment of Christianity the division between theory and practice was formed ... This great and beautiful idea ... must be carefully preserved, with all the other achievements of humanity under the influence of the old system, which must not be allowed to perish with that system.' ('Par l'établissement définitif du christianisme, la division de la théorie et de la pratique fut constituée ... Cette grande et belle conception ... doit être précieusement conservée, avec toutes les autres conquêtes que l'esprit humain a faites sous l'influence de l'ancien système, et qui ne sauraient périr avec lui.') Comte, *Plan*, p. 67.

43. '... les différentes branches de nos connaissances n'ont pas dû parcourir d'une vitesse égale les trois grandes phases de leur développement indiquées ci-dessus, ni, par conséquent, arriver simultanément à l'état positif'. Comte, *Philosophie positive*, vol. I, leçon 1 (Exposition), p. 18.

44. See note 23 above.

45. '[I]l ne saurait être question ici d'une suite de cours spéciaux sur chacune des branches principales de la philosophie naturelle ... [C]'est un *Cours de philosophie positive*, et non de sciences positives, que je me propose de faire. Il s'agit uniquement ici de considérer chaque science fondamentale dans ses relations avec le système positif tout entier, et quant à l'esprit qui la caractérise, c'est-à-dire, sous le double rapport de ses méthodes essentielles et de ses résultats principaux.' Comte, *Philosophie positive*, vol. I, leçon 1 (Exposition), pp. 25–6 (emphasis in original).

    The term *esprit* has many shades of meaning, with Littré, *Dictionnaire*, recording 29 principle senses in an entry nearly ten pages in length. I translate Comte's various uses of the term as 'essence', 'ethos', 'intellect', 'mind', 'spirit', and so forth, as appropriate in context.

46. 'En effet, les divisions que nous établissons entre nos sciences, sans être arbitraires, comme quelques-uns le croient, sont essentiellement artificielles. En réalité, le sujet de toutes nos recherches est un; nous ne le partageons que dans la vue de séparer les difficultés pour les mieux résoudre.' Comte, *Philosophie positive*, vol. I, leçon 1 (Exposition), pp. 43–4. For a similar view, see Comte, *Esprit positif*, p. 101.

    Grange, *Auguste Comte: La Politique et la Science*, p. 56, misleads regarding Comte's views on the essential unity of science. Kolakowski, *Positivist Philosophy*, p. 77, exaggerates Comte's admittedly considerable obsession with definiteness and order, regarding this and other contexts.

47. 'Les sciences sont devenues positives, l'une après l'autre, dans l'ordre ... du degré de complication plus ou moins grand de leurs phénomènes ... Ainsi,

les phénomènes astronomiques d'abord, comme étant les plus simples, et ensuite successivement, les physiques, les chimiques et les physiologiques, ont été ramenés à des théories positives; ceux-ci à une époque toute récente.' Comte, *Plan*, p. 80.

48. '. . . le but principal que l'on doit avoir en vue dans tout travail encyclopédique, c'est de disposer les sciences dans l'ordre de leur enchaînement naturel, en suivant leur dépendance mutuelle; de telle sorte qu'on puisse les exposer successivement, sans jamais être entraîné dans le moindre cercle vicieux'. Comte, *Philosophie positive*, vol. I, leçon 2, p. 76.

49. Comte first introduced the term 'sociologie' in *Philosophie positive*, vol. IV, leçon 47, p. 252, but declared it to be equivalent to the 'social physics' ('physique sociale') that he had used in the earlier *Plan. Ibid.*, n. He excused the introduction of the new term as necessary 'to meet the particular purposes of the work' ('pour correspondre à la destination spéciale de ce volume'). *Ibid.* Nevertheless, he continued to use the term 'physique sociale' elsewhere in this volume. See e.g. Comte, *Philosophie positive*, vol. IV, leçon 48, p. 411. For Comte's further comment on the need for the new term, see *Philosophie positive*, vol. IV, leçon 46, p. 7 n.; and for comment on this, see Grange, *La Philosophie d'Auguste Comte*, p. 243 n.5. On the question whether sociology is different in kind from the physical sciences, Grange offers mutually contradictory views within a single work, compare *Auguste Comte: La Politique et la Science*, p. 67 with *ibid.*, p. 86.

50. '. . . la dernière science fondamentale'. Comte, *Philosophie positive*, vol. IV, leçon 49, p. 534.

51. Harré, *Great Scientific Experiments*, p. 11.

52. Carr, *What is History?*, p. 11.

53. '. . . le noble but indiqué par Bacon'. *Philosophie positive*, vol. VI, leçon 56, p. 305.

54. 'Condorcet was the first to understand the true nature of the general task of raising politics to the level of the sciences of observation, but he carried it out in an utterly wrong-headed way . . . He entirely missed the point, first as regards theory and then as regards practice. Consequently, the work has to be rethought from the beginning.' ('Condorcet a conçu, le premier, la véritable nature du travail général qui doit élever la politique au rang des sciences d'observation mais il l'a exécuté dans un esprit absolument vicieux . . . Le but a été entièrement manqué, d'abord quant à la théorie, et par suite quant à la pratique. Ainsi, ce travail doit être de nouveau conçu en totalité.') Comte, *Plan*, p. 119. Condorcet had tried to apply probability theory, which Comte rejected, see Chapter 2.

55. 'Montesquieu, even Machiavelli, Adam Smith and the political economists universally, . . . Bentham, and all thinkers initiated by him, had a full conviction that social phenomena conform to invariable laws, the discovery and illustration of which was their great object as speculative thinkers. All that can be said is, that those philosophers did not get so far as M. Comte in discovering the methods best adapted to bring these laws to light. It was not, therefore, reserved for M. Comte to make sociological inquiries positive [– that is, to bring them within the ambit of positivist analysis].' Mill, *Auguste Comte and Positivism*, p. 52 (punctuation and spelling slightly changed). For 'speculative', see note 19 above.

2 The Structure of a Positive Science

1. 'Law' has the same linguistic roots as the German verb *legen* (to lay). See *OED*, vol. L, p. 113 cols 2–3. However, the modern German equivalent for law in the sense of a commandment set down by authority is *Gesetz*, which derives from the verb *setzen*, a different root but with a similar sense of placing or setting down.
2. *Ibid.*, p. 115 col. 3. Similarly, Mill states, 'the expression *law of nature* has generally been employed with a sort of tacit reference to the original sense of the word law, namely, the expression of the will of a superior'. *Logic*, p. 207 (italics in original).
3. Kepler stated this for the particular case of Mars in *Astronomia nova* and generalized it to all the planets in *Epitome astronomiae Copernicanae*.
4. For such a derivation, see Franck, *Dictionnaire*, p. 974. For seventeenth- and eighteenth-century usage, see *OED*, vol. L, p. 115 col. 3. I am not aware of any earlier use of 'law' in the scientific sense. Kurath and Kuhn, *Middle English Dictionary*, vol. 'L', pp. 699–708, give for the equivalent Middle English term *laue* all the familiar meanings of law in the juridical sense. While they also give the meaning 'A consistent principle controlling the action of material things, law of nature, physical law', all the illustrations that they quote in fact relate to entities obeying a direct divine prescription. Consequently, their evidence does not support their proposed meaning, which, as I argue in the text, is anachronistic. For the parallel French development, Huguet, *Dictionnaire*, vol. 5, pp. 53–4, gives for *loy* in the sixteenth century the senses of both juridical law and legal right. There is no sense at all of scientific law.

   Some writers resisted the scientific use of 'law' well into the nineteenth century, generally for political reasons. Thus, for example, John Austin, endeavouring to reinforce his argument that juridical laws were the commands of a lawgiver (see Chapter 7), dismissed 'laws determining the movements of inanimate bodies or masses' as 'rest[ing] upon a slender analogy and . . . merely metaphorical or figurative'. Austin, *The Province of Jurisprudence Determined*, p. 12.
5. Newton derived the elliptical motion of planets from the inverse-square law (under the simplifying assumption that the mass of each planet is negligible compared with that of the sun) in *Principia Mathematica*, vol. II, pp. 587–8 (Bk III, Prop. XIII, Th. XIII), relying on his demonstration that a body subject to a centripetal force varying as the inverse square of the distance moves in a conic section, *ibid.*, vol. I, p. 125 (Bk I, Sec. III, Prop. XIII, Cor. 1).
6. For example, Kepler sought to explain the relative dimensions of the planetary orbits in terms of the dimensions obtained by nesting the five regular (or platonic) solids one inside the other, as well as in terms of the lengths of strings that produce musical harmonies. See his aptly entitled *Harmonices mundi*.
7. The source is the past participle of the Latin *ponere* (to place, put or lay down). See *OED*, p. 1152 cols 2–3.
8. Pennington, 'Law, Legislative Authority, and Theories of Government', p. 425. For further discussion, see Finnis, 'The Truth in Legal Positivism', p. 195; Kuttner, 'Sur les origines du terme "droit positif"'.

9. Contrast with French, German and Latin, which respectively use *loi*, *Gesetz* and *lex* for the edict and *droit*, *Recht* and *ius* for the system, and so have *droit positif*, *positives Recht* and *ius positivum*. There is a considerable literature discussing the extent to which the terms used for the system incorporate notions of justice or moral right.
10. For a summary, see Scharff, *Comte after Positivism*, pp. 63–7.
11. Russell, *Portraits from Memory*, p. 20.
12. 'C'est par les mathématiques que la philosophie positive a commencé à se former: c'est d'elles que nous vient la *méthode*.' Comte, *Philosophie positive*, vol. I, leçon 3, p. 163 (emphasis in original).
13. '. . . sous le point de vue purement logique, cette science est . . . universelle. Car il n'y a pas de question quelconque qui ne puisse finalement être conçue comme consistant à déterminer des quantités les unes par les autres d'après certaines relations, et, par conséquent, comme réductible, en dernière analyse, à une simple question de nombres.' *Ibid.*, pp. 148–9.
14. '. . . pour se former une idée convenable de la science mathématique . . . il n'est pas moins indispensable de considérer maintenant les grandes limitations réelles qui, vu la faiblesse de notre intelligence, rétrécissent singulièrement son domaine effectif'. *Ibid.*, p. 151.
15. '. . . par la recherche chimérique d'une perfection impossible'. *Ibid.*, p. 162.
16. 'La première condition pour que des phénomènes comportent des lois mathématiques *susceptibles d'être découvertes*, c'est évidemment que les diverses quantités qu'ils présentent puissant donner lieu à des nombres fixes.' *Ibid.*, p. 152 (emphasis added).
17. '. . . un caractère éminemment propre aux phénomènes physiologiques . . . c'est l'extrême instabilité numérique qu'ils présentent . . . sous l'influence d'une foule de circonstances . . . en sorte que toute idée de nombres fixes, et, par suite, de lois mathématiques *que nous puissions espérer d'obtenir*, implique réellement contradiction avec la nature spéciale de cette classe de phénomènes'. *Ibid.*, p. 155 (emphasis added).
18. '. . . toute idée . . . de loi mathématique étant déjà interdite en biologie . . . elle doit être, à plus forte raison, radicalement exclue des spéculations encore plus compliquées de la sociologie'. Comte, *Philosophie positive*, vol. IV, leçon 49, p. 512. For 'spéculations', see Chapter 1, note 19.

    Some eighteenth-century thinkers had considered using probability theory to study social phenomena. However, as I discuss in the next section, for Comte the essence of science is to discover invariable laws, and he therefore rejects what he regards as 'a so-called calculus of probabilities, that implicitly presupposes the absence of any actual law governing certain events' ('. . . un prétendu calcul des chances, qui suppose implicitement l'absence de toute loi réelle à l'égard de certains évènements'). Comte, *Esprit positif*, p. 19.
19. '[C]haque science, en se développant, a fait subir à la méthode positive générale des modifications déterminées par les phénomènes qui lui sont propres . . . [C]'est seulement alors qu'elle a pris son véritable caractère définitif, qui ne doit jamais être confondu avec celui d'aucune autre science fondamentale.' Comte, *Philosophie positive*, vol. I, leçon 3, p. 163.
20. '. . . l'imminente désorganisation des études supérieures sous l'aveugle domination des inférieures'. Comte, *Politique positive*, vol. I, p. 51.

21. '. . . dans la disposition constante des plus éminents biologistes à concevoir la science sociale comme un simple corollaire ou appendice de la leur'. *Ibid.*
22. '. . . l'indispensable prépondérance de l'analyse historique'. *Philosophie positive*, vol. IV, leçon 49, p. 513.
23. '[N]os études réelles sont strictement circonscrites à l'analyse des phénomènes pour découvrir leurs *lois* effectives, c'est-à-dire, leurs relations constantes de succession ou de similitude, et ne peuvent nullement concerner leur nature intime, ni leur *cause*, ou première ou finale . . . [T]oute hypothèse qui franchit les limites de cette sphère positive, ne peut aboutir qu'a engendrer des discussions interminables, en prétendant prononcer sur des questions nécessairement insolubles pour notre intelligence.' Comte, *Philosophie positive*, vol. II, leçon 28, pp. 435–6 (emphasis in original).
24. [N]ous disons que les phénomènes généraux de l'univers sont *expliqués*, autant qu'ils puissent l'être, par la loi de la gravitation newtonienne, parce que, d'un côté, cette belle théorie nous montre toute l'immense variété des faits astronomiques, comme n'étant qu'un seul et même fait envisagé sous divers points de vue; la tendance constante de toutes les molécules les unes vers les autres en raison directe de leurs masses, et en raison inverse des carrés de leurs distances; tandis que, d'un autre côté, ce fait général nous est présenté comme une simple extension d'un phénomène qui nous est éminemment familier, et que, par cela seul, nous regardons comme parfaitement connu, la pesanteur des corps à la surface de la terre. Quant à déterminer ce que sont en elles-mêmes cette attraction et cette pesanteur, quelles en sont les causes, ce sont des questions que nous regardons tous comme insolubles, qui ne sont plus du domaine de la philosophie positive, et que nous abandonnons avec raison à l'imagination des théologiens, ou aux subtilités des métaphysiciens.' Comte, *Philosophie positive*, vol. I, leçon 1 (Exposition), pp. 15–16 (emphasis in original; wrongly repeated word removed).

    Comte anticipates Richard Rorty here. 'Comte's aims were social and political. The real argument against continuing metaphysical discussion, in his view, is that experience shows that it doesn't pay off; in this respect, however different his recommendations, Comte very much resembles that most recent "end-of-philosophy" philosopher Richard Rorty.' Putnam, 'The Question of Realism', in *Words and Life*, p. 295 at p. 296. For further discussion see Chapter 4.

    There is a considerable debate in the literature regarding whether Comte considered questions regarding original or ultimate causes to be not only futile but also meaningless. See e.g. Laudan, 'Reassessment of Comte's "Méthode Positive"', 39–41; Scharff, *Comte after Positivism*, p. 90. For the views of more recent positivism-inclined thinkers on this issue, see Kolakowski, *Positivist Philosophy*, pp. 242–4.
25. 'Le véritable esprit positif consiste surtout à substituer toujours . . . la détermination du *comment* à celle du *pourquoi*.' Comte, *Politique positive*, vol. I, p. 47 (emphasis in original).
26. See e.g. Comte, *Plan*, p. 120 for the use of 'cause' in the common sense, and the text quoted in note 30 below for *engendrer* (to give rise to).
27. For a brief account, with references to original sources, see Laudan, 'Reassessment of Comte's "Méthode Positive"', 46.

28. Thus, for example, Arthur Conan Doyle, in a work published in 1923, has Sherlock Holmes state as follows. 'One forms provisional theories and waits for time or fuller knowledge to explode them. A bad habit, . . . but human nature is weak. I fear that . . . [Dr Watson] has given an exaggerated view of my scientific methods.' 'The Adventure of the Sussex Vampire', p. 281. The plain implication is that with proper scientific method one would not form provisional theories.

29. '[Sans] l'introduction . . . des hypothèses en philosophie naturelle . . . la découverte effective des lois naturelles serait évidemment impossible . . . Mais, l'emploi de ce puissant artifice doit être constamment assujetti à une condition fondamentale . . . [qui] consiste à ne jamais imaginer que des hypothèses susceptibles, par leur nature, d'une vérification positive.' Comte, *Philosophie positive*, vol. II, leçon 28, p. 434.

30. Comte asks rhetorically about introducing the ether and like imaginary entities into the theory of physical phenomena: 'What could be the scientific use of these fantastic notions . . . ? Is this intimate mixture of the real and the chimerical not bound to give rise to pointless discussions . . . ? ('Quelle peut être l'utilité scientifique de ces conceptions fantastiques . . . ? Ce mélange intime de réalités et de chimères ne doit-il pas . . . engendrer des débats sans issue . . . ?') *Ibid.*, p. 439.

31. For discussion, see Laudan, 'Reassessment of Comte's "Méthode Positive"', 50–1.

32. See note 18 above.

33. '. . . la prévision scientifique convient évidemment au présent, et même au passé, aussi bien qu'à l'avenir'. Comte, *Esprit positif*, p. 21. Comte thus avoids the need for such neologisms as 'retrodiction' and 'postdiction'.

34. 'Soit qu'il s'agisse . . . d'expliquer ou de prévoir, tout se réduit toujours à lier: toute liaison réelle . . . découverte entre deux phénomènes quelconques, permet à la fois de les expliquer et de les prévoir l'un d'après l'autre.' *Ibid.*, pp. 20–21.

35. 'En réalité, tous les hommes, quelque peu avancés qu'on les suppose, font de véritables prédictions, toujours fondées sur le même principe, la connaissance de l'avenir par celle du passé. Tous prédisent, par exemple, les effets généraux de la pesanteur terrestre, et une foule d'autres phénomènes assez simples et assez fréquents pour que leur ordre de succession devienne sensible au spectateur le moins capable et le moins attentif. *La faculté de prévoyance, dans chaque individu, a pour mesure sa science.* La prévoyance de l'astronome qui prédit, avec une précision parfaite, l'état du système solaire un très-grand nombre d'années à l'avance, est absolument de même nature que celle du sauvage qui prédit le prochain lever du soleil. Il n'y a de différence que dans l'étendue de leurs connaissances.' Comte, *Plan*, p. 118 (emphasis added).

36. '. . . cette prévision rationnelle que nous avons vue constituer, à tous égards, le principal caractère de la vraie science'. Comte, *Esprit positif*, p. 28.

37. 'The ability to underwrite successful predictions is our best quality-control test of the adequacy of scientific theorizing. To be truly satisfactory, our scientific explanations must have a rationale that also engenders adequate predictions.' Nicholas Rescher, 'Prediction', in Honderich, *Oxford Companion to Philosophy*, p. 713 at p. 714. The issue of what constitutes an 'adequate' level

of predictive power in any given scientific context is much discussed. See
e.g. Kuhn, *Structure of Scientific Revolutions*, pp. 66–91.

38. Comte does offer predictive power as an affirmative test to distinguish positive science from sterile fact-gathering. 'Such a [capacity for] prediction . . .
does distinguish genuine science from that vain *erudition* that merely col-
lects facts without trying to relate them to one another.' ('Une telle prévision . . . ne permettra jamais de confondre la *science* réelle avec cette vaine
érudition qui accumule machinalement des faits sans aspirer à les déduire les
uns des autres.') *Esprit positif*, p. 16 (emphasis in original).

    Laudan, 'Reassessment of Comte's "Méthode Positive"', 36, relies on this
same text (in English translation) for the conclusion that Comte uses predictive power 'to draw a sharp contrast between scientific theories on the
one hand and, on the other, metaphysical or theological systems'. This is
wholly erroneous.

39. 'Toute science a pour *but* la prévoyance.' Comte, *Plan*, p. 118 (emphasis
added).

40. 'Ainsi, le véritable esprit positif consiste surtout à voir pour prévoir, à étudier
ce qui est afin d'en conclure ce qui sera, d'après le dogme général de l'in-
variabilité des lois naturelles.' Comte, *Esprit positif*, p. 17.

41. 'Si l'homme peut prédire, avec une assurance presque entière, les
phénomènes dont il connaît les lois . . . pourquoi regarderait-on comme une
entreprise chimérique, celle de tracer, avec quelque vraisemblance, le tableau
des destinées futures de l'espèce humaine, d'après les résultats de son histoire? . . . [L]es lois générales . . . qui règlent les phénomènes de l'univers,
sont nécessaires et constantes; et par quelle raison ce principe serait-il
moins vrai pour le développement des facultés intellectuelles et morales de
l'homme, que pour les autres opérations de la nature?' Condorcet, *Esquisse*,
p. 203 (punctuation slightly changed).

42. 'Il est donc évidemment très-conforme à la nature de l'esprit humain que
l'observation du passé puisse dévoiler l'avenir, en politique, comme elle le
fait en astronomie, en physique, en chimie, et en physiologie.' Comte, *Plan*,
p. 118.

43. 'La dernière perfection de la science, qui, vraisemblablement, ne sera jamais
atteinte d'une manière complète, consisterait, sous le rapport théorique, à
faire concevoir avec exactitude . . . la filiation des progrès d'une génération
à l'autre, soit pour l'ensemble du corps social, soit pour chaque science,
chaque art, et chaque partie de l'organisation politique; et sous le rapport
pratique, à déterminer rigoureusement, dans tous ses détails essentiels, le
système que la marche naturelle de la civilisation doit rendre dominant.'
Ibid., p. 136.

    Grange, *Auguste Comte: La Politique et la Science*, p. 87, misleadingly states
that Comte's view of prediction in the human sciences relates more to major
issues of customs and values than to details of social organization. Carr, *What
is History?*, p. 68, appears to take a similar view of Comte's thesis. Both are
in conflict with Comte's texts, to which neither of these writers cites in
support.

44. '. . . on doit concevoir l'étude de la nature comme destinée à fournir la véritable base rationnelle de l'action de l'homme sur la nature, puisque la connaissance des lois et des phénomènes, dont le résultat constant est de nous

les faire prévoir, peut seule évidemment nous conduire, dans la vie active, à les modifier à notre avantage les uns par les autres.' Comte, *Philosophie positive*, vol. I, p. 62.
45. 'En résumé, *science, d'où prévoyance; prévoyance, d'où action.*' *Ibid.*, p. 63 (emphasis in original).
46. '. . . régler le présent d'après l'avenir déduit du passé'. *Politique positive*, vol. IV, p. *618, p. *624.

3 Positivist Social Reorganization

1. 'La loi fondamentale qui régit la marche naturelle de la civilisation prescrit rigoureusement tous les états successifs par lesquels l'espèce humaine est assujettie à passer dans son développement général . . . [L]a marche de la civilisation qui en dérive est donc essentiellement inaltérable, quant au fond. En termes plus précis, aucun des degrés intermédiaires qu'elle fixe ne peut être franchi, et aucun pas rétrograde véritable ne peut être fait.' Comte, *Plan*, pp. 92–3.
2. '[O]n ne voit que les hommes, et jamais les choses qui les poussent avec une force irrésistible. Au lieu de reconnaître l'influence prépondérante de la civilisation, on regarde les efforts de ces hommes prévoyants comme les véritables causes des perfectionnements qui se sont opérés, et qui auraient eu également lieu, un peu plus tard, sans leur intervention . . . En un mot, suivant l'ingénieuse expression de madame de Staël, on prend les acteurs pour la pièce. Une telle erreur est absolument de même nature que celle des Indiens attribuant à Christophe Colomb l'éclipse qu'il avait prévue.' *Ibid.*, p. 94 (paragraph break suppressed). Comte's reference is to Germaine de Staël, *Considérations sur les principaux événements de la Révolution française* (1818).
3. 'Seulement, la marche de la civilisation est modifiable, en plus ou en moins, dans sa vitesse, entre certaines limites, par plusieurs causes physiques et morales, susceptibles d'estimation. Au nombre de ces causes, sont les combinaisons politiques. Tel est le seul sens dans lequel il soit donné à l'homme d'influer sur la marche de sa propre civilisation.' Comte, *Plan*, p. 93.
4. '. . . le but essentiel de la politique pratique est, proprement, d'éviter les révolutions violentes qui naissent des entraves mal entendues apportées à la marche de civilisation'. *Ibid.*, p. 96.
5. 'Depuis un demi-siècle que la crise révolutionnaire des sociétés modernes développe son vrai caractère . . . un esprit essentiellement rétrograde a constamment dirigé toutes les grandes tentatives en faveur de l'ordre, et les principaux efforts entrepris pour le progrès ont toujours été conduits par des doctrines radicalement anarchiques . . . Tel est le cercle profondément vicieux dans lequel s'agite si vainement la société actuelle.' Comte, *Philosophie positive*, vol. IV, leçon 46, p. 11.
6. 'L'ordre et le progrès, que l'antiquité regardait comme essentiellement inconciliables . . .' *Ibid.*, p. 9.
7. 'Aucun ordre réel ne peut plus s'établir, ni surtout durer, s'il n'est pleinement compatible avec le progrès; aucun grand progrès ne saurait effectivement s'accomplir, s'il ne tend finalement à l'évidente consolidation de l'ordre.' *Ibid.*, p. 10.

8. 'Aussi la politique positive sera-t-elle surtout caractérisée, dans la pratique, par son aptitude tellement spontanée à remplir cette double indication, que l'ordre et le progrès y paraîtront directement les deux aspects nécessairement inséparables d'un même principe.' *Ibid.*

9. '... la conciliation fondamentale entre l'ordre et le progrès constitue ... le privilège caractéristique du positivisme ... L'ordre devient alors la condition permanente du progrès, tandis que le progrès constitue le but continu de l'ordre.' Comte, *Politique positive*, vol. I, p. 105. For a restatement in similar terms, see Comte, *Esprit positif*, p. 56.

10. 'Envers chaque ordre d'évènements, ces lois doivent ... être distinguées en deux sortes, selon qu'elle [sic] lient par similitude ceux qui coexistent, ou par filiation ceux qui succèdent ... d'où résulte, dans toute science réelle, une différence fondamentale entre l'appréciation *statique* et l'appréciation *dynamique* d'un sujet quelconque.' Comte, *Esprit positif*, p. 20 (emphasis in original).

11. '... une heureuse combinaison de stabilité et d'activité, d'où résultent les besoins simultanés d'ordre et de progrès'. *Ibid.*

12. 'Whether it is a matter ... of explaining or predicting, everything always comes down to making connections. Every genuine connection, *whether static or dynamic*, discovered between any two phenomena allows both explanation and prediction of one in terms of the other.' ('Soit qu'il s'agisse ... d'expliquer ou de prévoir, tout se réduit toujours à lier: toute liaison réelle, *d'ailleurs statique ou dynamique*, découverte entre deux phénomènes quelconques, permet à la fois de les expliquer et de les prévoir l'un d'après l'autre.') *Ibid.*, pp. 20–21 (emphasis added).

    Comte insists that: 'The two kinds of relationships have explanatory and predictive power in equal measure, even though it might at first glance have been supposed that laws of similarity would have explanatory power but only laws of succession could have predictive power. ('Les deux genres de relations contribuent également à expliquer les phénomènes, et conduisent pareillement à les prévoir, quoique les lois d'harmonie semblent d'abord destinées surtout à l'explication et les lois de succession à la prévision.') *Ibid.*, p. 20.

13. 'La multiplicité des prétendues constitutions enfantées par les peuples, depuis le commencement de la crise, et l'excessive minutie de rédaction qui se rencontre plus ou moins dans toutes, suffiraient seules pour montrer ... combien la nature et la difficulté de la formation d'un plan de réorganisation ont été méconnues jusqu'à présent.' Comte, *Plan*, p. 61.

14. 'Quand une science quelconque se reconstitue d'après une théorie nouvelle ... le principe général se produit, se discute et s'établit d'abord; c'est ensuite par un long enchaînement de travaux qu'on parvient à former, pour toutes les parties de la science, une coordination que personne, à l'origine, n'aurait été en état de concevoir, par même l'inventeur du principe. C'est ainsi, par exemple, qu'après que Newton eut découvert la loi de la gravitation universelle, il fallut près d'un siècle de travaux très-difficiles ... pour donner à l'astronomie physique la constitution qui devait résulter de cette loi ... Si telle est évidemment la marche nécessaire et invariable de l'esprit humain dans des révolutions qui, malgré leur importance et leur difficulté, ne sont cependant que particulières, combien doit paraître frivole la marche

présomptueuse qui a été suivie jusqu'à présent dans la révolution la plus générale, la plus importante, et la plus difficile de toutes: celle qui a pour objet la refonte complète du système social!' *Ibid.*, pp. 61–2.

15. '... les peuples n'ont pas compris jusqu'à présent le grand travail de la réorganisation sociale. En cherchant à préciser en quoi la nature de ce travail a été méconnue, on trouve que c'est pour avoir regardé *comme purement pratique* une entreprise essentiellement *théorique*.' *Ibid.*, p. 63 (emphasis added, paragraph break suppressed).

16. 'La formation d'un plan quelconque d'organisation sociale se compose nécessairement de deux séries de travaux, totalement distinctes par leur objet, ainsi que par le genre de capacité qu'elles exigent. L'une, théorique ou spirituelle, a pour but le développement de l'idée-mère du plan ... et la formation du système d'idées générales destiné à servir de guide à la société. L'autre, pratique ou temporelle, détermine le mode de répartition du pouvoir et l'ensemble d'institutions administratives les plus conformes à l'esprit du système, tel qu'il a été arrêté par les travaux théoriques. La seconde série étant fondée sur la première ... c'est par celle-ci que, de toute nécessité, le travail général doit commencer. Elle en est ... la partie la plus importante et la plus difficile.' *Ibid.*, p. 63.

17. '... toutes les fois que, dans une direction particulière quelconque, la société a besoin de travaux théoriques, il est reconnu que c'est à la classe de savants correspondante qu'elle doit s'adresser'. *Ibid.*, p. 72.

18. 'Ces travaux étant théoriques, il est clair que ... les savants occupés de l'étude des sciences d'observation, sont les seuls dont le genre de capacité et de culture intellectuelle remplisse les conditions nécessaires ... [L]'éducation ... qui résulte de l'étude des sciences d'observation, est la seule qui puisse développer d'une manière convenable leur capacité théorique naturelle.' *Ibid.*, pp. 71–2.

19. 'Le dogme de la souveraineté du peuple ... a été créé pour combattre le principe du droit divin, base politique générale de l'ancien système.' *Ibid.*, p. 53.

20. 'L'opinion dominante dans l'esprit des peuples sur la manière dont la société doit être réorganisée ... se réduit à présenter, comme principes organiques, les principes critiques qui ont servi à détruire le système féodal et théologique.' *Ibid.*, pp. 51–2.

21. 'Le principe de cette doctrine, sous le rapport spirituel, est le dogme de la liberté illimitée de conscience ... Le dogme de la souveraineté du peuple est celui qui correspond, sous le rapport temporel, au dogme qui vient d'être examiné, et dont il n'est que l'application politique.' *Ibid.*, pp. 52–3 (paragraph breaks suppressed).

22. 'Le gouvernement n'est plus conçu comme le chef de la société, destiné à unir en faisceau et à diriger vers un but commun toutes les activités individuelles. Il est représenté comme un ennemi naturel.' *Ibid.*, p. 52.

23. 'Le premier [le dogme de la souveraineté du peuple] ne peut pas plus être la base politique de la réorganisation sociale, que le second [le dogme de la liberté de conscience] n'en peut être la base morale. Nés tous deux pour détruire, ils sont également impropres à fonder.' *Ibid.*, pp. 53–4.

24. '... la réorganisation politique se présente de plus en plus comme nécessairement impossible sans la reconstruction préalable des opinions et des

mœurs. Une systématisation réelle de toutes les pensées humaines constitue donc notre premier besoin social, également relatif à l'ordre et au progrès.' Comte, *Politique positive*, vol. I, pp. 2–3.

25. 'Il n'y a point de liberté de conscience en astronomie, en physique, en chimie, en physiologie, dans ce sens que chacun trouverait absurde de ne pas croire de confiance aux principes établis dans ces sciences par les hommes compétents. S'il en est autrement en politique, c'est parce que les anciens principes étant tombés, et les nouveaux n'étant pas encore formés, il n'y a point, à proprement parler, dans cet intervalle, de principes établis. Mais convertir ce fait passager en dogme absolu et éternel, en faire une maxime fondamentale, c'est évidemment proclamer que la société doit toujours rester sans doctrines générales... [U]n tel dogme mérite... les reproches d'anarchie.' Comte, *Plan*, p. 53.

Comte also argues that allowing freedom of conscience makes it impossible to reach any fixed decision. 'To always be examining without ever deciding... is, in its nature, radically anarchic, in that if it were allowed to continue indefinitely it would preclude any true theoretically structured social reorganization.' ('Examiner toujours sans se décider jamais... est, par sa nature, radicalement anarchique, en ce que, si elle pouvait indéfiniment persister, elle empêcherait toute véritable organisation spirituelle.') Comte, *Philosophie positive*, vol. IV, leçon 46, pp. 54–5 (footnote omitted, punctuation changed). For the equivalence of theoretical and spiritual, see note 16 above.

26. '... les diverses mesures propres à faciliter cette reconstruction fondamentale'. Comte, *Politique positive*, vol. I, p. 111.

27. '[Les savants] seuls exercent, en matière de théorie, une autorité non contestée. Ainsi, indépendamment de ce que seuls ils sont compétents pour former la nouvelle doctrine organique, ils sont exclusivement investis de la force morale nécessaire pour en déterminer l'admission. Les obstacles que présente pour cela le préjugé critique de la souveraineté morale, conçue comme un droit inné dans tout individu, seraient insurmontables à tout autre qu'à eux.' Comte, *Plan*, p. 73.

28. 'On ne passionnera jamais la masse des hommes pour un système quelconque, en leur prouvant qu'il est celui dont la marche de la civilisation, depuis son origine, a préparé l'établissement, et qu'elle appelle aujourd'hui à diriger la société... Le seul moyen... consiste à présenter aux hommes le tableau animé des améliorations que doit apporter dans la condition humaine le nouveau système, envisagé sous tous les points de vue différents, et abstraction faite de sa nécessité et de son opportunité.' *Ibid.*, p. 105 (paragraph break suppressed).

29. 'Telle est la part spéciale réservée aux beaux arts dans l'entreprise générale de la réorganisation sociale.' *Ibid.*, p. 106. In giving such a role to the artists, Comte reflects a longstanding debate in French intellectual society regarding the role of the arts in supporting the moral foundation of society. This was closely associated with the *querelle des anciens et des modernes*, see Chapter 1, note 16.

Involving the fine arts raises for Comte the issue of artistic freedom. Referring to the artistic imagination, he states: 'Its effects will not be socially troublesome if it operates along the lines that the scientists have established at the theoretical stage and if it works towards the adoption of the system that the positivist polity has determined on, rather than inventing some system itself. As long as it keeps to these terms, the artistic imagination should have free rein. Indeed, the freer the artistic imagination then is, the more complete and beneficial will be its indispensable social influence.' ('Son action ne saurait avoir aucun inconvénient, puisqu'elle s'exercera dans la direction établie par les travaux scientifique, puisqu'elle se proposera pour but, non l'invention du système à constituer, mais l'adoption de celui qui aura été déterminé par la politique positive. Ainsi lancée, l'imagination doit être entièrement livrée à elle-même. Plus son allure sera franche et libre, plus l'action indispensable qu'elle doit exercer sera complète et salutaire.') Comte, *Plan*, pp. 105–6. One can only guess at what this might have meant in practice for the creative arts.

30. 'Ainsi concurrent à cette vaste entreprise toutes les forces positives; celle des savants, pour déterminer le plan du nouveau système; celle des artistes, pour provoquer l'adoption universelle de ce plan; celle des industriels, pour mettre le système en activité immédiate, par l'établissement des institutions pratiques nécessaires. Ces trois grandes forces se combineront alors entre elles pour constituer le nouveau système, comme elles le feront, quand il sera formé, pour son application journalière.' *Ibid.*, p. 106.

31. '...de toutes les portions de la société actuelle, le peuple proprement dit doit être, au fond, la mieux disposée...à accueillir favorablement la nouvelle philosophie, qui finalement doit trouver là son principal appui, aussi bien mental que social'. Comte, *Esprit positif*, p. 83. It is clear from the context that by *le peuple proprement dit* Comte means the proletariat (*les prolétaires*). For purposes of the present discussion, we can regard Comte as using 'the proletariat' (*les prolétaires*), 'the people' (*le peuple*) and other such terms more or less interchangeably. For references to Comte's texts on this, see Grange, *Le vocabulaire de Comte*, pp. 43–5; Grange, *August Comte: La Politique et la Science*, pp. 118–19.

32. See Littré, *Auguste Comte et la Philosophie Positive*, p. 592.

33. See Simon, *European Positivism*, p. 75.

34. '[L]'opinion publique...doit devenir le principal appui de la morale, non-seulement sociale, mais aussi privée, et même personnelle, parmi des populations où chacun sera de plus en plus poussé à vivre au grand jour, de manière à permettre au public le contrôle efficace de toute existence quelconque. La chute irrévocable des illusions théologiques rend cette force spécialement indispensable, pour compenser, chez la plupart des hommes, l'insuffisance de la moralité naturelle, même sagement cultivée.' Comte, *Politique positive*, vol. I, pp. 139–40 (paragraph break suppressed). Note that in Comte's scheme this public social structure is applicable only to men, not to women; see note 60 below and accompanying text.

35. '...l'empire de l'opinion publique'. Comte, *Politique positive*, vol. I, p. 139.

36. See note 25 above. Grange, *Auguste Comte: La Politique et la Science*, pp. 124–9, presents Comte's empire of public opinion as a space for vigorous debate on a broad range of issues, comparing it to a scientific society such as the Royal Society. This is utterly misleading. Grange gives no citation to Comte's works for any part of her discussion on this point.

37. See the article *Athéisme* in Voltaire, *Dictionnaire Philosophique*, drawing on Bayle's observations in his *Dictionnaire historique et critique*.
38. '... l'esprit positif ... [a une] aptitude spontanée à systématiser enfin la morale humaine, ce qui constituera toujours la principale application de toute vraie théorie de l'humanité'. *Esprit positif*, p. 62.
39. '... la pensée théologique est, de sa nature, essentiellement individuelle, et jamais directement collective. Aux yeux de la foi, surtout monothéique, ... la société humaine ne peut alors offrir immédiatement qu'une simple agglomération d'individus ... occupés chacun de son seul salut.' *Ibid.*, p. 74.
40. '[L]a prépondérance générale de la méthode historique proprement dite dans les études sociales a ... l'heureuse propriété de développer spontanément le sentiment social, en mettant dans une pleine évidence ... cet enchaînement nécessaire des divers événements humains qui nous inspire aujourd'hui ... un intérêt immédiat, en nous rappelant l'influence réelle qu'ils ont exercée sur l'avènement graduel de notre propre civilisation ... Il importe ... de ne pas confondre un tel sentiment de la solidarité sociale avec cet intérêt sympathique que doivent exciter spontanément tous les tableaux quelconques de la vie humaine, et que de simples fictions peuvent même pareillement inspirer. Le sentiment dont il s'agit ici est à la fois plus profond ... et plus réfléchi, comme résultat surtout d'une conviction scientifique.' Comte, *Philosophie positive*, vol. IV, leçon 48, pp. 455–6.
41. '... l'esprit positif ... [est] seul susceptible de développer directement le sentiment social, première base nécessaire de toute saine morale'. Comte, *Esprit positif*, p. 72.
42. 'Réservée d'abord à des esprits d'élite, cette nouvelle forme du sentiment social pourra ensuite appartenir, avec une moindre intensité, à l'universalité des intelligences, à mesure que les résultats généraux de la physique sociale deviendront suffisamment populaires.' Comte, *Philosophie positive*, vol. IV, leçon 48, p. 457.
43. 'L'esprit positif ... est directement social, autant que possible ... Pour lui, l'homme proprement dit n'existe pas, il ne peut exister que l'humanité, puisque tout notre développement est dû à la société, sous quelque rapport qu'on l'envisage. Si l'idée de *société* semble encore une abstraction de notre intelligence, c'est surtout en vertu de l'ancien régime philosophique: car, à vrai dire, c'est à l'idée d'*individu* qu'appartient un tel caractère, du moins chez notre espèce.' Comte, *Esprit positif*, p. 74 (emphasis in original).
44. '... diviser [l'ordre humain] définitivement dans ses deux modes nécessaires, l'un collectif, l'autre individuel, qui constituent respectivement l'existence sociale et l'existence morale'. Comte, *Politique positive*, vol. II, p. 432.

    There is considerable debate as to whether Comte thought in terms of human society as a collective subject, see e.g. Wernick, *Auguste Comte and the Religion of Humanity*, pp. 201–6. Grange, *Auguste Comte: La Politique et la Science*, p. 131, conclusively asserts that Comte did think in this way, without giving any citation to his works in support.
45. '[I]l faut, d'une part, déterminer exactement ce qu'exige, en chaque cas, l'utilité générale, et, d'une autre part, développer partout les dispositions correspondantes. Ce double office continu réclame surtout une doctrine fondamentale, une éducation convenable, un esprit public bien dirigé. Il doit donc dépendre principalement de l'autorité philosophique que le posi-

tivisme vient installer au sommet de la société moderne.' Comte, *Politique positive*, vol. I, p. 164.

46. '... le plus complet exercice possible des penchants généraux deviendra la principale source de la félicité personnelle'. Comte, *Esprit positif*, p. 75.

47. 'Tous ceux qui les subiront les auront volontairement adoptées par l'éducation, et leur observance habituelle conservera le mérite de la liberté.' Comte, *Politique positive*, vol. I, p. 163 (paragraph breaks suppressed).

48. For various observations on Comte's view of the relationship between the individual and society, see also Grange, *Auguste Comte: La Politique et la Science*, pp. 74–5, p. 131; Wernick, *Auguste Comte and the Religion of Humanity*, pp. 11–13, pp. 201–6.

49. 'Here now are the seven essential hierarchical stages: mathematics, astronomy, physics, chemistry, biology, sociology, and finally moral science. From now on these will constitute my great encyclopaedic scale.' ('[O]n obtient les sept degrés essentiels, mathématique, astronomique, physique, chimique, vital, social et enfin moral, qui composeront désormais ma grande échelle encyclopédique.') Comte, *Politique positive*, vol. II, p. 433.

50. '[L]'office propre de la philosophie consiste à coordonner entre elles toutes les parties de l'existence humaine, afin d'en ramener la notion théorique à une complète unité ... [L]a politique [est] seule arbitre légitime de toute évolution pratique. Entre ces deux fonctions principales du grand organisme, le lien continu et la séparation normale résident à la fois dans la morale systématique, qui constitue naturellement l'application caractéristique de la philosophie et le guide général de la politique.' Comte, *Politique positive*, vol. I, pp. 8–9.

51. '[L]es préceptes moraux se trouveront ainsi ramenés enfin à de véritables démonstrations, susceptibles de surmonter toute discussion, d'après la vraie connaissance de notre nature personnelle et sociale, dont les lois permettent d'apprécier exactement, dans la vie réelle, privée ou publique, l'influence quelconque ... de chaque affection, pensée, action, et habitude. Les convictions correspondantes peuvent devenir aussi profondes que celles qu'inspirent aujourd'hui les meilleures preuves scientifiques.' *Ibid.*, p. 99.

52. 'Mais en développant, à un degré jusqu'alors impossible, la puissance de la démonstration, la nouvelle philosophie évitera toujours d'exagérer son importance pour l'éducation morale ... Quelque saines que soient désormais de telles études, *leur point de vue ne saurait être directement moral*, puisque chacun y appréciera nécessairement la conduite d'autrui plutôt que la sienne, suivant les conditions d'impartialité et de netteté propres à la contemplation vraiment scientifique, qui doit toujours rester objective et non subjective.' *Ibid.*, p. 100 (emphasis added).

53. 'Notre année de vertueuse tendresse réciproque ...' *Ibid.*, Dédicace, p. XVI.

54. 'La vraie philosophie se propose de systématiser, autant que possible, toute l'existence humaine, individuelle et surtout collective, contemplée à la fois dans les trois ordres de phénomènes qui la caractérisent, pensées, sentiments, et actes.' *Ibid.*, p. 8.

55. '... la coordination positive, sans cesser d'être théorique et pratique, doit aussi devenir morale, et puiser même dans le sentiment son vrai principe d'universalité'. *Ibid.*, p. 13.

56. 'L'amour pour principe, l'ordre pour base, et le progrès pour but; tel est . . . le caractère fondamental du régime définitif que le positivisme vient inaugurer en systématisant toute notre existence, personnelle et sociale, par une combinaison inaltérable entre le sentiment, la raison, et l'activité.' *Ibid.*, p. 321.
57. ' . . . la parfaite unité que procure à la morale positive son principe unique de l'amour universel'. *Ibid.*, p. 94.
58. ' . . . les trois degrés essentiels de notre existence, d'abord personnelle, puis domestique, et enfin sociale, représente spontanément l'éducation graduelle du sentiment fondamental'. *Ibid.*
59. Thus, Comte declares that 'all women have one basic mission in life: to love' ('les femmes n'ont toutes, au fond, qu'une même mission, celle d'aimer'). *Ibid.*, p. 254. For Comte's discussion of the nature and role of women, see *ibid.*, pp. 206–66.
60. 'On this subject, the true general sense of human progress demands that the life of women be increasingly directed towards the family and removed from all outside work. This will better assure that they fulfil their loving purpose.' ('Tel est donc, à ce sujet, le vrai sens général de la progression humaine: rendre la vie féminine de plus en plus domestique, et la dégager davantage de tout travail extérieur, afin de mieux assurer sa destination affective.)' *Ibid.*, p. 249.
61. ' . . . les pensées doivent être systématisées avant les sentiments, et ceux-ci avant les actes'. *Ibid.*, p. 21.
62. ' . . . l'immuable nécessité extérieure'. *Ibid.*, p. 24.
63. 'L'esprit n'est pas destiné à régner, mais à servir.' *Ibid.*, p. 16.
64. '[L]'intelligence . . . est souvent disposée à méconnaître sa destination nécessaire au service continu de la sociabilité . . . L'univers doit être étudié, non pour lui-même, mais . . . pour l'humanité. Tout autre dessein serait, au fond, aussi peu rationnel que peu moral . . . Hors de ce domaine, *déterminé par la sociabilité*, nos connaissances resteront toujours autant imparfaites qu'oiseuses.' *Ibid.*, pp. 35–6 (emphasis added).

    Seemingly to indicate the idea of the social orientation of love, Comte introduces the term *sociabilité* (social feelings) essentially in place of previous terms that I have translated uniformly as 'feelings'. In fact he uses various terms for the three aspects of human existence that I translate uniformly as 'thoughts' or 'the intellect', 'feelings' and 'actions'. Among others, he uses *pensées, raison, domaine spéculatif* and *intelligence* for 'thoughts', and *sentiments, sociabilité, domaine affectif, amour* and *le cœur* for 'feelings'. He seems to treat some of each set as synonyms, while others may indicate a development of his ideas, as appears to be the case with *sociabilité*.
65. 'Le positivisme érige donc désormais en dogme fondamental, à la fois philosophique et politique, la prépondérance continue du cœur sur l'esprit.' *Ibid.*, p. 17. Putting Comte's view of the role of women in regard to feelings (love) together with his view of the primacy of feelings (love) gives women a crucial role in the positivist socio-political order. One might seek the germ of an essentialist feminist theory in this, but even those who would welcome such a theory would, given Comte's intended restrictions on women, derive only a very wretched version from his works.

4 Comte and Mill

1. For an account of Mill's attitudes to Comte's work in his earlier years, with references to original sources, see Pickering, *Auguste Comte*, pp. 509–20.
2. For the context, see Simon, *European Positivism*, p. 174, and sources cited therein.
3. Mill, *Autobiography*, p. 162. The correspondence was conducted in French. The letters from Mill are reproduced in Mineka, *The Earlier Letters of John Stuart Mill*. The letters from Comte are generously excerpted in Littré, *Auguste Comte et la Philosophie Positive*, Pt II, Ch. X, pp. 403–21 (letters on the social position of women), and Ch. XI, pp. 422–66 (other letters).
4. For a complete list of Mill's references to Comte in the *Logic*, with comparisons between the first (1843) and eighth (1872) editions, see Simon, *European Positivism*, pp. 275–9.
5. Mill, *Autobiography*, p. 205. For 'speculations', see Chapter 1, note 19.
6. These are the first part of Mill, *Auguste Comte and Positivism* (the first part is entitled *The Cours de Philosophie Positive*), and Mill, *Autobiography*.
7. Mill, *Auguste Comte and Positivism*, p. 53 (typographical error corrected).
8. *Ibid.*, pp. 33–46.
9. *Ibid.*, p. 43 n.
10. See Chapter 1, note 46, and accompanying text.
11. For Comte's law, see Chapter 1, Section iii. For Mill's discussion of it, see *Auguste Comte and Positivism*, pp. 9–33.
12. Mill, *Logic*, p. 606. Mill included this tribute in successive editions of the *Logic*, from first to last, although he altered a number of references to Comte. See Simon, *European Positivism*, p. 278.
13. Mill, *Autobiography*, p. 132.
14. Mill, *Auguste Comte and Positivism*, p. 86.
15. *Ibid.*, p. 106.
16. *Ibid.*, p. 124.
17. Mill, *Logic*, pp. 545–622 (Bk VI).
18. Mill, *Autobiography*, p. 132.
19. *Ibid.*, p. 138.
20. Mill, *Logic*, p. 546, p. 622.
21. See Chapter 3, note 25, and accompanying text.
22. Mill, *Autobiography*, p. 162 (emphasis added).
23. *Ibid.*, p. 192. Mill concludes: 'with this [system of education, the voting proposal] . . . would perhaps not be needed'.
24. *Ibid.*, pp. 162–3. Mill and Comte had already disagreed on the capacities and roles of women.
25. *Ibid.*, pp. 132–3.
26. See Chapter 3, note 34, and accompanying text.
27. Many years after Comte's death the positivist Grégoire Wyrouboff observed that it was essential to positivist philosophy that there could be only one proper positivist view on any fundamental matter in any field whatsoever, just as (according to positivist doctrine) there could be only one proper scientific view on any fundamental matter in physics or chemistry. He concludes that 'if two different views are expressed, one or the other must be

illusion'. ('If faut donc que d'un côté ou d'un autre on se fasse illusion.')
Wyrouboff, *Stuart Mill et la philosophie positive*, p. 59. However, he does not
go on to make my point in the text, that it is equally essential to positivist
philosophy that there should be a 'scientific' way to determine which of two
differing views is valid and which is illusion, just as (according to positivist
doctrine) there is with chemistry or physics.

28. T. H. Huxley, *Fortnightly Review* (Feb. 1869), cited in Congreve, *Essays*, vol. I,
    p. 262 (non-emphatic italics suppressed).
29. Comte did not formally adhere to any established religion. He considered
    Catholicism to represent the theological stage of the social order, and
    Protestantism with its notions of individual conscience to represent the
    transitional, metaphysical stage. See *Philosophie positive*, vol. IV, leçon 46,
    pp. 14–15.
30. Mill, *Logic*, p. 39. Mill himself employed the term 'empiricism' to denote a
    different viewpoint of no relevance here (and one that he insisted he did
    not hold). For discussion, see Anschutz, 'The Logic of J. S. Mill', p. 60.
31. Mill, *Logic*, p. 420.
32. For a survey of the ideas considered here in the context of positivist episte-
    mologies, see Putnam, 'The Idea of Science', in *Words and Life*, p. 481 at
    p. 484.
33. 'There is a sort of bad faith involved in acknowledging and living by certain
    beliefs in day-to-day life and denying these beliefs in the study.' C.A.J. Coady,
    'Common sense', in Honderich, *Oxford Companion to Philosophy*, p. 142.
34. 'I dine, I play a game of back-gammon, I converse, and am merry with my
    friends; and when after three or four hours' amusement, I wou'd return to
    these speculations, they appear so cold, and strain'd, and ridiculous, that I
    cannot find in my heart to enter into them any farther.' Hume, *Treatise of
    Human Nature*, Bk I, Pt IV, Sec. VII, p. 269.
35. Mill, *Logic*, p. 138.
36. Among the many critiques of the idea of observation unmediated by theory,
    see Russell, *Inquiry into Meaning and Truth*, pp. 15 *et seq.*; Hesse, *Structure of
    Scientific Inference*, chap. 1.
37. Horton, 'Tradition and Modernity Revisited', p. 228.
38. *Ibid.*, pp. 229–30 (paragraph break suppressed).
39. *Ibid.*, p. 228. As an anthropologist, Horton perceives these differences obtain-
    ing 'as between community and community, culture and culture'. *Ibid.* He
    correspondingly downplays differences between one worldview and another
    within a 'community' or 'culture'. *Ibid.*, p. 223. For my purposes, only the
    existence and conceptual scopes of the various 'dictionaries' of Horton's
    thesis are relevant. I am not concerned with the societal range of any given
    'dictionary'.
40. Kuhn, *Structure of Scientific Revolutions*, p. 10. Kuhn particularly focuses on
    the societal context formed by the community of any given scientific disci-
    pline. However, this is not a conceptual restriction on the use of the term
    'paradigm' in Kuhn's sense, and so does not affect the discussion here.
41. Mill, *Logic*, pp. 374–5.
42. *Ibid.*, p. 205.
43. *Ibid.*, p. 185.
44. See *ibid.*, p. 209.

45. *Ibid.*, pp. 208–9.
46. For Hume's sceptical discussïon of induction, see particularly *Treatise of Human Nature*, Bk I, Pt iii, Secs 6, 7 and 15. Mill does not associate this problem with Hume by name, but my discussion in the text will show that he had some sense of it. His careful, although ultimately limited, attempt to avoid the problem undermines claims (such as in Scharff, *Comte after Positivism*, pp. 63–4 n. 49) that he did not care about it.
47. Mill, *Logic*, p. 201.
48. *Ibid.*, p. 208.
49. *Ibid.*, p. 209.
50. *Ibid.*, p. 525.
51. *Ibid.*, pp. 525–6. Mill approves Bacon's analysis in *Novum Organum*, Bk I, Aphorism LX, where Bacon critiques the medieval misuse of the notion of *humidum* ('wet') in much the manner that Mill adopts with regard to 'hard.' Mill uses the 'hard' analogy to criticize Bacon's analysis of 'heat'. Mill does not specify the reference to Bacon's discussion of heat, but it is in fact *Novum Organum*, Bk II, Aphorism 20.
52. Mill, *Logic*, p. 146. Mill notes that the development of a science as deductive does not deny his principle that every deduction relies on induction. *Ibid.*, p. 144.

    What Mill calls experimental science is essentially what Comte calls sterile fact-gathering; see Chapter 2, note 38.
53. Kuhn, *Structure of Scientific Revolutions*, p. 28. Boyle's Law states that for any gas at a constant temperature, the product of the volume and the pressure remains constant.
54. For example, French has *eau dure* and *un cœur dur* for 'hard water' and 'a hard heart', respectively. German has *hartes Wasser* and *ein hartes Herz* for these, and also *ein harter Knoten* for 'a hard knot'. In each case the usage is similar to English usage.
55. I discussed Mill's empiricism in Section ii. Note that empiricism in this standard sense differs from Comte's use of the cognate *empirisme* to mean sterile fact-gathering, see *Esprit positif*, p. 16, and note 52 above.
56. '[L]e véritable esprit philosophique consiste surtout dans l'extension systématique du simple bon sens à toutes les spéculations vraiment accessibles.' Comte, *Esprit positif*, p. 45. Comte also uses here the expression 'common sense' ('la raison commune'). For 'esprit', see Chapter 1, note 45, and for 'spéculations', see Chapter 1, note 19.

    Grange devotes considerable space to Comte's epistemology. See *La philosophie d'Auguste Comte*, pp. 45–89 (chapter entitled *L'épistémologie de Comte*), and *Auguste Comte: La Politique et la Science*, pp. 35–91 (chapter entitled *Épistémologie générale*). However, there is little overlap between her analysis and mine. Note also that she shifts between different senses of 'epistemology' ('épistémologie'), 'theory of knowledge' ('théorie de la connaissance') and other related terms, often without clear definitions to warn the reader or close correlation with Comte's texts.
57. 'Il ne saurait exister aucune astronomie chez une espèce aveugle, quelque intelligente qu'on la supposât.' Comte, *Esprit positif*, p. 14.
58. 'Tous les bons esprits répètent, depuis Bacon, qu'il n'y a de connaissances réelles que celles qui reposent sur des faits observés. Cette maxime fonda-

mentale est évidemment incontestable, si on l'applique, comme il convient, à l'état viril de notre intelligence. Mais en se reportant à la formation de nos connaissances, il n'en est pas moins certain que l'esprit humain, dans son état primitif, ne pouvait ni ne devait penser ainsi. Car, si d'un côté, toute théorie positive doit nécessairement être fondée sur les observations, il est également sensible, d'un autre côté, que, pour se livrer à l'observation, notre esprit a besoin d'une théorie quelconque. Si en contemplant les phénomènes, nous ne les rattachions point immédiatement à quelques principes, non seulement il nous serait impossible de combiner ces observations isolées, et par conséquent, d'en tirer aucun fruit, mais nous serions même entièrement incapables de les retenir; et, le plus souvent, les faits resteraient inaperçus sous nos yeux.' Comte, *Philosophie positive*, vol. I, Exposition, pp. 8–9. He restates much the same point in *Esprit positif*, p. 6.

59. Comte's philosophy of the analysis of mental processes is in his *Philosophie positive*, vol. III. For Comte's determination to bring the analysis of mental processes within the positivist programme, see Simon, *European Positivism*, p. 122.

60. '. . . pressé entre la nécessité d'observer pour se former des théories réelles, et de la nécessité . . . de se créer des théories quelconques pour se livrer à des observations suivies, l'esprit humain, à sa naissance, se trouverait enfermée dans un cercle vicieux . . . s'il ne se fût heureusement ouvert une issue naturelle par le développement spontané des conceptions théologiques.' Comte, *Philosophie positive*, vol. I, Exposition, p. 9.

61. Thus, for example, the sense of phenomena preceding theory appears in: 'Our intelligence, driven by its blind instinct to make connections, yearns to connect together virtually any pair of phenomena' ('Dans son aveugle instinct de liaison, notre intelligence aspire presque à pouvoir toujours lier entre eux deux phénomènes quelconques.') Comte, *Esprit positif*, p. 22. See also Laudan, 'Reassessment of Comte's "Méthode Positive"', 42.

62. '. . . dans nos recherches positives . . . il importe . . . de sentir que cette étude des phénomènes, au lieu de pouvoir devenir aucunement absolue, doit toujours rester relative à notre organisation et à notre situation'. Comte, *Esprit positif*, p. 13.

63. 'Si la perte d'un sens important suffit pour nous cacher radicalement un ordre entier de phénomènes naturels, il y a tout lieu de penser, réciproquement, qu'l'acquisition d'un sens nouveau nous dévoilerait une classe de faits dont nous n'avons maintenant aucune idée, à moins de croire que la diversité des sens . . . se trouve poussée, dans notre organisme, au plus haut degré que puisse exiger l'exploration totale du monde extérieur, supposition évidemment gratuite, et presque ridicule.' *Ibid.*, p. 14.

64. Note that ontology in this standard sense differs from Comte's use of the cognate *ontologie* to mean the metaphysical mode of explaining events in terms of ultimate causes. See e.g. *ibid.*, p. 9.

65. The first quotation is '[le] monde extérieur, base immuable de toute la philosophie naturelle'. Comte, *Philosophie positive*, vol. VI, leçon 56, p. 303. My translation of 'philosophie naturelle' captures Comte's meaning. The second quotation refers to a goal of 'notre science' as producing '[une] exacte représentation du monde réel'. Comte, *Esprit positif*, p. 24. The third quota-

tion is 'une incontestable réalité'. Comte, *Politique positive*, vol. II, p. 48. For the fourth quotation, see Chapter 3, note 62.

66. 'La méthode [positive] . . . n'est pas susceptible d'être étudiée séparément des recherches où elle est employée . . . Tout ce qu'on en peut dire de réel, quand on l'envisage abstraitement, se réduit à des généralités tellement vagues, qu'elles ne sauraient avoir aucune influence sur le régime intellectuel . . . [et] on connaît beaucoup moins nettement la méthode que celui qui a étudié, d'une manière un peu approfondie, une seule science positive.' Comte, *Philosophie positive*, vol. I, Exposition, p. 39.

67. Mill, *Auguste Comte and Positivism*, p. 58 n.

68. *Ibid.*, pp. 55–6; Mill, *Autobiography*, p. 161.

69. Regarding Mill's *Logic*, then recently published in its first edition, Comte states: 'The last seven chapters of the first volume contain an admirable, rationally structured development of inductive logic. It is both profound and enlightening, and I dare to promise that it will never be better understood or better described, within the limitations of the point of view that the author has taken.' ('Les sept derniers chapitres du tome premier contiennent une admirable exposition dogmatique, aussi profonde que lumineuse, de la logique inductive, qui ne pourra jamais, j'ose l'assurer, être mieux conçue ni mieux caractérisée en restant au point de vue où l'auteur s'est placé.') *Esprit positif*, p. 17 n. 1. My translation may bring out the point that I make in the text somewhat more strongly than it appears in the French original, but it is reasonable to suppose that Comte would carefully veil such a comment on an admirer and supporter.

70. Mill, *Auguste Comte and Positivism*, p. 19.

71. '. . . [le] jeu varié des nombreuses divinités indépendantes qui avaient été imaginées primitivement.' Comte, *Philosophie positive*, vol. I, Exposition, p. 5.

72. See text at note 25 above.

73. The only general role that Comte prescribes for experience is to make us aware of the limited extent of our abilities, and thereby to divert us from inaccessible ontological problems towards those that we can reasonably hope to resolve. *Philosophie positive*, vol. I, Exposition, p. 10.

74. Putnam, 'The Question of Realism', in *Words and Life*, p. 295 at pp. 309–10. See also Scharff, *Comte after Positivism*, pp. 95–111. The comparison between Comte and Rorty illustrates Bertrand Russell's observation that there is no logical connection between a person's views regarding epistemology and social questions. Russell, 'Reply to Criticisms', p. 727.

75. See text at note 25 above.

76. Mill, *Autobiography*, p. 161.

5. The Critic and the Disciple

1. 'J'ai une très haute estime pour ses travaux en ce qui regarde la théorie de la méthode positive, mais je suis très éloigné de sa manière d'appliquer cette méthode aux questions sociales. La plupart de ses opinions sociologiques sont diamétralement opposées aux miennes.' Letter from John Stuart Mill to Émile Littré (22 December 1848), in Mineka, *Earlier Letters*, p. 741 at p. 742.

2. Mill, *Autobiography*, p. 205.
3. In *Pride and Prejudice*, Jane Austen's satire is apparent in having the parodically sententious, humourless, moralistic and conceited Mr Collins address the far wiser and more insightful Elizabeth Bennet: 'I consider myself more fitted by education and habitual study to decide on what is right than a young lady like yourself.' *Pride and Prejudice*, p. 139.
4. In *Hard Times*, Charles Dickens presents as the parodic representative of the scientific approach to social organization 'Thomas Gradgrind . . . [a] man of facts and calculations . . . ready to weigh and measure any parcel of human nature, and tell you exactly what it comes to'. *Hard Times*, Bk 1, Chap. II, p. 6. Gradgrind – hardware merchant turned educator – applies his rigid educational system to his daughter, stifling her imagination and leading inexorably to her emotional devastation, so that in the end he sees her, 'the pride of his heart and *the triumph of his system* lying, an insensible heap, at his feet'. *Ibid.*, Bk 2, Chap. XII, p. 141 (emphasis added). Meanwhile, his son, subjected to the same educational system, has turned to crime, but applies the science of social behaviour to deny personal responsibility. 'So many people are employed in situations of trust; so many people, out of so many, will be dishonest. I have heard you talk, a hundred times, of its being a law. How can I help laws? You have comforted others with such things, father. Comfort yourself!' *Ibid.*, Bk 3, Chap. VII, p. 181.
5. See e.g. Chapter 4, text at notes 22–3.
6. 'Indeed, though the mode of thought expressed by the terms Positive and Positivism is widely spread, the words themselves are, as usual, better known through the enemies of that mode of thinking than through its friends; and more than one thinker who never called himself or his opinions by those appellations, and carefully guarded himself against being confounded with those who did, finds himself, sometimes to his displeasure, though generally by a tolerably correct instinct, classed with Positivists, and assailed as a Positivist.' Mill, *Auguste Comte and Positivism*, p. 2.
7. 'La positivisme se compose essentiellement d'une philosophie et d'une politique, qui sont nécessairement inséparables, comme constituant l'une la base et l'autre le but d'un même système universel.' Comte, *Politique positive*, vol. I, p. 2.
8. Mill, *Auguste Comte and Positivism*, p. 185.
9. *Ibid.*, pp. 199–200.
10. 'I have often received praise . . . for the greater practicality which is supposed to be found in my writings, compared with those of most thinkers who have been equally addicted to large generalizations.' Mill, *Autobiography*, p. 149. As an example of contemporaneous public criticism of 'systems' that deny common sense, in *Hard Times* Dickens describes a supporter of Gradgrind's educational system (see note 4 above) as 'a government officer . . . always with a system to force down the general throat like a bolus . . . ready to fight all England . . . certain to knock the wind out of common sense, and render that unlucky adversary deaf to the call of time'. Bk 1, Chap. II, pp. 7–8.
11. 'La conséquence est la première qualité d'un philosophe; et, sans elle, philosopher est une chétive besogne.' Littré, *Auguste Comte et Stuart Mill*, p. 4.

12. Mill, *Auguste Comte and Positivism*, p. 199. Comte's more bizarre views, including the one cited, appear in his *Logique positive*; for a summary, see Mill, *ibid.*, pp. 196–8.

    Comte's deteriorating mental condition in his last years was well recognized. Thus, Littré 'notes with all appropriate solicitude that such lapses of M. Comte towards the end of his life were attributable to weaknesses brought on by overwork'. *Auguste Comte et la Philosophie Positive*, Préface, p. V. ('. . . j'indiquerai avec tous les ménagements nécessaires que ces manquements de M. Comte, dans la fin de sa vie, sont imputables à des affaiblissements produits par l'excès du travail').

13. The silence was a reaction to social and political propositions that the admirers of the *Philosophie positive* found offensive and even dangerous. Grange offers a reasonable additional explanation, although she seems to present it as the whole explanation, which is not the case. 'Challenging the primacy of the economic system, calling into question the supremacy of the state as political form – this is what makes Comte inflammatory, this is what explains the silence surrounding his political thought.' Grange, *Auguste Comte: La Politique et la Science*, p. 98. ('Récuser la primauté de l'économie, mettre en cause la suprématie de l'État comme forme politique, voilà qui fait de Comte un provocateur: Voilà qui explique le silence qui entoure sa pensée politique.')

14. Thus, while Littré saw in Comte's *Politique positive* a betrayal of the structure set up in the *Philosophie positive*, he did not suggest that it might have been the product of mental deterioration. I discuss Littré's criticisms in the next section.

15. Mill, *Auguste Comte and Positivism*, p. 5.

16. *Ibid.*, p. 62.

17. Mill, *Autobiography*, p. 205.

18. '. . . surtout à manifester la parfaite harmonie des efforts qui caractérisèrent ma jeunesse avec les travaux qu'accomplit ma maturité'. Comte, *Appendice général du Système de Politique positive*, p. I.

19. A good contemporaneous source for biographical information on Littré is Sainte-Beuve, *Notice sur M. Littré*. Aquarone, *The Life and Works of Émile Littré*, benefits from more recently available materials.

20. 'Son livre me subjugua. Une lutte s'établit dans mon esprit entre mes anciennes opinions et les nouvelles. Celles-ci triomphèrent, d'autant plus sûrement que, me montrant que mon passé n'était qu'un stage, elles produisaient non pas rupture et contradiction, mais extension et développement. Je devins dès lors disciple de la philosophie positive, et je le suis resté.' Émile Littré, *Auguste Comte et la Philosophie Positive*, Préface, p. I.

21. 'Ces . . . théologies ont . . . un . . . vice irrémédiable qui les rend absolument impropres au service exigé par l'état international du monde; c'est leur immobilité. Aucun mouvement, aucun développement, aucune progression ne leur est possible . . . Il faut quelque chose d'aussi vivant, d'aussi croissant que l'esprit positif.' Littré, 'De la Situation théologique du monde', 171.

22. 'M. Comte, en fondant la philosophie positive, en étendant la méthode positive à l'ensemble de la connaissance humaine, a mis, dans le domaine public, un instrument puissant dont il est le créateur sans doute, mais qui ne lui appartient pas exclusivement. Cette méthode le domine aussi bien que

tout autre . . . Quand Newton et Leibnitz eurent institué le calcul différentiel, ils devinrent aussitôt sujets de ce calcul . . . De même ici la méthode positive est un juge impersonnel destiné à prononcer sur tout ce qui s'est fait par le maître, sur tout ce qui se fera par les disciples.' Littré, *Auguste Comte et la Philosophie Positive*, p. 530.

23. '[C]ette œuvre . . . arrivait peu après le tourbillon de 1848 et dans les menaces diverses qui suivirent; elle s'annonçait comme décisive à la fois sur le présent et sur l'avenir. Jamais auditeur ne fut mieux préparé; évidemment j'attendais pour la politique quelque chose d'aussi neuf et d'aussi lumineux que l'avait été pour moi, dix ans auparavant, la philosophie positive.' *Ibid.*, pp. 527–8.

24. 'Dans la méthode subjective, le point de départ est une conception de l' esprit, qui pose, *à priori* . . . un certain principe métaphysique d'où il déduit . . . [L]es conséquences sont métaphysiques comme le point de départ . . . et ne trouvent ni requièrent les confirmations *à posteriori* de l'expérience.' *Ibid.*, p. 532. For *esprit*, see Chapter 1, note 45.

25. The first quotation is: 'subjective ou métaphysique (c'est la même chose)'. Littré, *Auguste Comte et la Philosophie Positive*, p. 534. The second is: 'M. Comte . . . en réinstallant la méthode subjective qui n'a aucune place dans les sciences . . . défait lui-même ce qui fit sa gloire et sa puissance philosophiques.' *Ibid.*, p. 536.

26. '. . . un des principes les mieux assurés de la philosophie positive, un de ceux que M. Comte a le plus fermement posés, et qui lui font le plus d'honneur, c'est que, plus une science est élevée hiérarchiquement, plus la faculté de déduire est diminuée'. *Ibid.*, p. 533. When Littré speaks of deduction he generally embraces induction as well (see *ibid.* p. 536 for his statement that they are conjoined). In effect, he means the positive scientific method, as I discussed in Chapters 1 and 2.

27. 'La méthode subjective, étant, elle, soumise non aux vérifications de l'expérience, mais seulement aux vérifications par la liaison de prémisses à conséquences, a devant elle un champ illimité; rien ne l'arrête ni ne la borne . . . Au contraire, la méthode déductive n'offrait que lenteurs et obstacles . . . Enserré dans ce dilemme, M. Comte glissa dans la voie de prémisses et des conséquences, voie trompeuse dans les sciences élevées et particulièrement dans la sociologie, la plus élevée de toutes.' Littré, *Auguste Comte et la Philosophie Positive*, p. 534.

28. For a summary see Aquarone, *The Life and Works of Émile Littré*, Appendix F, pp. 158–61.

29. 'Je ne voudrais pas que de cette prédiction on tirât trop grande conclusion; car le même M. Comte a prédit que la république ne serait pas détruite en France et que la grande guerre n'éclaterait pas en Europe. L'insuccès de telles prévisions montre . . . *l'impossibilité où l'on est de pousser bien loin la déduction en matière politique et sociale.*' Littré, *Auguste Comte et la Philosophie Positive*, p. 592 (emphasis added). Whether Littré's reasoning supports his conclusion is irrelevant here.

30. See Chapter 2, note 46, and accompanying text.

31. 'Je suis un disciple de la philosophie positive; M. Mill en est un critique.' Littré, *Auguste Comte et Stuart Mill*, p. 3.

32. '. . . constituer la sociologie fut pour M. Comte un moyen, non un but; le but était la philosophie positive'. *Ibid.*, p. 16.

33. 'The question is whether positive philosophy has come into being or is yet
to come into being. I thought more than twenty-five years ago that it had
come into being. I still think so, despite M. Mill.' ('Il s'agit de savoir si la
philosophie positive est venue ou est à venir. J'ai pensé, il y a maintenant
plus de vingt-cinq ans, qu'elle était venue; je le pense encore, même contre
M. Mill.') *Ibid.*, p. 18.
34. 'In all areas . . . the method is yet more important than the doctrine itself.'
('En tous genres . . . la méthode est encore plus importante que la doctrine
elle-même.') Littré, *Auguste Comte et la Philosophie Positive*, p. 529, quoting
Comte, *Philosophie positive*, vol. I, leçon 46, p. 177 (Littré adds emphasis
without noting the fact).
35. '. . . la sociologie est constituée quand on a saisi la loi suivant laquelle le
corps social transmet d'âge en âge l'accumulation héréditaire'. Littré, *Auguste
Comte et la Philosophie Positive*, p. 303.
36. '[L]a méthode déductive, en sociologie, . . . signale, dans les événements successivement accomplis, ceux qui appartiennent à l'ordre de développement
régulier, et les sépare de ceux qui appartiennent à la catégorie des perturba-
tions . . . c'est ainsi qu'elle achève la philosophie de l'histoire et en assure les
lois. Semblable est son rôle pour les événements de l'avenir . . . Mais, comme
les événements à venir n'existent pas encore, et que, en raison de la com-
plexité de la sociologie, elle ne peut les deviner que dans la limite la plus
restreinte, il lui faut attendre qu'ils se produisent.' *Ibid.*, p. 537.
37. 'Son office, et c'en est un de suprême importance qu'elle seule peut remplir,
consiste alors à montrer aux gouvernements et aux peuples de quels de ces
événements il faut favoriser l'évolution, et quels il faut étouffer à leur
naissance.' *Ibid.*

6 The Structure of the Legacy of Positivism

1. See Chapter 5, note 6.
2. Mill, *Auguste Comte and Positivism*, p. 153. The context was Comte's development of positivism into a religion, but Mill plainly intended a general
criticism.
3. Popper, *Objective Knowledge*, p. 321.
4. Thus, for example, one writer states that 'the scientific positivisms of Auguste
Comte, John Stuart Mill, . . . and many others . . . , in supposing that there
can be universal principles of observation, identification, and explanation,
suppose as well that scientific observation can be (more or less) value free'.
Schauer, 'Positivism as Pariah', p. 49 n. 6. As I discuss in the text in the
present section and the next section, this is a reasonable summary of the
position of Mill but not of Comte.
5. See Chapter 4, note 58, and accompanying text.
6. The positivist Richard Congreve was particularly influential in setting up
these churches. See Simon, *European Positivism*, pp. 48–50. Against Huxley's
gibe (see Chapter 4, text at note 28), Congreve retorted: 'Instead of "Catholicism *minus* Christianity", I recommend to his notice "Catholicism *plus*
Science".' Congreve, *Essays*, vol. I, p. 265 (italics in original).
7. Pease, *History of the Fabian Society*, p. 14.

8. Simon, *European Positivism*, p. 12.

9. In England, a few positivist churches survived into the twentieth century. It was still possible to write in 1910 that 'a number of prominent Positivists have carried out Comte's original idea of a Church of Humanity with ritual and organization. The chief building (in . . . London) is adorned with busts of the saints of humanity, and regular services are held. Positivist hymns are sung and addresses delivered.' Anonymous Author, 'Positivism', p. 173. The last of the English churches closed its doors in the 1930s; see Simon, *European Positivism*, p. 62. The religion of humanity appears now to be largely confined to a sprinkling of adherents in France and a few small organizations in Latin America. For the latter, see note 18 below.

10. For a brief introduction to the leading figures of the Vienna Circle, the forerunner of logical positivism, see Simon, *European Positivism*, pp. 258–62; Johnston, *The Austrian Mind*, pp. 181–95. For modern logical positivism, see Ayer, *Language, Truth and Logic*.

11. I discussed Comte's views on these matters in previous chapters. For Hegel's views, see *Philosophie der Geschichte*, p. 51, pp. 59–60, p. 69.

    Gustave d'Eichthal, a friend and admirer of Comte in his earlier years and an acquaintance of Hegel, introduced an early version of Comte's *Plan* to Hegel and Hegel's works to Comte in the expectation that they would find much in common. However, Hegel gave only limited praise to Comte's work, and although Comte recognized similarities between Hegel's work and positivism he found Hegel too metaphysical. For an account, with references to original sources including the letters of d'Eichthal, see Pickering, *Auguste Comte*, pp. 296–301. For further reference, see Littré, *Auguste Comte et la Philosophie Positive*, pp. 152–3.

12. 'Ich studiere jetzt nebenbei Comte, weil die Engländer und Franzosen soviel Lärm von dem Kerl machen. Was sie daran besticht, ist das Enzyklopädische, la synthèse. Aber das ist jammervoll gegen Hegel . . . Und dieser Scheißpositivismus erschien 1832!' Letter from Karl Marx to Friedrich Engels, 7 July 1866, in Marx & Engels, *Karl Marx – Friedrich Engels: Ausgewählte Briefe*, p. 211 at p. 212. I am not aware of any work of Comte published in exactly 1832. However, the tenor of Marx's comments suggests that he was reading *Philosophie positive*, vol. I, published in 1830.

13. Lenzer, *Auguste Comte and Positivism*, p. lv, pp. lvi–lvii, p. xlii.

14. See Chapter 3, note 30.

15. Comte, *Politique positive*, pp. 154–6.

16. For a brief bibliography of works comparing Comte with Marx or Hegel, see Simon, *European Positivism*, p. 239.

17. Gabino Barreda, a Mexican intellectual who as a young man attended Comte's lectures in Paris and studied his works, introduced a positivist curriculum largely based on Comte's works into Mexican education in the late 1860s. Notably, he also included Mill's *Logic* in the curriculum to provide a general theory of induction; see my discussion of induction in Chapter 4.

18. There is a vast literature on positivism in Latin America. For the intellectual and political context into which positivism was introduced in the Spanish-speaking countries, see Safford, 'Politics, ideology and society in post-Independence Spanish America', pp. 383–417. For the intellectual and political context in which positivism developed and was ultimately abandoned,

see Hale, 'Political ideas and ideologies in Latin America', pp. 143–86. The articles in Woodward, *Positivism in Latin America*, focus on the reconcilability of order and progress, and there is also a useful bibliography. Zea, *El positivismo en México* and Zea, *Pensamiento Positivista Latinoamericano* offer unique insights into the Mexican experience with positivism.

In Brazil, the present national flag, adopted in 1889, bears the motto *Ordem e Progresso* (*Order and Progress*). For the history of the flag, including explicit attribution of the motto to the Brazilian positivists and Comte, see the website of the National Observatory of Brazil, http://www.on.br/glossario/alfabeto/b/bandeirabrasil.html (visited 31 January 2005). The positivist religion gained a particular hold in Brazil, and continued to flourish there long after its decline in Europe. The positivist Templo da Humanidade (Temple of Humanity) in Rio de Janeiro was inaugurated in 1897 and was still functioning at the beginning of the twenty-first century. The Chapelle de l'Humanité (Chapel of Humanity) in Paris, the only surviving positivist chapel in Europe at the beginning of the twenty-first century, has been since its inauguration in 1903 a venture of the Brazilian positivists.

19. Similar observations ultimately apply to the attempts in the late nineteenth and early twentieth centuries to implement positivism politically in Turkey. For the history of this, see Lewis, *The Emergence of Modern Turkey*, particularly Chapter VII; Ramsaur, *The Young Turks*.
20. Berlin, 'Historical Inevitability', pp. 41–2.
21. Carr, *What is History?*, pp. 84–6.
22. Berlin, 'Historical Inevitability', p. 43.
23. See text at Chapter 2, note 11, and Chapter 4, notes 12–20.
24. See Chapter 1, note 49.
25. Geertz, *The Interpretation of Cultures*, p. 24, p. 42 (paragraph breaks suppressed).
26. Geertz, *Local Knowledge*, p. 22.
27. See Chapter 4, note 60, and accompanying text.
28. Carr, *What is History?*, pp. 95–6.
29. *Ibid.*, pp. 68–9.
30. See Chapter 5, note 36, and accompanying text.
31. Mazower, 'The dangers of pick'n'mix history' (paragraph break suppressed).
32. See Chapter 1, note 46, and accompanying text.
33. See text at Chapter 1, note 52.
34. Comte, *Philosophie positive*, vol. I, Exposition, pp. 27–9.
35. 'Qu'une classe nouvelle de savants, préparés par une éducation convenable, sans se livrer à la culture spéciale d'aucune branche particulière de la philosophie naturelle, s'occupe uniquement, en considérant les diverses sciences positives dans leur état actuel, à déterminer exactement l'esprit de chacune d'elles, à découvrir leurs relations et leur enchaînement, . . . en se conformant sans cesse aux maximes fondamentales de la méthode positive.' *Ibid.*, p. 30. For 'esprit', see Chapter 1, note 45.
36. Berger and Luckmann, *The Social Construction of Reality*, pp. 13–14.
37. Carr, *What is History?*, p. 86.
38. See Cassese and Weiler, *Change and Stability in International Law-making*, p. 149 (emphasis in original).
39. See Chapter 5, note 37, and accompanying text.

40. Carr, *What is History?*, p. 69.
41. Universal Declaration of Human Rights, G.A. Res. 217A (III), UN GAOR, 3rd Sess., pt 1, p. 71, UN Doc. A/810 (1948). At the time of the AAA 1947 Statement, the proposed United Nations Declaration was provisionally entitled 'Declaration on the Rights of Man', and the AAA 1947 Statement naturally refers to it as such. For consistency of reference I nonetheless refer to it throughout as the Universal Declaration of Human Rights.
42. AAA, *1999 Declaration*. This document has no page numbers, so there will be no notes in the text to further references to it.
43. AAA, *1947 Statement*, pp. 539–40.
44. For Comte's view, see Chapter 3, note 25, and accompanying text. For Mill's view, see text at Chapter 4, note 22.
45. Compare my comments on Horton's position, in Chapter 4, note 39, and accompanying text.
46. AAA, *1947 Statement*, p. 543.
47. It is common to distinguish positive morality ('the morality actually accepted and shared by a given social group') from critical morality ('the general moral principles used in the criticism of actual social institutions including positive morality'). See Hart, *Law, Liberty, and Morality*, p. 20. It is often not clear whether this is intended as a distinction between theory (critical morality) and practice (positive morality), or rather as a distinction between two kinds of theoretical principles, with one kind being employed to assess the other kind. If it is intended as a distinction between theory and practice, it of course fits with Comte's scheme and my discussion can be taken as referring to critical morality. However, if it is intended as a distinction between two kinds of theoretical principles, it does not fit with Comte's scheme, in which the idea of dividing a science into two kinds of principles in this way would be no more possible in morality than in physics. In this case, my discussion can be taken as referring to critical and positive morality harmonized and conjoined.
48. A social science may of course be concerned with training its own practitioners in what is right for them to do the course of their investigations. This is usually regarded as an aspect of the professional 'ethics' of the science. Thus, for example, the AAA 1999 Declaration exhorts professional anthropologists as follows: 'Anthropology's cumulative knowledge of human cultures ... entails an ethical commitment to the equal opportunity of all cultures.' For a general discussion, see Giddens, *Sociology*, pp. 683–6.
49. See Chapter 1, note 13, and accompanying text.
50. Proponents of utilitarianism in fact viewed it as providing a scientific foundation for morality. Thus, Mill commented of Jeremy Bentham: 'He introduced into morals and politics those habits of thought and modes of investigation, which are essential to the idea of science; and the absence of which made those departments of inquiry, as physics had been before Bacon, a field of interminable discussion, leading to no result.' Mill, 'Bentham', p. 57. Mill appears to have overstated the effects on moral discourse of Bentham's contributions.
51. Hart, *Law, Liberty, and Morality*, p. 71.
52. When in Chapter 2, Section iv I based a discussion on imagining a scientist about to begin an investigation, it was merely to illustrate a process, not to attempt to justify a substantive conclusion.

53. Clearly, my point here is connected with the distinction made between theoretical and practical reason, particularly in the work of Aristotle and as developed by Kant. However, theoretical reason as it has traditionally been understood is not scientific reasoning, as it slides too easily towards a naïve realism that, as I discussed in Chapters 2 and 4, has little to do with the epistemology of the modern sciences. It may be worth pursuing the idea that the classical distinction between theoretical and practical reason has shifted under the influence of the legacy of positivism into the distinction I draw here between scientific and moral reasoning.

7 The Legacy of Positivism in the Autonomy of Law

1. Consider, for example: 'Legal positivism shares something of the spirit and motivation of positivism in the general sense, and originated at about the same time, but in fact has developed rather independently.' Alan Lacey, 'Positivism', in Honderich, *Oxford Companion to Philosophy*, p. 705 at p. 706.
2. '[L]es instincts qui nous poussent à l'isolement ou aux conflits sont naturellement plus énergiques que ceux qui nous disposent à la concorde. Or, telle est la destination générale propre à la force de cohésion sociale désignée partout sous le nom de *gouvernement*, qui doit à la fois contenir et diriger.' Comte, *Politique positive*, vol. II, pp. 294–5 (emphasis in original). Compare Comte's observations on government that I quoted in Chapter 3, note 22.
3. '. . . il n'existe pas davantage de société sans gouvernement que de gouvernement sans société'. *Ibid.*, p. 267.
4. '. . . les légistes . . . possèdent exclusivement la capacité réglementaire, qui est une des grandes capacités nécessaires à la formation du nouveau système social'. Comte, *Plan*, p. 71, n.1.
5. Austin, *The Uses of the Study of Jurisprudence*, p. 379. This work, first published in 1863, is purportedly the text of the opening lectures in Austin's courses on jurisprudence in the 1820s.
6. See Savigny, *Vom Beruf unserer Zeit für Gesetzgebung und Rechtswissenschaft*.
7. See e.g. Austin, *The Province of Jurisprudence Determined*, p. 11.
8. The text quoted in note 4 above continues: '. . . et qui sera mise en jeu aussitôt que la partie purement spirituelle du travail général de réorganisation sera terminée, ou même suffisamment avancée'. Comte, *Plan*, p. 71, n.1. For the equivalence of 'spiritual' ('spirituelle') and 'theoretical' ('théorique'), see Chapter 3, note 16.
9. The first quotation is: 'Faisant profession de chercher des moyens pour persuader une opinion quelconque, plus ils acquièrent, par l'exercice, d'habileté dans ce genre de travail, plus ils deviennent impropres à coordonner une théorie d'après ses véritables principes.' Comte, *Plan*, p. 70. The second is: 'étrangers à toute idée théorique positive'. *Ibid.*, p. 71.
10. '. . . the need to divide theoretical from practical tasks . . . primarily derives from the weakness of the human intellect' ('. . . la nécessité de la division en travaux théoriques et travaux pratiques . . . [est] principalement motivée sur la faiblesse de l'esprit humain'). Comte, *Plan*, p. 67. For 'esprit', see Chapter 1, note 45.
11. The full text quoted with elision in note 4 above begins: '. . . lawyers, especially those who have thoroughly studied positive law, are the only people

who really understand working with rules' ('. . . les légistes, et surtout ceux d'entre eux qui ont fait une étude approfondie du droit positif, possèdent exclusivement la capacité réglementaire'). Comte, *Plan*, p. 71, n.1.

12. See Chapter 4, note 58 and accompanying text.

13. See note 9 above and accompanying text.

14. 'Thus a physician, a judge or a statesman can formally understand many fine pathological, juridical or political rules . . . and nonetheless easily slip up in trying to apply them.' ('Ein Arzt daher, ein Richter, oder ein Staatskundiger kann viel schöne pathologische, juristische oder politische Regeln im Kopfe haben . . . und wird dennoch in der Anwendung derselben leicht verstoßen.') Kant, *Kritik der reinen Vernunft*, Bk II, Introduction, p. 140 (A 133–4/B 172–3) (spelling amended to Reform usage). For the terminology of 'rules' ('Regeln') as Kant has it and 'laws' as I have it in the text, see my discussion earlier in this section and in Chapter 2, Section i. My translation of 'Staatskundiger' is based on Grimm, *Deutsches Wörterbuch*, vol. X.II.I, p. 309. My translation of 'schöne . . . Regeln' as 'fine . . . rules' brings out the potential for irony in the German; compare the common ironical expression *schöne Worte* (fine words). See *ibid.*, vol. IX, p. 1464 at p. 1485, for such ironical uses of *schön* from the early eighteenth century onwards.

   For a reference in Comte's texts to Kant's work demonstrating familiarity with it, see Comte, *Philosophie positive*, vol. I, leçon 3, p. 150.

15. Kant's text quoted in the previous note continues: '. . . entweder, weil es ihm an natürlicher Urteilskraft . . . mangelt, . . . oder auch darum, weil er nicht genug durch Beispiele und wirkliche Geschäfte zu diesem Urteile abgerichtet worden'. Kant, *Kritik der reinen Vernunft*, Bk II, Introduction, p. 140 (A 134 / B 173) (spelling amended to Reform usage).

16. Comte may have had in mind an aspect of a traditional view of Roman law practice. Thus, Austin, quoting Savigny in translation, refers to the Roman lawyers as having their theory 'so thoroughly worked out as to be fit for immediate application'. Austin, *The Uses of the Study of Jurisprudence*, p. 377.

17. See e.g. McDougal and Reisman, *International Law Essays*, p. 201, pp. 274–5, p. 358.

18. As Otto von Bismarck is anecdotally reputed to have said: 'The less that people know about how sausages and laws are made, the better they sleep.' ('Je weniger die Leute davon wissen, wie Würste und Gesetze gemacht werden, desto besser schlafen sie.')

19. For a discussion with references to original sources, see Vile, *Constitutionalism and the Separation of Powers*, especially Chapter 4 (discussing Montesquieu), Chapter 5 (dealing with English doctrines in the period following Montesquieu, particularly regarding Blackstone and Bentham) and Chapter 8 (dealing with the growth of hostility to institutional separation of powers in nineteenth-century England).

20. See *ibid.*, Chapter 4.

21. For a survey of early comparisons, see Shapiro, 'Law and Science in Seventeenth Century England'.

22. For the first use, see Austin, *The Province of Jurisprudence Determined*, p. 126. For the second, see *ibid.*, p. 61, where Austin's specific reference is to 'the science of Ethics or Deontology'.

23. See Sutherland, *The Law at Harvard*, p. 175, for this quotation from an 1886 address by Langdell.
24. *Ibid.* Note that some writers use the term 'science of law' to mean jurisprudence, in the sense of the analysis of the underlying philosophy of law; see e.g. Dias, *Jurisprudence*, p. 489.
25. For Langdell's statement, see Sutherland, *The Law at Harvard*, p. 175. For Carr's argument, see text at Chapter 6, note 21.
26. Pound, 'Mechanical Jurisprudence', 608.
27. Pollock, *Essays in Jurisprudence and Ethics*, p. 238.

8 Aspects of the Legacy of Positivism in Law

1. Austin, *The Province of Jurisprudence Determined*, p. 184.
2. For a survey of some of the major factions, their rivalries and their conflicts with opponents of positivism, see Simon, *European Positivism*, pp. 19–70.
3. John Gardner asserts that for work in the history of ideas (rather than philosophy) it is enough to observe that legal positivism is 'attached to a broad intellectual tradition, distinguished by an emphasis on certain aspects of legal thought and experience (namely the empirical aspects)' and that 'there is no need to identify any distinctive proposition that was advanced or accepted by all those designated as "legal positivists", for the label attaches by virtue of common themes rather than common theses'. Gardner, 'Legal Positivism: $5^1/_2$ Myths', 199. However, the term 'empirical' (or its cognates) has undergone so many shifts of meaning over the centuries that to connect ideas historically merely on the basis of being 'empirical' may well be misleading. In general, overly broad definitions of ideas may allow one to miss valid connections while misleadingly suggesting invalid ones. Moreover, many scholars would not agree that legal positivists are such 'by virtue of common themes rather than common theses'. The acrimonious debates in defence of various supposedly pure versions of legal positivism evidence this. Consequently, I must disagree with Gardner here.
4. *Ibid.*, 199. Gardner later modifies his proposition to make it clear that, according to legal positivism, in a constituted legal system the merit of the accepted source of a norm is irrelevant to the validity of the norm. *Ibid.*, 201. Note that Gardner's sense of 'norm' is essentially equivalent to 'law, rule or decision' if one takes into account my discussion of 'law' and 'rule' in Chapter 2.
5. For discussion, see Dyzenhaus, 'The Genealogy of Legal Positivism', 41.
6. Gardner, 'Legal Positivism: $5^1/_2$ Myths', 199–200.
7. *Ibid.*, 215–6 (paragraph break suppressed).
8. As one among a vast number of possible examples, see Scalia, *Common-Law Courts in a Civil-Law System*, pp. 97–8 (demanding that judges restrict themselves to a 'textualist' interpretation of statutes without regard to 'broader social purposes').
9. Gardner, 'Legal Positivism: $5^1/_2$ Myths', 215.
10. *Ibid.*, 219–20. Gardner acknowledges that '[i]nsofar as law-making agents are to be treated as *authorities* regarding the norms they made, there is a reason

to apply to those norms the interpretative norms that were knowably applicable to them *at the time when they were made'. Ibid.*, 220 (emphasis in original). But he concludes that this constraint is 'so limited as to be rarely worthy of any real moral anxiety'. *Ibid.*, 221.

11. *Ibid.*, 219.
12. *Ibid.*, 220.
13. *Ibid.*, 226–7.
14. *Ibid.*, 202.
15. *Ibid.*, 219.
16. '[L]aw must not become too scientific for the people to appreciate its workings.' Pound, 'Mechanical Jurisprudence', 606.
17. I do not consider here the relationship between law and morality under legal positivism in any context other than adjudication. Thus, I do not consider whether there is a moral dimension to the idea of law and the rule of law, whether there is a moral obligation to obey the law, whether there is a moral obligation to disobey a law when obedience would conflict with morality, and so forth. For discussion, see e.g. Hart, 'Positivism and the Separation of Law and Morals', 615–21. Nor do I consider whether, or to what extent, the political lawmaking body should endeavour to enact the society's moral sentiments into law. For discussion, see e.g. Hart, *Law, Liberty, and Morality*, and Devlin, *The Enforcement of Morals*.
18. Hart, 'Postscript', p. 272.
19. Hart, 'Positivism and the Separation of Law and Morals', 609. Hart and other writers give additional reasons for indeterminacy and incompleteness, but the character of language is sufficient for my arguments.
20. Hart, 'Postscript', p. 272 (emphasis in original).
21. Austin, *'The Province of Jurisprudence Determined'*, p. 191.
22. Hart, 'Postscript', p. 273.
23. Thus, for example, Gardner stipulates that a judge may introduce moral considerations only if an 'existing legal norm . . . plays a nonredundant . . . role in the argument'. Gardner, 'Legal Positivism: $5^1/_2$ Myths', 216. See also text at note 7, above.
24. See e.g. Gardner, 'Legal Positivism: $5^1/_2$ Myths', 215–7.
25. For a brief and clear summary by Dworkin of his views, see Dworkin, 'Indeterminacy in law', in Honderich, *Oxford Companion to Philosophy*, p. 399. The American Legal Realist school took a view in some respects similar, see Horwitz, *The Transformation of American Law 1870–1960*, p. 209. I discuss the Realists further in the next section. For Hart's rejection of this approach, see 'Positivism and the Separation of Law and Morals', 614, and 'Postscript', pp. 272–6.
26. See Hart, 'Postscript', pp. 273–4; Gardner, 'Legal Positivism: $5^1/_2$ Myths', 215–6.
27. Raz asserts that whenever moral reasoning fails to cover a case, legal reasoning somehow becomes available – in his words, 'legal doctrine takes on a life of its own' – and decides the case independently of moral considerations. He describes the legal interpretive principles that come spontaneously into life in such cases as 'an artificial system of reasoning' that, apparently, emerges specifically for such cases. Raz, *Ethics in the Public Domain*, pp. 339–40.

Even if one accepts this, the obvious question is why these 'artificial' legal principles should not simply serve in all cases, so that moral reasoning is never needed. Raz rejects this, but his rejection is unpersuasive. He declares that 'artificial' principles 'should always give way to moral considerations when they conflict with them'. *Ibid.* He attempts to justify this claim as follows:

> I am taking it to be a necessary truth . . . that whatever people do they do because they believe it to be good or valuable, however misguided or reckless their beliefs may be. Given that the courts are manned by people who will act only in ways they perceive to be valuable, principles of adjudication will not be viable, will not be followed by the courts, unless they can reasonably be thought to be morally acceptable, even though the thought may be misguided.

Ibid., pp. 333–4 (footnote omitted).

However, what Raz claims to be 'a necessary truth' is contentious. Perhaps people may do something they believe to be morally reprehensible for the sake of a salary that they find good and valuable. Without empirical evidence, one really has no idea whether Raz's statement is true either in general or specifically in regard to the behaviour of courts. Moreover, he offers no reason to suppose that these so-called 'artificial' legal principles will in fact be found morally unacceptable – especially since he allows the views of morally misguided people to determine how they are assessed.

In sum, Raz's proposed solution in terms of 'artificial' legal principles that substitute for moral reasoning when the latter is unavailable, but are otherwise inadmissible, must be rejected.

28. *Ibid.*, p. 340.
29. See note 27 above.
30. Thus, Gardner in a detailed example admits moral reasoning interstitially when the relevant legal rule is inapplicable 'in the technical sense'. Gardner, 'Legal Positivism: $5\frac{1}{2}$ Myths', 216. Hart associates his 'core' of the settled meaning of a legal rule with purely deductive reasoning. Hart, 'Positivism and the Separation of Law and Morals', 608.
31. Raz notes that this is not the practice of English courts. Raz, *Ethics in the Public Domain*, p. 253.
32. Horwitz, *The Transformation of American Law 1870–1960*, p. 209.
33. *Muller* v. *Oregon*, 208 US 412 (1908).
34. *Ibid.*, 419 n. In US jurisprudence, a sociologically focused brief of this kind is generally called a Brandeis brief, after the author of the brief in this case.
35. *Ibid.*
36. *Ibid.*, 421.
37. Friedenthal and Singer, *The Law of Evidence*, pp. 283–4. The discussion in this and the following paragraph draws on this text.
38. *Brown* v. *Board of Education*, 347 US 483 (1954).
39. *Ibid.*, 494.
40. Thayer, *A Preliminary Treatise on Evidence at the Common Law*, p. 279.
41. For critical comment in this vein on a case of judicial notice of legislative facts in which the justices of the US Supreme Court expressed what the

authors ironically describe as 'certain knowledge as to what symptoms of disharmony are fatal to human relationships ... in the criminal fringe of society', see Friedenthal and Singer, *The Law of Evidence*, p. 166.
42. Horwitz, *The Transformation of American Law 1870–1960*, p. 209 (emphasis added).
43. Thus, I wholly reject such views as that of Walker and Monahan, that 'courts may properly treat social science methodology as law and accord it the effect of common law precedent'. Walker and Monahan, 'Social Facts: Scientific Methodology as Legal Precedent', 896. Note that although the authors cite certain US Supreme Court and federal appellate court cases as taking the view that they propose, these cases do not in fact support that view in the full generality that the authors claim.

Bibliography

American Anthropology Association. *Declaration on Anthropology and Human Rights*. Adopted by AAA membership June 1999. Available at http://www.aaanet.org/stmts/humanrts.htm [cited as AAA, *1999 Declaration*].

American Anthropology Association. 'Statement on Human Rights'. *American Anthropologist*, vol. 49 (1947), 539–43 [cited as AAA, *1947 Statement*].

Anonymous Author. 'Positivism', in *Encyclopaedia Britannica*. New York, 11th edn, 1910, vol. 22, p. 172.

Anschutz, R. P. 'The Logic of J. S. Mill', in J. B. Schneewind, ed., *Mill: A Collection of Critical Essays*. University of Notre Dame Press, 1969, pp. 46–83.

Aquarone, Stanislas. *The Life and Works of Émile Littré*. Sythoff, Leyden, 1958.

Austen, Jane. *Pride and Prejudice*. London, 1813; Penguin English Library, 1972 [cited to latter edition].

Austin, John. *The Province of Jurisprudence Determined*. John Murray, 1832; in *The Province of Jurisprudence Determined* and *The Uses of the Study of Jurisprudence*, Hackett, Indianapolis, Indiana, 1998 [cited to latter edition].

Austin, John. *On the Uses of the Study of Jurisprudence*. John Murray, 1863; in *The Province of Jurisprudence Determined* and *The Uses of the Study of Jurisprudence*, Hackett, Indianapolis, Indiana, 1998, beginning at p. 365 [cited to latter edition].

Ayer, Alfred Jules. *Language, Truth and Logic*. Victor Gollancz, London, 2nd edn, 1946.

Bacon, Francis. *Novum Organum*. London, 1620.

Bayle, Pierre. *Dictionnaire historique et critique*. Leers, Rotterdam, 1697.

Berger, Peter L. and Luckmann, Thomas. *The Social Construction of Reality*. Anchor Books, New York, 1967.

Berlin, Isaiah. 'Historical Inevitability', in *Four Essays on Liberty*. Oxford University Press, 1969, pp. 41–117. This essay is a reprint of the first Auguste Comte Memorial Trust Lecture, London School of Economics and Political Science, 1953.

Carr, E. H. *What is History?* Pelican Books, 1964.

Cassese, Antonio and Weiler, Joseph H. H. *Change and Stability in International Law-making*. De Gruyter, Berlin, 1988.

Comte, Auguste [Isidore-Auguste-Marie-François-Xavier]. *Cours de Philosophie positive*. 6 volumes, Bachelier, Paris, 1830–42 [cited as Comte, *Philosophie positive*]. Comte retrospectively refers to this work as the *Système de philosophie positive*. Émile Littré also occasionally does so. To avoid confusion stemming from this, I have not followed the common English-language usage of referring to Comte's treatise as the *Cours*. In the original publication the volumes are described as *tomes* in the title pages but also referred to as *volumes* in the text. I use these terms interchangeably. Each *volume* is made up of a number of *leçons* numbered in a single sequence through the volumes. To assist the reader in tracking down quotations in other, differently paginated editions I give the number of the *leçon*. The second edition (Bachelier, 1852) is marked on the title page as 'identical to the first' ('identique à la première'). However, while the text appears to be identical to that of the first edition, the pagination is not. The main current complete edition (Hermann, Paris, 2 vols 1975, reprinted 1990) is not widely available. In quotations from this and other French works of and before the nineteenth century I have for clarity and consistency changed the variant plural spellings *–ens* and *–ans* (of nouns and adjectives ending in *–ent* and *–ant,* respectively) to the modern usage, without noting this in each instance.

Comte, Auguste. *Correspondance inédite d'Auguste Comte.* Première Série. Au Siège de la Société Positiviste, 1903.

Comte, Auguste. *Discours sur l'esprit positif.* Carilian-Goeury et Victor Dalmont, Paris, 1844 [cited as Comte, *Esprit positif*]. This work is also published as the first part of Comte, *Traité philosophique d'astronomie populaire.* Carilian-Goeury et Victor Dalmont, Paris, 1844. I cite to this latter edition.

Comte, Auguste. *Leçons sur la Sociologie* (Juliette Grange, ed.). Flammarion, Paris, 1995 [cited as Comte, *Leçons*]. *Leçons sur la Sociologie* is the title given in the title page of the book. The title on the front and back covers is *Leçons de sociologie.* This is a full-text reprint of all but the first *leçon* of volume IV of the *Philosophie positive,* together with introduction and notes by Grange.

Comte, Auguste. *Plan des travaux scientifiques nécessaires pour réorganiser la société* [cited as Comte, *Plan*]. This essay first appeared in 1822 with the title *Prospectus des travaux scientifiques nécessaires pour réorganiser la société* within a work of Saint-Simon. Two years later Comte revised the essay and published it separately under the title *Système de politique positive.* It is sometimes confused with Comte's far more extensive work under a similar title, in this Bibliography. Comte revised it again and gave it its final title, as given here, and republished it as the third *Opuscule* in *Appendice Général du Système de Politique Positive: Tous les Opuscules Primitifs de l'Auteur sur la Philosophie Sociale* (Paris, 1854). My citations to the *Plan* are to this latter edition.

Comte, Auguste. *Synthèse subjective, ou Système universel des conceptions propres à l'état normal de l'humanité.* Vol. I: *Système de logique positive, ou Traité de philosophie mathématique.* Paris, 1856 [cited as Comte, *Logique positive*].

Comte, Auguste. *Système de politique positive, ou Traité de sociologie instituant la religion de l'Humanité.* 4 vols, Paris, 1851–54 [cited as Comte, *Politique positive*]. An asterisk before the page number indicates that the citation is to the edition denominated as *Réimpression de l'édition 1851–1881* (Otto Zeller, Osnabrück 1967).

Conan Doyle, Arthur. 'The Adventure of the Sussex Vampire', in *The Second Sherlock Holmes Illustrated Omnibus.* John Murray, Jonathan Cape, London, 1979, pp. 277–88. This is a facsimile edition of the original *Strand Magazine* publication.

Condorcet, marquis de (Marie-Jean-Antoine-Nicolas Caritat). *Esquisse d'un tableau historique des progrès de l'esprit humain.* Paris, 1793–4; (O.H. Prior and Yvon Belaval, eds), Librairie Philosophique J. Vrin, Paris, 1970 [cited to latter edition as Condorcet, *Esquisse*].

Congreve, Richard. *Essays: Political, Social, and Religious.* Vol. I., Longmans, Green, London, 1874; Vol. II, Reeves & Turner, London, 1892.

Devlin, Patrick. *The Enforcement of Morals.* Oxford University Press, 1968.

Dias, R. W. M. *Jurisprudence.* Butterworths, London, 4th edn, 1976.

Dickens, Charles. *Hard Times*. Bradbury & Evans, London, 1854; *Hard Times: An Authoritative Text* (Fred Kaplan and Sylvère Monod, eds), Norton, 2001 [cited to latter edition].

Dyzenhaus, David. 'The Genealogy of Legal Positivism'. *Oxford Journal of Legal Studies*, vol. 24 (2004), 39–67.

Finnis, John. 'The Truth in Legal Positivism', in Robert P. George, ed., *The Autonomy of Law: Essays on Legal Positivism*. Clarendon Press, Oxford, 1996, pp. 195–214.

Franck, Adolphe. *Dictionnaire des Sciences Philosophiques*. Librairie Hachette, Paris, 3rd edn, 1885 [cited as Franck, *Dictionnaire*].

Friedenthal, Jack H. and Singer, Michael. *The Law of Evidence*. Foundation Press, Mineola, New York, 1985.

Gardner, John. 'Legal Positivism: $5^1/_2$ Myths'. *American Journal of Jurisprudence*, vol. 46 (2001), 199–227.

Geertz, Clifford. *Local Knowledge: Further Essays in Interpretive Anthropology*. Basic Books, New York, 1983.

Geertz, Clifford. *The Interpretation of Cultures*. Basic Books, New York, 1973.

Giddens, Anthony. *Sociology*. Polity Press, Oxford, 1989.

Gouhier, Henri. *La jeunesse d'Auguste Comte et la formation du positivisme*. 3 vols, Vrin. Paris, 1933–41.

Grange, Juliette. *Auguste Comte: La Politique et la Science*. Odile Jacob, Paris, 2000.

Grange, Juliette. *La philosophie d'Auguste Comte: science, politique, religion*. Presses Universitaires de France, Paris, 1996.

Grange, Juliette. *Le vocabulaire de Comte*. Ellipses, Paris, 2002.

Grimm, Jacob and Grimm, Wilhelm. *Deutsches Wörterbuch*. Hirzel, Leipzig, 1897.

Hale, Charles A. 'Political ideas and ideologies in Latin America, 1870–1930', in Bethell, Leslie, ed., *Ideas and Ideologies in Twentieth-Century Latin America*. Cambridge University Press, 1996, pp. 133–206.

Hall, A. R. 'The Scientific Movement and its Influence on Thought and Material Development', in *The New Cambridge Modern History*, Vol. X: *The Zenith of European Power: 1830–70*. Cambridge University Press, 1960, pp. 49–75.

Harré, Rom. *Great Scientific Experiments*. Oxford University Press, 1983.

Hart, H. L. A. *The Concept of Law*. Oxford University Press, 1961; 2nd edn, with postscript, 1994 [cited to 1st edn, except for postscript to 2nd edn, which is cited as 'Postscript'].

Hart, H. L. A. *Law, Liberty, and Morality*. Oxford University Press, 1968.

Hart, H. L. A. 'Positivism and the Separation of Law and Morals'. *Harvard Law Review*, vol. 71 (1958), 593–629.

Hegel, G. W. F. *Vorlesungen über die Philosophie der Geschichte*. Reclam, Stuttgart 1961. This work was collated from Hegel's writings after his death.

Hesse, Mary. *The Structure of Scientific Inference*. University of California Press, 1974.

Honderich, Ted. *Oxford Companion to Philosophy*. Oxford University Press, 1995.

Horton, Robin. 'Tradition and Modernity Revisited', in Martin Hollis and Steven Lukes, eds, *Rationality and Relativism*. MIT Press, 1982, pp. 201–60.

Horwitz, Morton J. *The Transformation of American Law, 1870–1960: The Crisis of Legal Orthodoxy*. Oxford University Press, 1992.

Huguet, Edmond. *Dictionnaire de la Langue Française du Seizième Siècle*. Librairie M. Didier, Paris, 1973 [cited as Huguet, *Dictionnaire*].

Hume, David. *A Treatise of Human Nature*. 1739; (L.A. Selby-Bigge and P.H. Nidditch, eds), Oxford University Press, 1978.

Johnston, William M. *The Austrian Mind: An Intellectual and Social History 1848–1938*. University of California Press, 1972.

Kant, Immanuel. *Kritik der reinen Vernunft*. Hartknoch, Riga, 1781, revised edn 1787; (Benno Erdmann, ed.), Leopold Voss, Hamburg and Leipzig 1889 [cited to latter edition, with standard references to original editions].

Kepler, Johannes. *Astronomia nova*. Vogelin, Heidelberg, 1609.

Kepler, Johannes. *Epitome astronomiae Copernicanae*. Linz/Frankfurt, 1618–1621.

Kepler, Johannes. *Harmonices mundi libri V*. Linz, 1619. The title translates loosely as *Five Books on the Harmony of the Universe*.

Kolakowski, Leszek. *Positivist Philosophy: From Hume to the Vienna Circle*. Pelican Books, Harmondsworth, 1972.

Kuhn, Thomas S. *The Structure of Scientific Revolutions*. University of Chicago Press, 2nd edn, 1970.

Kuttner, Stephan. 'Sur les origines du terme "droit positif"'. *Revue historique de droit français et étranger*, vol. 15 (1936), 728–40.

Kurath, Hans and Kuhn, Sherman M., eds. *Middle English Dictionary*. University of Michigan Press, 1954.

Laudan, Larry. 'Towards a Reassessment of Comte's "Méthode Positive"'. *Philosophy of Science*, vol. 38 (March 1971), 35–53.

Lenzer, Gertrud, ed. *Auguste Comte and Positivism*. Transaction Publishers, New Brunswick, New Jersey, 1998.

Lewis, Bernard. *The Emergence of Modern Turkey*. Oxford University Press, 3rd edn 2002.

Littré, Émile. *Auguste Comte et la Philosophie Positive*. Hachette, Paris, 2nd edn, 1864.

Littré, Émile. *Auguste Comte et Stuart Mill*. *Revue des Deux Mondes*, 15 August 1866; Germer Baillière, Paris, 1867 [cited to latter edition].

Littré, Émile. *Conservation, Révolution et Positivisme*. Ladrange, Paris, 1852; 2nd edn, augmentée, 1879.

Littré, Émile. 'De la Situation théologique du monde'. *La Philosophie Positive*, vol. 19 (September-October 1877), 161.

Littré, Émile. *Dictionnaire de la Langue Française*. (Jean-Jacques Pauvert, ed.), Paris, 1956 [cited as Littré, *Dictionnaire*]. This is a reprint of the edition published 1863–72.

Martineau, Harriet. *The Positive Philosophy of Auguste Comte*. 3 vols 1853. This work was reissued in 1896 (George Bell, London) with an 1895 introduction by Frederic Harrison. I cite to this latter edition.

Marx, Karl and Engels, Friedrich. *Karl Marx – Friedrich Engels: Ausgewählte Briefe*. Besorgt vom Marx-Engels-Lenin-Stalin Institute beim ZK der SED, Dietz, Berlin, 1953.

Mazower, Mark. 'The dangers of pick'n'mix history'. *Financial Times*, London, 10 January 2005, p. 13

McDougal, Myres S. and Reisman, W. Michael. *International Law Essays*. Foundation Press, Mineola, New York, 1981.

Mill, John Stuart. *A System of Logic, Ratiocinative and Inductive*. Eight edns by Mill, 1843–72; University Press of the Pacific, Honolulu, 2002 (reprint of 1891 edn) [cited as Mill, *Logic* to latter edition].

Mill, John Stuart. *Auguste Comte and Positivism*. N. Trübner, London, 1865.

Mill, John Stuart. *Autobiography*. Longmans, Green, London, 1873; (John M. Robson, ed.), Penguin Books, 1989 [cited to latter edition].

Mill, John Stuart. 'Bentham', in Mary Warnock, ed., John Stuart Mill, *Utilitarianism* and *On Liberty*, Blackwell, Malden, Massachusetts, 2nd edn 2003, pp. 52–87.

Mineka, Francis E., ed. *The Earlier Letters of John Stuart Mill, 1812–1848*. Collected Works of John Stuart Mill, vol. XIII: *The Letters 1838–1848*. University of Toronto Press, 1963.

Montesquieu, Charles-Louis de Secondat. *De l'Esprit des Loix*. Barillot, Geneva, 1748.

Morley, John and anonymous author. 'Comte', in *Encyclopaedia Britannica*. New York, 11th edn, 1910, vol. 6, p. 814.

Newton, Isaac. *Philosophiae Naturalis Principia Mathematica*. 3rd edn, 1726; (Alexandre Koyré and I. Bernard Cohen, eds), Cambridge University Press, 1972 [cited to latter edition].

Oxford English Dictionary. Clarendon Press, Oxford, 1933 [cited as *OED*].

Pease, Edward R. *The History of the Fabian Society*. Fifield, London, 1916.

Pennington, K. 'Law, Legislative Authority, and Theories of Government, 1150–1300', in J. H. Burns, ed., *The Cambridge History of Medieval Political Thought*. Cambridge University Press, 1988, pp. 424–53.

Pickering, Mary. *Auguste Comte: An Intellectual Biography*, vol. I. Cambridge University Press, 1993.

Pollock, Frederick. *Essays in Jurisprudence and Ethics*. Macmillan, London, 1882.

Popper, Karl R. *Objective Knowledge: An Evolutionary Approach*. Oxford University Press, revised edn, 1979.

Pound, Roscoe. 'Mechanical Jurisprudence'. *Columbia Law Review*, vol. 8 (1908), 605–23.

Putnam, Hilary. *Words and Life*. (James Conant, ed.), Harvard University Press, 1994. The essay 'The Question of Realism', p. 295 in this volume, is a revised version of the Auguste Comte Memorial Trust Lecture, London School of Economics and Political Science, 1993.

Ramsaur, Ernest Edmondson. *The Young Turks; prelude to the revolution of 1908*. Russell & Russell, New York, 1970.

Raz, Joseph. *Ethics in the Public Domain*. Oxford University Press, revised paperback edn 1995.

Rousseau, Jean-Jacques. *Discours qui a remporté le Prix à l'Académie de Dijon en l'année 1750, Sur cette Question proposée par la même Académie: Si le rétablissement des Sciences et des Arts a contribué à épurer les mœurs*. Barillot & fils, Geneva, n.d. (c.1750) [cited as Rousseau, *Discours sur les sciences et les arts*].

Russell, Bertrand. *An Inquiry into Meaning and Truth*. George Allen & Unwin, London, 1940.

Russell, Bertrand. *Portraits from Memory and Other Essays*. George Allen & Unwin, London, 1956.

Russell, Bertrand. 'Reply to Criticisms', in Paul Schilpp, ed., *The Philosophy of Bertrand Russell*. Northwestern University Press, 1944, p. 681.

Safford, Frank. 'Politics, ideology and society in post-Independence Spanish America', in Leslie Bethel, ed., *The Cambridge History of Latin America*, vol. III. Cambridge University Press, 1985, pp. 347–422.

Sainte-Beuve, Charles-Augustin. *Notice sur M. Littré, sa vie et ses travaux*. Hachette, Paris, 1863.

Savigny, Friedrich Carl von. *Vom Beruf unserer Zeit für Gesetzgebung und Rechtswissenschaft*. Mohr and Zimmer, Heidelberg, 1814.

Scalia, Antonin. *Common-Law Courts in a Civil-Law System: The Role of United States Federal Courts in Interpreting the Constitution and Laws*. The Tanner Lectures on Human Values, Princeton University, 1995.

Scharff, Robert C. *Comte after Positivism*. Cambridge University Press, 1995.

Schauer, Frederick. 'Positivism as Pariah', in Robert P. George, ed., *The Autonomy of Law: Essays on Legal Positivism*. Clarendon Press, Oxford, 1996, pp. 31–55.

Scott, John A. *Republican Ideas and the Liberal Tradition in France 1870–1914*. Octagon Books, New York, 1966.

Shapiro, Barbara J. 'Law and Science in Seventeenth-Century England'. *Stanford Law Review*, vol. 21 (1968–9), 727–66.

Simon, W. M. *European Positivism in the Nineteenth Century: An Essay in Intellectual History*. Cornell University Press, 1963.

Sutherland, Arthur E. *The Law at Harvard: A History of Ideas and Men, 1817–1967*. Belknap Press of Harvard University Press, 1967.

Thayer, James Bradley. *A Preliminary Treatise on Evidence at the Common Law*. Little, Brown, Boston, 1898.

Vile, M. J. C. *Constitutionalism and the Separation of Powers*. Liberty Fund, Indianapolis, 2nd edn, 1998.

Voltaire, François-Marie Arouet de. *Dictionnaire Philosophique*. Amsterdam, 1764.

Walker, Laurens and Monahan, John. 'Social Facts: Scientific Methodology as Legal Precedent'. *California Law Review*, vol. 76 (1988), 877–96.

Wernick, Andrew. *Auguste Comte and the Religion of Humanity: The Post-Theistic Program of French Social Theory*. Cambridge University Press, 2001.

Wheeler, Harvey. 'The Invention of Modern Empiricism: Juridical Foundations of Francis Bacon's Philosophy of Science'. *Law Library Journal*, vol. 6 (1983), 78–120.

Woodward, Ralph Lee, Jr, ed. *Positivism in Latin America, 1850–1900*. Heath, London, 1971.

Wyrouboff, Grégoire Nicolaevitch. *Stuart Mill et la philosophie positive*. Germer Baillière, Paris, 1867. This work is published as the second part of Littré, *Auguste Comte et Stuart Mill*, beginning at p. 57.

Zea, Leopoldo, ed. *Pensamiento positivista latinoamericano*. Biblioteca Ayacucho, Caracas, Venezuela, 1980.

Zea, Leopoldo. *El positivismo en México*. El Colegio de México, 1943; 2nd edn, 1953.

Index

abstract stage 11
accident, element of 97
actions 33, 45–6, 162
actual possibilities 23
adjudication 115–16, 131, 141, 178
Alembert, J. d' 7
American Anthropological
    Association 103–6, 142
  Declaration (1999) 103–6, 174
  Statement (1947) 103–6, 174
American Legal Realist school 116,
    139, 178
Anglican Protestant mind-set 55
Anschutz, R.P. 164
anthropology 16, 94–5, 103–5, 108,
    142
Aquarone, S. 169, 170
Aristotle/Aristotelian 8, 9, 19, 20,
    25, 63, 175
arts/artists, role of 39, 158–9
astronomy x, 9, 19–20, 25, 26, 30,
    36, 38, 52, 65
atheism/atheists 13, 14, 41, 147
Austen, J. 73, 168
Austin, J. 118, 124–5, 136, 150, 175,
    176
  law, legacy of positivism in
      128–30, 132–3, 177, 178
autonomy 82, 97–100, 132–3, 134,
    135
  epistemological 135, 137, 138,
      140–1
  see also autonomy of law
autonomy of law 113–27, 175–6
  claim of law as a science 122–7
  law in Comte's positivism 117–22
  Part III, introduction to 113–16
Ayer, A.J. 172

Bacon, F. 8, 17, 63, 65, 108–9, 126,
    144, 165
Barreda, G. 172
Bayle, P. 41, 160
Bentham, J. 128, 149, 174
Berger, P.L. 173
Berlin, I. 90–3, 143, 173
biology x, 15, 17, 24

Bismarck, O. von 176
Brazil 173
Brown v. *Board of Education* 140,
    142

calculus of probabilities 151
Carr, E.H. 17, 125, 149, 154, 177
  structure of the legacy of positivism
    92, 96–7, 99, 101, 103, 173,
    174
Cassese, A. 173
causal laws 22
causes 24–6, 27, 96, 152
certainty 86
  and indecision, opposition between
    10
Chapel of Humanity 173
chimerical 10
Christianity 148
  see also Protestantism; Roman
    Catholicism
Church of Humanity 172
circularity/circle, vicious 16, 34,
    61–2, 66, 95
classification 62–4
Coady, C.A.J. 164
Columbus, C. 33
Comte, A. *see Table of Contents and*
    entries for specific topics
Conan Doyle, A. 153
Condorcet, marquis de 7, 9, 17, 30,
    144, 145, 149, 154
Congreve, R. 143, 171
conscience, freedom of 37–8, 87,
    158
Conservation, Révolution et Positivisme
    (Littré) 80
constant conjunction 61
context-dependency 70
Cours de Philosophie positive 3
critique of the legacy of positivism
    97, 99–100, 102–7, 109–10
culture/cultural groups 104, 164

deduction 27, 28, 79, 81, 124
Descartes, R. 74, 144
Devlin, P. 178

Dias, R.W.M.   177
Dickens, C.   73, 168
Diderot, D.   7
direction, vigilant   69
discord   51–5
Dworkin, R.   136, 178
dynamic analysis   35
Dyzenhaus, D.   177

education   xi, 43, 47, 54, 172
Eichthal, G. d'   172
emphasis, Comte's shifts in   5
empiricism   22, 55–60, 164, 165, 177
Engels, F.   89
England   7, 51, 87, 123, 128
Enlightenment   7
epistemology/epistemological   55, 57
   autonomy   121, 135, 137, 138,
      140–1
   of Comte   65–7
   context-sensitive   68
   differences   59, 73
   and experience   69
   framework   56
   Grange on   165
   law   133, 136
   of Mill   55–8
   and perception   58
   questions   100
   relativism   66–7
   and science   81–2, 88, 93, 94
   similarities between Comte and
      Rorty   70
   theory   66
   two-level   58–60, 65
   variations   86, 120
esprit   148
Esprit des Loix, De l' (Montesquieu)
   123
état   146
ether   153
Europe   128
exercise   121
experience   62, 69, 167
experiment   8, 9, 28, 63, 64, 79, 109
   see also scientific: experiments
explanation   29, 81–2, 92, 96–7,
   156

faith   7, 41, 80, 87, 145
'Fallacies of Generalisation'   62–3
family   xi, 60
feedback loop structure   134–5
feelings   45–6, 162

Finnis, J.   150
France   viii, 7, 33–4, 41, 51, 172
Franck, A.   150
Friedenthal, J.H.   139–40, 179, 180
futile and useful, contrast between
   10, 145

Galileo Galilei   144
Gardner, J.   115, 130–5, 177, 178,
   179
Geertz, C.   94–5, 173
Giddens, A.   174
Gouhier, H.   144
government   117–18
   power   40
   see also politics/political
Grange, J.   143, 144, 148, 149, 154,
   159, 160, 161, 165, 169
'great notion of Deity'   11

Hale, C.A.   173
harmony   51–5
Harré, R.   16–17, 149
Harrison, F.   143
Hart, H.L.A.   109, 135–6, 174, 178,
   179
Hegel, G.W.F.   88, 172
Hellenion   147
hierarchical classification   xii, 52, 79,
   82, 93, 100–1
   autonomy of law   114–15, 120,
      124, 125
   epistemology of positive science
      23, 24
   positivist morality in theory and
      practice   44, 47
   scientific thought, evolution of
      16–17
   social reorganization   161
history   17, 32–3, 41, 52, 81, 88–90,
   92, 93, 96–7, 98
Hobbes, T.   109, 128
Honderich, T.   153, 164, 175
Horton, R.   58–9, 60, 64, 69, 164,
   174
Horwitz, M.T.   178, 179, 180
human development   30–1, 66, 68–9,
   70–1
human differences   104
human progress, inevitability of   7
human rights   103, 105, 142
human sciences   xi, xvi, xvii, 16,
   30–1, 32, 92, 96, 101
   autonomous   99

human sciences – *continued*
  autonomy of law   113, 114, 116,
      122, 123, 124
  and epistemology   93
  inter-scientific claims   100
  and law   134, 138–42
  and neutral and objective science
      94
  positive   *see* science
  predictive capacity   30–1, 32,
      79–83, 96–8, 154
  prescriptive   xi, xvi–xvii, 18, 33–4,
      38, 47, 53, 82, 102–7
human thought   11–12
humanity   14
  benefit to   xvi, 100–2, 103, 104–5,
      108, 133
  notion of   12
  see human sciences
Hume, D.   26, 57, 61–2, 91, 103,
      128, 164, 165
Huxley, T.H.   55, 143, 164, 171
hypothesis   27, 109
hypothetico-deductive method   27,
      28

indecision and certainty, opposition
      between   10
individual
  action, freedom of   70–1
  interests   42–3
  and society   40–3
induction   26, 28, 60–4, 67–71, 81,
      124, 125
intellect   46–7, 162
interpretive principles   124
inverse-square law of gravitational
      attraction   20, 25, 28, 29, 36, 43,
      91, 150

Johnston, W.M.   172
judgement, exercise of   121
judicial
  notice of legislative facts   140–1
  system   116
juridical
  context   xvii
  laws   19–22, 113, 120, 121

Kant, I.   7, 114, 121, 175, 176
Kepler, J.   20, 21, 144, 150
kinesis   63
knowledge   ix, x, xii, 7
  progress of   62

synthesis of   11
  theory of   165
Kolakowski, L.   143, 148, 152
Kuhn, S.M.   150
Kuhn, T.S.   59–60, 63–4, 66, 99, 154,
      164, 165
Kurath, H.   150
Kuttner, S.   150

Lacey, A.   175
Langdell, C.C.   125–7, 133, 177
Latin America   xv, 90, 172
Laudan, L.   145, 152, 153, 154, 166
law   40, 128–42, 150, 177–80
  from legacy of positivism to legal
      positivism   128–35
  and human sciences   138–42
  incompleteness of   137–8
  indeterminacy of   137–8
  and morality in adjudication
      135–8
  and morality, relationship between
      130, 178
  as a science   133
  of three stages   ix–x, xii, 11–15,
      52, 53, 66, 70, 92–3, 95
  see also autonomy of law
laws   27, 60, 119
  and causes   24–6
  of nature   19–20, 30
legal
  positivism   xviii, 113, 115–16, 119,
      128–35, 175
  reasoning   137–8, 141, 178
Leibnitz   74, 78
Lenzer, G.   172
Lewis, B.   173
liberty, individual   xii
Littré, É.   xii–xvii, 39, 134, 159, 163
  autonomy of law   113–14, 122–4
  as disciple   77–83, 167, 168, 169,
      170, 171
  Mill as critic   72–3, 75
  philosophy of positivism   143,
      145
  structure of the legacy of positivism
      84–5, 96–7, 102–5, 107, 172
logic   72
Logic (Mill)   51, 53, 68, 167
logic, science of   60
logical
  induction, theory of   xii
  positivism   xv, 88
  possibilities   23

love   45–6, 78, 162
Luckmann, T.   173

Machiavelli, N.   41, 149
Martineau, H.   143
Marx, K.   xv, 89–90, 172
materialism   24
mathematics   x, 22–3, 93
Mazower, M.   173
McDougal, M.S.   176
metaphysical mode of thought   ix, x,
    11, 12–13, 14, 52, 53
method   xvi, 94
Mexico   172
Mill, J.S.   xii–xiii, 38, 79, 113, 149,
    165, 167, 168, 169
  philosophy of positivism   14,
      17–18
  positive science, structure of   22,
      27, 150
  structure of the legacy of positivism
      85–7, 91, 93–4, 104, 171, 174
Mill, J.S. and Comte   51–71, 163–7
  empiricism of Mill   55–60
  epistemology of Comte   65–7
  harmony and discord   51–5
  induction, differences over   67–71
  induction theory of Mill   60–4
Mill, J.S. as critic   72–6, 167–71
Monahan, J.   180
monotheism   41
Montesquieu, C.-L. de S.   123–4,
    149
moral/morality   xi–xii, xiv, 41, 107,
    122, 135–8
  and adjudication   131
  critical   174
  existence   42
  and law, relationship between
      130, 178
  matters   73
  non-science, legacy in   xvii,
      107–10
  objective and subjective aspects of
      47
  positive   174
  reasoning   108–9, 116, 178–9
  role of   82
  science   16, 44, 47, 82, 83, 161
  sense, internal   40
  social   42
  subjective   119
  in theory and practice   43–7
Muller v. *Oregon*   139, 142

nationality   101
natural science   *see* physical science
negative   10–11
neutral science   86, 94
Newton, I.   9, 20, 25, 28, 35–6, 43,
    78, 91, 144, 150
norm   21–2

objective science   79, 86, 94
observation   28, 66, 67–8, 70, 86,
    94–5, 109, 125
  categories   58
ontology   67, 166
order   32–5, 45–6, 78, 90
organization   *see* social organization

paradigm   59–60, 64, 66
  positivist   67
Pease, E.R.   171
Pennington, K.   150
Philosophie der Geschichte (Philosophy
    of History) (Hegel)   88
Philosophie positive   15, 16, 51, 76,
    77, 79, 80–1, 88, 89, 149
philosophy/philosophical   47, 73
  aspects   72, 74, 76, 77
  debates   84
  of positivism   3–18, 143–9; Comte
      and his works   3–6; law of
      three stages   11–15; positivist
      philosophy, origins of   7–11;
      scientific thought, evolution of
      15–18
  reasons   85–6, 88
  structures   44
  theme   3, 6, 7, 11, 12
physical sciences   35–6, 54–5, 91, 92,
    96, 124
  accuracy/certainty/precision   86,
      91–2
  epistemology   93
  and neutral and objective science
      94
  predictive capacity   29–31, 79, 92,
      126, 153–4
Pickering, M.   143, 163, 172
placing or setting down   19, 21
planetary motion, first law of   20
Plato   8, 63
politics/political   47, 73
  bodies   122–3
  conservatism, extreme   xv, 88, 90
  critiques   87
  debates   84

politics/political – *continued*
  law-making process   123
  organization   51
  reasons   85–6, 88
  scheme   54
  sphere   82
  structures   44
  thought: Latin America   90
  see also socio-political aspects
Politique positive   45, 73, 75–6, 78,
    79
Pollock, F.   126, 177
Popper, K.R.   86, 171
positif   viii, ix, 9–10
positive
  law   21, 120
  method   xiv, 67, 70, 81, 93–5
  science   18, 32, 34, 38
  science, structure of   19–31, 150–5;
      epistemology of   22–4;
      juridical and scientific laws
      19–22; laws and causes   24–6;
      predictive power   26–31
  stage   x, xii, 11, 12, 15, 16
positivist
  churches   87, 172
  philosophy, origins of   7–11
Pound, R.   126, 177, 178
practical reason   175
practice stage   82, 89, 119, 121, 148,
    149, 174
precision   10, 86
predictive power of science   26–31,
    33, 79–81, 92, 96–9, 154, 156
previous experience   56
primary theory   59, 60, 65, 66, 69
principles   21–2, 91
progress   32–5, 45–6, 78, 87, 90
Protestantism   55, 164
Putnam, H.   70, 152, 164, 167

Raz, J.   137–8, 178–9
real, that which is   10
Realist doctrine   140
reality, perception of   57–8
reasoning   ix, xvii, 7, 98, 113
  legal   137–8, 141, 178
  moral   108–9, 116, 178–9
  practical   175
Reform Bill (1859)   53
Reisman, W.M.   176
religion   70
  of humanity   xv, 3, 12, 77, 87–8,
    173
  see also Protestantism; religious;
      Roman Catholicism/Roman
      Catholic Church
religious
  aspects   4
  faith   41
  ideas   6
  reason   85–6, 87
  thought   52
reorganization
  of society   99, 119, 124
  see also social reorganization
Rescher, N.   153
respect   104–5
revolution   xi, 7, 33–4, 35, 79, 80
  Comte's aversion to   87
Roman Catholicism/Roman Catholic
    Church   14, 19, 55, 164
Rorty, R.   70, 152, 167
Rousseau, J.-J.   9, 144, 145
rules   21–2, 60, 117–18, 119–20, 121,
    122, 176
Russell, B.   22–3, 93, 151, 164, 167

Safford, F.   172
Saint-Simon, H. de   7
Sainte-Beuve, C.-A.   169
Savigny, F.C. von   118, 175, 176
Scalia, A.   177
Scharff, R.C.   144, 146, 147, 151,
    152, 165, 167
Schauer, F.   171
science   7–8, 9, 51–2, 82, 115, 122,
    124
see also human sciences, physical
    sciences, positive science
science positive   9
scientific
  approach   20–1
  autonomy   xvi, 97–100, 126–7,
      130
  experiments   8, 9, 28, 63, 79
  laws   x, 19–22, 28, 29, 34–5
  method   xiv, 81, 99
  mind-set   26–7
  prediction (*prévision*)   *see*
      predictive power of science
  proof   44
  reasoning   108, 116, 138
  stage   *see* positive
  theory   61
  thought   15–18
secondary theory   59, 60, 62, 64, 65,
    66, 69, 70

separation-of-powers doctrines
124
Shapiro, B.J. 176
similarity/harmony, laws of 35
Simon, W.M. 159, 163, 166, 172,
177
Smith, A. 149
sociabilité (social feelings) 162
social
awareness (*sentiment social*) 41–2
control xiii
development 12–13
existence 42
morality 42
order 38, 69, 70, 81, 118–19, 123,
124
new 40
organization 51, 70, 87, 102,
135
pressure 119
reorganization 12, 72–3, 84–5, 87,
89
reorganization, positivist xi, xii,
xiii, xv, 32–47, 155–62;
morality in theory and practice
43–7; order and progress
32–5; practice of 38–40;
pressure 40; society and the
individual 40–3; theory of
35–8; *see also* reorganization of
society
sciences 53, 54–5, 64, 108, 174
socio-political aspects xi, 3, 4, 6, 13,
34, 77, 84–5, 90
autonomy of law 114, 116
framework xiii
and induction 68–9
law and positivism 133, 134,
142
and philosophical aspects 72, 74,
76
philosophy of positivism 148
Rorty's view on 70
theoretical phase 37
sociology x, xii, xiii, 16, 24, 42,
149
and autonomy 100
findings 139–40
and history 98, 99
law and positivism 142
Littré's views on 80–2, 83
Mill's views on 52, 63, 74, 76
and morality 44, 107–8

as positive science xiv, 38, 74
as predictive science *see* human
sciences, predictive capacity
as prescriptive science xi, 18, 34,
47
sovereignty of the people 37, 87
specialization 98
speculation 145
Staël, G. de 33, 155
'stage'/'state' 146
static analysis 35
structure of the legacy of positivism
84–110, 171–5
benefit to humanity 100–2
method 93–6
moral non-science 107–10
positivism as creed: diversions from
the legacy 84–90
prescriptive human science
102–7
received view of the legacy
90–3
scientific autonomy 97–100
structured explanation 96–7
structured explanation xvi, 96–7
subjective principle 78–9, 82, 83,
107
substantive
principle 109
problem 26
succession, laws of 35
superstition 7
Sur, S. 102
Sutherland, A.E. 177
syllogism 57, 60
systematization 85–6
Système de politique positive 3

Temple of Humanity 173
terminological problem 25–6
textual issue 4
Thayer, J.B. 179
theological stage ix, x, 11, 13, 14,
69
theoretical
phase 36–7
plan 89
reason 175
theory stage 38, 67–8, 70, 82, 89,
119, 121, 148–9, 174
thoughts 45–6, 70, 162
training 121
Turkey 173

United Nations
  Commission on Human Rights
      103
  General Assembly   106
United States
  judicial system   116, 140
  Supreme Court   139, 140, 179, 180
  see also American
Universal Declaration of Human
      Rights   103, 105–6, 174
usage, Comté's shifts in   5
useful and futile, contrast between
      10, 145
utilitarianism   174

vagueness   10, 11
Vaux, C. de   45–6

verification process   28
Vile, M.J.C.   176
Voltaire, F.-M.A. de   41

Walker, L.   180
Weiler, J.H.H.   173
Wernick, A.   160, 161
'what the law is'/'what the law ought
      to be'   129
women, role of   xi, 46, 87, 159, 162,
      163
Wyrouboff, G.N.   163–4

Yale policy-science school   123

Zea, L.   173